中國一东盟法律评论

2012年 第2卷 • 第1期

China-ASEAN Law Review Volume II Dec.2012 Number 1

■ 张晓君 主编
Zhang Xiaojun Editor-in-Chief

■ 中国—东盟法律研究中心 主办
Sponsored by China-ASEAN Legal Research Center

厦门大学出版社 XIAMEN UNIVERSITY PRESS | 国家一级出版社 全国百佳图书出版单位

中國一东盟法律评论

韩德培

Bình luận pháp luật Trung quốc – Asean

越南—中国—东盟法律信息咨询中心主任陈大兴用越南文字为《中国—东盟法律评论》题写刊名

Journal Undang Undang Asean-China

冯正仁

马来西亚联邦法院前大法官、第五届“中国—东盟法律合作与发展高层论坛”组委会主席冯正仁先生以马来语为《中国—东盟法律评论》题写刊名。

ទស្សនាវដ្តី ច្បាប់ ចិន-អាស៊ាន

អង្គ វ៉ាន់ វឌ្ឍនា
រដ្ឋមន្ត្រីក្រសួងយុត្តិធម៌ កម្ពុជា

柬埔寨司法部大臣昂翁·瓦塔纳用高棉语为《中国—东盟法律评论》题写刊名

中国—东盟法律研究中心：

法学之花盛开！

佟晓玲
驻东盟大使
二〇一二年五月七日

Advisory Committee

目 录

学术综述

附录

Contents

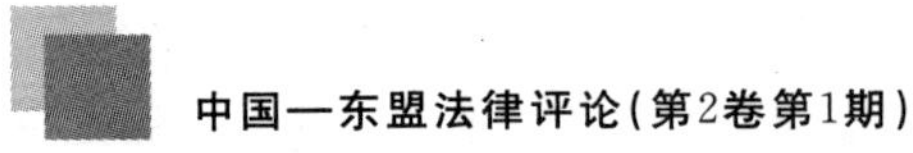

LEGAL SYSTEM ISSUES OF CHINA AND ASEAN COUNTRIES

ACADEMIC SUMMARY

APPENDIX

发刊词

刘 飏

2011年是中国和东盟建立对话关系20周年。回首往昔，中国和东盟国家齐心协力，克服艰难险阻，成功走出了一条具有亚洲特色的区域合作之路，实现了前所未有的发展与繁荣。2011年也是《落实中国—东盟面向和平与繁荣的战略伙伴关系联合宣言的第二个五年行动计划》的开局之年。展望未来，中国和东盟国家的多样性必将转化为加强交流合作的活力和动力，在相互学习和相互借鉴中增进彼此的理解和信任，实现各领域合作的深化和拓展。在这样一个承前启后的特殊时期，我欣喜地看到，由中国—东盟法律研究中心编辑的、汇集了来自东盟和中国法律法学界专家研究成果的《中国—东盟法律评论》正式出版。

伴随中国—东盟自贸区货物贸易、服务贸易、投资等领域一体化进程的深入，自由贸易区内各种复杂新颖的法律问题层出不穷。在此背景下，加强中国和东盟法学、法律界的交流与合作，对于保障自由贸易区顺畅运作、深化区域合作的内涵，加强和充实中国—东盟战略伙伴关系，具有迫切的现实意义。

《中国—东盟法律评论》要为本地区的法制建设提供一个常态化的交流平台。来自不同国家和不同领域的专家学者可以实时关注本地区出现的可能影响自贸区顺畅运转的各种问题，积极为中国—东盟自贸区涉及的法制建设献言建策，探究一整套适应国际规则和惯例，符合自由贸易区实际需要，能够被自由贸易区成员普遍接受的自贸区经贸和投资保障机制、司法协助体系、民商事争议解决机制以及法律协调机制，以防止和减少商贸风险和投资纠纷，逐步完善成员方各自的经贸法律规范，为推动中国—东盟自由贸易区法制建设进程做出有益贡献。

《中国—东盟法律评论》的出版，更为中国与东盟间政界、法学、法律界和商业界架设起一座文化沟通的桥梁。《中国—东盟法律评论》的作者来自东盟国家和中国的政界、法学、法律界和商业界，广泛代表各自所在国家、组织和职

业团体的观点和意见，不同思想和观念之间的碰撞与协调，必将增进中国与东盟之间法律的相互理解，为促进本地区政治、经济和文化等各方面的和谐发展尽绵薄之力。

“中国—东盟法律合作与发展高层论坛”自创立以来，一直秉承“合作、发展、共赢”的精神，积极致力于中国—东盟间的法律交流与合作，并于2010年结出累累硕果：“中国—东盟法律研究中心”在中国法学重镇——西南政法大学成立。在中国法学会的大力支持下，《中国—东盟法律评论》的创刊出版，为“中国—东盟法律研究中心”的实体化建设写下了浓墨重彩的篇章。

我期待着，研究中心能够以《中国—东盟法律评论》出版为契机，围绕自贸区经贸、投资、争端解决机制，以及各国法律协调和区域法制建设中具有全局性、战略性、前瞻性和实践性的重大法律理论和实践课题，进行深入的研究、探讨和交流，为促进本地区的法律法学合作和交流作出不懈的努力，为本地区的和平、稳定与繁荣作出积极贡献。

2011年9月

An Inaugural Statement in Honor of the First Issue of China-ASEAN Law Review

Liu Yang
Executive Vice-president of China Law Society
Chairman of China-ASEAN Legal Research Center

The year 2011 marks the 20th anniversary of the China-ASEAN dialogue relations. Looking back at the past decades, China and ASEAN countries have come a long way together from removal of misgivings and obstacles to successful opening of a regional cooperation with Asian identity, and achieved mutual growth and prosperity unseen in history. The year 2011 as well witnesses the beginning of The Second Five-year Plan of Action to Implement the Joint Declaration on ASEAN-China Strategic Partnership for Peace and Prosperity. Looking ahead to the future, there is no doubt that the common pursuit of peace and prosperity and the gaps in reality and individual diversities existed between China and ASEAN countries will turn into the incentive and motivation for enhancing exchange and cooperation, and China and ASEAN countries will push forward mutual understanding and trust in the process of learning from each other and further deepen and expand the cooperation in all areas. In such an extraordinary year inheriting the past and ushering in the future, I am absolute delightful to witness the official first issue of China-ASEAN Law Review, which is edited by the China-ASEAN Legal Research Center and will collect the findings of professionals of law from China and ASEAN countries.

Along with the speeding up of the integration process of the trade in goods, service and investment in China-ASEAN Free Trade Area (CAFTA), unprecedented legal problems are therefore on the increase accordingly. Under such cir-

cumstance, to strengthen the exchanges and cooperation in the field of law in the region will attach practical significance to the smooth functioning of CAFTA, enrichment of regional cooperation and promotion of China-ASEAN strategic partnership.

China-ASEAN Law Review will provide a persistent communication platform for the construction of local legal system, on which professionals and scholars from different nations in various domains will be able to follow up problems that may affect the normal operation of CAFTA in time and actively put forward proposals and ideas in legal system construction, concerning the making of a whole set of legal systems in China-ASEAN FTA, including FTA trade and investment guarantee mechanism, judicial assistance and civil and commercial dispute settlement mechanisms as well as legal coordination mechanism, which are in line with the international rules and practices, to the practical requirement of FTA and generally acceptable to FTA members, to prevent and reduce business risks and investment disputes ultimately, to gradually improve individual business rules of law of each member as well as to facilitate the progress of China-ASEAN FTA legal system construction. Furthermore, the publication of China-ASEAN Law Review will open up a new channel available for exchange of ideas among government officials, legal professionals and entrepreneurs from China and ASEAN countries. Since the authors of China-ASEAN Law Review come from ASEAN countries and Chinese government, law sectors and business world, their viewpoints will broadly represent that of their respective countries, organizations and professional societies, accordingly, the collision and merger of diverse ideas and concepts will for sure enhance mutual understanding, promote mutual trust and support so as to exert a vital and positive influence in facilitating the harmonious development of local politics, economy and culture. The China-ASEAN Forum on Legal Cooperation and Development, since its initiation, has been adhering to the idea of "Cooperation, Development and Win-win" and engaging in the legal communication and cooperation between China and ASEAN, out of which great success has been achieved. In the year 2010, China-ASEAN Legal Research Center was founded in Southwest University of Political Science and Law—a dominant quarter for legal studies around China. The publication of China-ASEAN Law Review will open a brand new chapter for the construction of the Legal Research Center in operation.

I sincerely hope that the China-ASEAN Law Review will grasp every opportunity and find out its own characteristic in a profound perspective, in the mean time, lead in the academic frontier, advocate theory innovation, follow closely to the judicial process and seek new channels for cooperation based on CAFTA major topics of general, strategic and foresighted importance in principle as well as in practice, to make it into the most influential domestic and international authoritative publication and to provide legal and intellectual support for the development of regional integration in an all-around and sound way.

Finally, I honestly wish that the China-ASEAN Law Review will gain success on every step!

September 2011

序 言

《评论》第2卷第1期开设了四大栏目,包括中国—东盟自贸区法律问题专论、中国—东盟自贸区争端解决机制专论、中国及东盟法律制度问题各论和学术综述,主要收录了来自中国、文莱、马来西亚、印度尼西亚、新加坡、泰国、越南等七国作者在第五届"中国—东盟法律合作与发展高层论坛"以及印度尼西亚举行的东盟法律协会第十一次全体会议上的演讲稿或参会论文共计16篇,突出地反映了中国及东盟国家法律人士对本区域经贸合作及法制发展中存在问题的前沿性研究成果。

在"中国—东盟自贸区法律问题专论"中,中国法学会对外联络部主任谷昭民先生以及海南省法学会常务副会长施文先生共同倡议建立CAFTA仲裁中心并对其设立的必要性、可行性、职能作用及组织机构做了具体阐述。商务部条约法律司副司长杨国华教授认为WTO《服务贸易总协定》为实现法律服务贸易自由化奠定了规则层面的基础。就中国—东盟自贸区而言,应该有更高程度的法律服务贸易开放水平。越南司法部官员、国际法律司副司长Nguyen Thanh Tu博士阐述了其提出的,法律服务自由化既是一个国家满足国际承诺的要求,也可以创造一个有竞争力的法律服务市场。西南政法大学副校长刘想树教授通过对当前形势的分析,认为设立中国—东盟自贸区仲裁中心的可能性及机遇已经具备。西南政法大学国际法学院张晓君教授和刘彬副教授阐述了区域贸易协定战略实施中的统筹安排,认为我国在积极推动自由贸易区实践的同时,应结合中国与东盟自由贸易区等成功范例,制订系统的自由贸易区战略。

在"中国—东盟自贸区争端解决机制专论"中,重庆大学法学院教授曾文革与研究生包李梅同学,在分析CAFTA争端解决机制现状的基础上,提出了其在今后发展中可能出现的挑战,并进行了前瞻性的分析。泰国外交部条约和法律事务司官员 Vilawan Mangklatanakul 着重通过审视 WTO 和 CAFTA 下的争端解决机制及在两种机制下的国家间争端和跨国公司与国家间争端的运行情况，探讨了国际贸易与投资领域不同类型的条约争端及其解决机制。中国外交部条法司参赞马新民先生就条约争端的含义，中国参加或缔结的条约对解决条约争端的规定，以及中国解决条约争端的特点与基本精神进行了阐释。马来西亚总检察长办公室官员 Datuk Azailiza Mohd Ahad 以国际贸易领域的争端解决为视角，探讨了国际争端的出现及其司法解决方面的问题。

在"中国、东盟国家法律制度问题各论"中，北京大学常务副校长吴志攀教授论述了中国"有余文化"对法律体系和金融政策的影响。印度尼西亚 Zatil Aqilah Metassan 先生通过解释为何由东盟达成的国际条约之所以应被视为其由东盟订立，并且据此所产生的权利义务被直接归属于作为一个独立实体的东盟的原因，以及进一步分析东盟机关的组织运行，以评估东盟是否可以实施其决议并探寻东盟将如何实施国际条约。司法部研究室主任、司法研究所所长王公义先生对中国律师服务业对外开放的进程以及今后的发展做了独到的阐述。印度尼西亚 Melli Darsa 则认为统一东盟成员国之间的投资法是实现东盟经济共同体前景的先决条件，只有东盟各国在一个更加开放的贸易和投资制度下，才能促进更有利的贸易和投资环境。新加坡律师钟庭辉先生阐释了新马两国白礁岛主权的争端和争端通过海牙国际法院得以解决的过程及其借鉴意义。云南财经大学法学院杨静、高学慧教授探讨了云南农村产品加工业对东盟贸易中的专利战略。

"学术综述"栏目则主要介绍了由中国—东盟法律研究中心秘书处的张晓君教授与宋继瑛博士共同整理的第五届"中国—东盟法律合作与发展高层论坛"学术综述。此次论坛以"合作共赢"为主题，围绕"中国—东盟自由贸易区条约争端"、"中国—东盟自由贸易区内的仲裁中心——机遇和挑战"、"中国—东盟自贸区货物、服务和投资贸易现状与未来趋势"和"中国—东盟自由贸易区下的法律服务自由化"四个分主题展开讨论，充分体现了自贸区内各国对通过开展和加强区域合作寻求共同发展的期望与信心。

《评论》蒙中国法学会会长韩杼滨先生为本刊题写了刊名，柬埔寨司法部大臣昂翁·瓦塔纳先生，马来西亚联邦法院前大法官冯正仁先生，缅甸最高检察院副检察长吴吞吞乌先生，泰国中央知识产权与国际贸易法院院长帕塔撒·万纳颂先生，越南—中国—东盟法律信息咨询中心主任陈大兴用越南文字为《中国—东盟法律评论》题写的刊名以及中国驻东南亚国家联盟前大使佟晓玲女士为本刊题字,厦门大学出版社给予大力支持,中心咨询单位和咨询委员,以及西南政法大学国际法学院研究生实验班及外语学院部分同学在翻译及校对等方面给予了热情关心和帮助。对此,编辑部对他们表示诚挚的谢意!

《中国—东盟法律评论》编辑部
2012 年 9 月

Editors' Note

Four columns are set up in the second volume of the China-ASEAN Legal Review (CALR), including CAFTA legal issues, dispute settlement mechanism for CAFTA, legal system issues of China and ASEAN countries and academic overview. The CALR mainly presents sixteen articles collected from speeches or forum papers in the 5th China-ASEAN Top Forum on Legal Cooperation and Development and the 11th plenary meeting of ASEAN Law Associationwhich was hold in Indonesia, of authors from China, Brunei, Malaysia, Indonesia, Singapore, Thailand and Vietnam. Those papers to a great extent reflect latest research achievements of China and ASEAN countries' lawyers on local and regional Economic and trade cooperation problems.

In the CAFTA legal issues column, Mr. Gu Zhaomin, the director of the International Liaison Department of the China Law Society, and Mr. Shi Wen, deputy president from Hainan Law Society, suggest establishing CAFTA arbitration center and analyze its necessity, feasibility and function. Mr. Yang Guohua, deputy director of the Department of Treaty and Law, Ministry of Commerce, belive that the General Agreement on Trade in Services (GATS) set a foundation for achieving liberalization of trade in legal services. As for CAFTA, there should be a higher degree of opening on trade in services. Dr. Nguyen Thanh Tu, vice-chief of the Department of International Law, Ministry of Justice of Vietnam, elaborates that liberalization of legal services are not only a country's obligation to meet the requirements of international commitments, but also contribute to create a competitive market for legal services. Through analyzing the current situation, Pro-

fessor Liu Xiangshu, vice-president from Southwest University of Political Science and Law, exams the possibility and feasibility to establish CAFTA Arbitration Center. Professor Zhang Xiaojun and Dr. Liu Bin from Southwest University of Political Science and Law, explore overall arrangements for the implementation of the strategy of regional trade agreements, and suggest to formulate systematic FTA Strategy combining with the successful example of China and the ASEAN Free Trade Area, as a result, facilitate the practice of free trade zone.

In the dispute settlement mechanism for CAFTA column, professor Zeng Weng of Chongqing University and his student Bao Limei put forward the challenges that may arise in the future and make a prospective analysis. Mr. Vilawan Mangklatanakul, official from Department of Treaties and Legal Affairs, Ministry of Foreign Affairs, Thailand, explore different types of treaty disputes and dispute settlement mechanism in the field of international trade and investment by the way of examining the dispute settlement mechanism under the WTO and CAFTA and the settlement of disputes between nations and between nations and multinational corporations. Mr. Ma Xinmin, counselor from Treaty and Legal Affairs of the China Foreign Ministry, review the meaning of treaty disputes, analyzes the treaties about how to solve treaty dispute under the international treaties which China had entered into or acceded to, as well as the feature and spirit of China's practice. Mr. Datuk Azailiza Mohd Ahad, officer from International Affairs Division Attorney General's Chambers explore the emergence of international dispute and its judicial settlement in the view of dispute settlement of international trade.

In the legal system issues of China and ASEAN countries column, Professor Wu Zhipan, vice-chancellor of Beijing University, discusses China's surplus culture and financial law. Mr. Zatil Aqilah Metassan from Indonesia argues why an international agreement concluded by ASEAN should be regarded as agreements by ASEAN, and why the rights and obligations from those agreements for ASEAN should be regarded as an independent entity. He further analyzes the functioning of ASEAN organizations. Mr. Wang Gongyi, director from justice department, gives an outline about process of

Chinese lawyers opening up of service and its development in the future. Dr. Melli Darsa from Indonesia, explores that harmonization of the investment laws among the ASEAN countries is assumed to be a prerequisite for implementing the vision of ASEAN Economic Community, where it is believed that a more liberalized trade and investment regime in ASEAN would encourage a more favorable trade and investment climate in the region. Mr. Zhang Tinghui, attorney from Singapore, descripts the process of formation and resolution of the dispute over sovereignty of Pedra Branca, and its significance. Ms. Yang Jing and Ms. Gao Chonghui from Law School of Yunnan University of Finance and Economics, explore the patent strategy of Yunnan agricultural product processing industry in its trade with ASEAN.

The academic overview column introduces summary of The 5th China-ASEAN Top Forum on Legal Cooperation and Development arranged by professor Zhang Xiaojun and Dr. Song Jiying .

The editorial board would like to express sincere gratitude to Mr. Han Zhubin , president of China Law Society, and Mr. Ang Vong Vathan, Minister of Justice of Cambodia. Our thanks go to Mr. Tan Sri James Foong, Justice of the Federal Court of Malaysia, Mr. U Tun Tun Oo, Deputy attorney Qeveval of Attoruey Gereual's Chambers and Mr. Tran Dai Hung, Director-General of Center for Vietnam-China-ASEAN Legal Information and Consultancy, and Ms. Tong Xiaoling , former Chinese ambassador to ASEAN, for their generous inscription for CALR. We are also grateful to Xiamen University Press for their generous support, to the Advisory Organizations as well as Advisory Members of the Center, for offering us a great deal of constructive advices during the publication of our CALR.

Editorial Board of China-ASEAN Law Review
September 2012

中国—东盟自贸区

法律问题专论

CAFTA LEGAL ISSUES

中国—东盟自由贸易区法律服务自由化

杨国华*

内容提要 从现在和可预测的将来来看，经济全球化已成为任何国家和社会发展的发展趋势，法律服务贸易自由化是经济全球化的必然产物。世贸组织项下《服务贸易总协定》为实现法律服务贸易自由化奠定了规则层面的基础。对于中国—东盟自贸区，我们有理由期待更高程度的法律服务贸易开放水平。

一、法律服务贸易自由化是经济全球化的必然产物

从现在和可预测的将来来看，经济全球化已成为任何国家和社会发展不可或缺的发展趋势。法律服务作为服务贸易的一个部门，其全球化与自由化也是必然的。国际贸易、投资、金融等跨国经济活动，都要以法律作为先导和保障。比如，一家中国公司要在马来西亚投资设立工厂，最基本的环节即需要向律师了解当地的法律环境，同时还需要律师为其提供投资决策的法律意见、参与谈判、审定合同、解决纠纷等。律师的服务伴随着国际经济活动的方方面面。随着各国经济联系的日益紧密，法律服务贸易的国际化、自由化范围将越来越广、程度将越来越深。

我们不难发现，经济全球化不仅加快了国际间经济贸易的活跃程度，也促进了国际法律服务需求的迅速提升，使得法律服务贸易正在全球范围内以较高的态势增长。同时，法律服务的开放和自由化程度也在不断加强，WTO 乌拉圭回合的谈判结果显示，有 45 个成员作出了法律服务自由化方面的承诺。中国在加入 WTO 的法律文件中对法律服务的开放承诺也比之前有了新的扩

---

* 杨国华，男，商务部条约法律司副司长，法学博士，西南政法大学兼职教授。

展，如承诺在加入WTO一年后取消对外国律师事务所在华设立代表处的地域和数量限制、扩大允许从事的业务范围等。此外，法律服务贸易国际法律制度正在逐渐形成与发展，WTO《服务贸易总协定》(GATS)中有关市场准入、非歧视待遇、透明度等基本原则为国际法律服务贸易自由化提供了国际法的依据；《美加自由贸易协定》、《北美自由贸易协定》等多双边协定也对法律服务贸易作出了规定。初具轮廓的法律服务贸易国际法律制度为法律服务贸易的国际化和自由化创造了更为宽广的发展空间。

但与此同时，和其他的服务部门相比，法律服务具有的鲜明特点。它具有属地性。当地律师无论是在对当地法律和社会环境的熟悉程度上，还是在与当事人的沟通能力上，均比外国律师有较大优势。同时，法律服务在一定程度上还具有政治性。刑事诉讼和行政代理等方面的法律活动，与国家地域、主权密切相关，承担着维护法律权威、促进司法公正的重要职责，属于上层建筑的范畴。因此，在开放法律服务问题上，各国采取了相对谨慎的态度，一般会在市场准入和国民待遇方面设置一定的限制，如执业资格、组织形式、业务范围等方面。

各国设置这些限制的目的或是为了保证法律服务执业素质、维护当事人权益和社会公共利益，或是为了维护本国司法管辖权的独立性，或是为了保护本国法律服务产业的健康发展，或是为了在与发达国家竞争中促进本国法律服务进出口贸易平衡。但是，也应该看到，过多过细的限制，在一定程度上将形成贸易壁垒，阻碍法律服务贸易自由化的发展，同时也会对经济全球化和本国经济繁荣造成不利影响。

经济全球化对法律服务提出的在形式、内容、规模等方面提出的新需求，只有在一个高水平、高层次的国际法律服务市场中才能够得以实现，并有赖于各国法律服务市场的开放程度及其法律服务提供者的水平。如果一国的法律服务市场开放程度过低，外国法律服务难以进入，会在很大程度上影响有此需求的国际经济活动的开展。所以说，法律服务贸易自由化既是经济全球化的必然产物，也是经济全球化进一步发展和本国经济繁荣的必备要件。

二、《服务贸易总协定》为实现法律服务贸易自由化奠定了规则层面的基础

众所周知，GATS是针对服务贸易全球化趋势制定的。为有效消除国际服务贸易壁垒，继续推动国际服务贸易自由化进程，GATS对各成员采取的

各项影响服务贸易的政策措施作出了规制，其中也为国际法律服务贸易设定了多边规则。

在GATS中，最惠国待遇原则、具体承诺、市场准入以及国民待遇对WTO成员的影响最为直接和深远：

最惠国待遇原则可消除成员对外国法律服务进入的歧视待遇，任何成员之间达成了服务自由化协议，其他成员都可适用。在这样的机制推动下，随着WTO成员之间法律服务贸易谈判的推荐，国际法律服务贸易自由化水平也会得到普遍提高。

具体承诺是GATS的核心部分，包含了各成员在服务贸易的市场准入、国民待遇等方面的具体权利义务。离开具体承诺，GATS的其他规则就是无本之木。在法律服务的具体承诺问题上，各成员都采取谨慎的态度，作出具体承诺的多是发达国家，不过没有提出承诺的成员并非完全不对外国律师开放本国法律服务市场，而是单方规定开放程度。

市场准入和国民待遇是各成员根据具体承诺承担的特定义务，而非普遍义务。各成员可根据自身情况，在具体承诺中给予其他成员特定的市场准入和国民待遇。这样可以使分歧较小的成员早日达成协议，也不会强迫发展中国家以他们难以接受的程度和方式开放服务市场。某一成员法律服务市场的开放程度，取决于其在具体承诺中关于市场准入和国民待遇的内容。

GATS所构建的法律服务贸易多边规则体系，对推进法律服务贸易自由化进程意义重大：

首先，GATS有助于法律服务贸易限制措施的削减。GATS提倡贸易自由化的主要重点就是削减和取消贸易限制措施，以提供更好的市场准入和国民待遇。同时，成员所作的多边承诺，使得相关政策变得明确和可预见，减少了其领土内不合理制度产生的可能性；

其次，GATS有助于形成法律服务贸易自由化的持续推动力。GATS要求各成员进行连续回合的谈判，一旦取得成果，就会形成作出承诺的成员的新义务。在这样的机制下，随着谈判的不断开展，法律服务贸易必然以渐进的方式迈向更高的自由化空间；

最后，GATS使发展中国家在法律服务自由化进程中获得更多的发展机会。GATS给予了发展中国家较大的灵活性和选择空间，并在市场准入、信息提供等方面规定了许多有利于发展中国家的条款。发展中国家可以充分地利用，在扩大开放的同时，将国内法律服务的水平逐渐向世界水平靠拢。

三、中国—东盟自贸区法律服务贸易发展的趋势

长期以来,为了互相减少贸易壁垒,建立一个稳定、透明、可预见的贸易制度环境,中国和东盟积极寻求实现区域经济一体化。《中国—东盟全面经济合作框架协议》以及《服务贸易协议》正是在此背景下签署的。《框架协议》的序言和对服务贸易谈判确定的目标与基本原则,说明了在中国—东盟自贸区实现服务贸易自由化,将在GATS规则的框架下进行。而《服务贸易协议》的内容,也正是基于GATS下的各项义务和承诺而制定的。

不仅如此,就《服务贸易协议》所覆盖的范围和所涉及的内容而言,更是对GATS的超越。东盟成员国都属于WTO成员。《服务贸易协议》受益主体的扩大是自贸区服务贸易自由化程度更高的体现。在具体承诺上,如新增了承诺开放的服务部门、对已承诺的服务部门放宽条件等,是自贸区服务贸易自由化推进的具体表现。

随着自贸区诸如金融、电信、旅游、海运等领域双边贸易和投资的快速增长,法律服务的需求也在日益增长。作为服务贸易自由化的组成部分,自贸区的法律服务贸易自由化也应当在GATS、《框架协议》和《服务贸易协议》确定的原则、目标和义务下进行推进。

与此同时,我们还需要认真分析自贸区法律服务贸易的特点,为下一步规划提供参考:

一方面,在中国—东盟自贸区内,虽不乏服务贸易自由化程度较高的成员国,但多数为逐步开放的发展中国家,总体上开放的服务贸易部门不多,普遍存在较多限制。而《服务贸易协议》并未涉及法律服务部门。因此,自贸区的法律服务贸易目前仍限于GATS的内容与承诺,且自由化程度不高。

另一方面,由于英、美等发达国家的法律服务相当成熟,其在国际金融、投资等诸多领域的竞争力非常强,这些国家的法律服务开放程度较高;而发展中国家法律服务相对竞争力较弱,因而开放程度较低,GATS还专门设置了发展中国家的优惠条款。但是,在自贸区内,由于成员国以发展中国家居多,不需要面对发达国家的竞争压力,法律服务贸易自由化的潜力反而比GATS下更大。

根据这些特点,结合前面所作的分析,本文认为自贸区法律服务贸易发展的趋势是:逐步加速的自由化进程。

首先,自由化是全球趋势。如前所述,法律服务贸易自由化是经济全球化

的必然结果,更是全球经济进一步发展、繁荣的必备要件。任何融入全球经济的国家,都无法回避。

其次,逐步自由化是GATS确定的原则。GATS序言中规定要在"透明和逐步自由化的条件下"扩大服务贸易。这一方面考虑到不同的服务贸易形态难以一时间达到全面开放的程度,另一方面也是给予发展中国家一定的灵活性,以促进他们服务贸易的发展。自由化进程取决于一国的国家政策目标和自身发展水平,以中国—东盟自贸区而言,多数成员国的法律服务行业尚未达到可以全面开放的程度,自由化必然是个渐进的过程。

最后,法律服务在自贸区范围内的自由化将是一个加速运动。WTO允许区域一体化安排作为最惠国原则的例外,自贸区外的WTO成员无法享受自贸区内的优惠安排。正是如此,我们自贸区的各成员国无需担心发达国家的竞争,为推进法律服务自由化减少了后顾之忧;同时,各成员国发展水平总体相当,相互之间有许多值得借鉴、交流的地方,在法律的观念、体系上也有不少共性,这都是法律服务自由化进一步推进的良好基础;此外,自贸区内的法律服务自由化,将有利于各成员国律师服务素质和服务理念的提高,从而促进国内法律服务业的发展。通过在自贸区范围内的不断积累经验,各成员国的法律服务业将得到区域化的成长,并最终得以走向国际,与发达国家的同行展开竞争。我们可以预见,在这样的有利条件下,随着各种限制的逐步削减,中国—东盟自贸区法律服务自由化的推进速度必然不断提升,各成员国的法律服务业以及区域经济一体化将因此获得更大的发展。

在经济全球化的大背景下,以GATS构建的法律服务贸易多边规则体系为依托,通过我们多方共同努力,因地制宜,中国—东盟自贸区的法律服务自由化必将富有特色、卓有成效地向前推进。

Liberalization of Legal Services of the CAFTA

Yang Guohua

The liberalization of legal services is an inevitable outcome of the economic globalization. *General Agreement on Trade in Services* (GATS) laid the basis for achieving the liberalization of trade in legal services. Looking at the China-ASEAN Free Trade Area, we have the reason to expect a higher openness level on trade in legal services.

1. The liberalization of trade in legal services is aninevitable outcome of the economic globalization

As a department of the trade in services, the globalization and liberalization of the legal services is certain. Trade in legal services is growing worldwide. In the meantime, the degree of openness and liberalization of legal services has also been strengthened. Therefore, the regime of the international law on trade in legal services is gradually formed and developed. Legal services have distinctive characteristics. For example, it has the feature of territoriality. To some extent, it also has political identity. Therefore, on the issue of opening up legal services, all the countries adopt a relatively cautious approach. However, we should also notice that, if there are so many limitations which might be caused form the trade barriers cumulating to a certain degree, as a result, it would hinder the development of the liberalization of the trade in legal services and would adversely affect the economic globalization and the country's economic prosperity as well. Hence, the liberalization of the trade in legal services is not only the inevitable outcome of economic globalization, but also the essential element of the further devel-

opment of the economic globalization and economic prosperity for all countries.

2. GATS lays the foundation for achieving the liberalization of trade in legal services

GATS is developed for the globalization of the trade in services. MFN principle, specific commitments, market access and national treatment have the most direct and far-reaching effect on WTO members. GATS builds a multilateral system of rules of trade in legal services which is of great significance for promoting the process of liberalization of trade in legal services:

(1)GATS contributes to the reduction of the restrictions on the trade in legal services;

(2)GATS contributes to the establishment of a sustained driving force for the liberalization of the trade in legal services;

(3)GATS provides more opportunities for the developing countries in the process of liberalization.

3. The developing trend of the legal services in FTA

To achieve the liberalization of trade in services of CAFTA, it should be carried out under the framework of the GATS. And the *Agreement on Trade in Services* is developed based on the obligations and commitments under the GATS. It also goes beyond the GATS according to its scope and contents.

At the same time, we also need a careful analysis on the characteristics of the trade in legal services in FTA. On the one hand, the trade in legal services is still restricted by the content and commitments of the GATS, and the degree of liberalization is relatively low. On the other hand, since the majority of Member States are developing countries and there is no risk for them to face the competitive pressures from the developed countries, there is a greater potential of development for the liberalization of trade in legal services in the FTA than that under GATS.

According to the analysis above, I think the developing trend for the trade in legal services in the FTA is a gradually accelerated liberalization process.

(1)Liberalization is a a global trend;

(2)Progressive liberalization is the principle settled by GATS;

(3)The liberalization will be an accelerated movement.

Member states do not have to worry about competition from the developed countries, should have greatly reduced the worries on promoting the liberalization of legal services. Besides, the member countries have a comparable level of economic development, they could learn from each other and boost cooperation and exchanges. Moreover, they have a lot of similarities in the legal concepts and legal systems. All the aspects stated above lays the good foundations for further advancing the liberalization of legal services. The accumulation of experience within the scope of the FTA, the legal services in the Member States would grow regionally which would finally go international and compete with the counterparts in developed countries.

Under the background of economic globalization, on the basis of the multilateral system of rules of trade in legal services built under GATS, the liberalization of legal services of the CAFTA will certainly move forward distinctively and effectively in the joint efforts of member states.

建立中国—东盟自由贸易区仲裁中心的设想

谷昭民*　施　文**

内容提要　中国—东盟自由贸易区(以下简称 CAFTA)的建成与发展，催生着大量商事仲裁的迫切需求。现行的 CAFTA 争端解决机制无法满足市场多元主体的法律需求。据此，本文倡议建立 CAFTA 仲裁中心并对其设立的必要性、可行性、职能作用及组织机构做了具体阐述。旨在建立一个覆盖中国—东盟 11 个成员国的争端解决平台，弥补现行机制的缺憾，以适应 CAFTA 形势发展的紧迫需要。建议将 CAFTA 仲裁中心设驻在中国(海南)并详述了其主要理由。

2010 年 1 月 1 日，中国—东盟自由贸易区(CAFTA)如期建成。此前一日，中国颁布了《国务院关于推进海南国际旅游岛建设发展的若干意见》，建设海南国际旅游岛正式提升为国家战略。在此背景下，我们提出在中国(海南)建立 CAFTA 仲裁中心的设想。

一、建立 CAFTA 仲裁中心的必要性和可行性

1. 建立 CAFTA 仲裁中心是形势发展的必然选择

随着 CAFTA 的建成，中国与东南亚地区已形成一个由 11 个国家参与、拥有 19 亿消费者、6 万亿美元国内生产总值、4.5 万亿美元的贸易总量的自由

---

* 谷昭民，男，公共管理学硕士，美国 HOFSTRA 大学访问学者。历任中华全国青年联合会国际部部长、副秘书长。现任中国法学会对外联络部部长、中国法学会学术交流中心主任。

** 施文，男，民商法学硕士。海南省法学会常务副会长，海口仲裁委员会主任。兼任中国法学会理事，中国—东盟法律研究中心理事，海南大学教授。

贸易区。它是世界上人口最多且由发展中国家组成的最大的自由贸易区,覆盖接近全球30%的人口,拥有世界40%的外汇储备,国内生产总值和对外商品贸易额分别占世界总额的10%左右。CAFTA庞大的经济规模、迅猛的发展势头、频繁的合作往来必然会产生各类摩擦与争端,诸如国际贸易纠纷、国际投资纠纷、国际劳资纠纷、国际知识产权纠纷、环境保护纠纷、垄断及不正当竞争纠纷等。这些纠纷的救济渠道,除了事前的预防、事中的协调等自我救济之外,相当数量的纠纷需要通过仲裁途径予以解决。

实践表明,面对跨国的或异国的商事争端,大多数当事人在主权色彩浓厚、程序繁多的司法程序和相对中立、便利快捷的仲裁程序面前,都会理智地选择仲裁。目前最大问题就是在CAFTA体系内没有一个相对统一的常设仲裁机构,故而,大量的商事争端,不得不在CAFTA体系之外寻求各类分散的诉讼或仲裁途径加以解决。因此建立一个CAFTA常设仲裁机构不仅符合整个亚洲经济发展的大方向,亦符合世界均衡发展的总体趋势。纵观近现代世界历史,时至今日,全世界大多数的仲裁都在西半球进行。东方各国的当事人要么远渡重洋赶赴仲裁,要么需支付昂贵的费用让西方的仲裁员来到东方国家进行仲裁,这似乎已成为定势和惯性思维。国际仲裁客观上为西方所把控,这与当今世界经济的发展格局极不相称,东方国家有理由也有能力构建起属于东方的法律平台,作自己的主人。我们之所以倡议在中国设立这样一个常设仲裁机构,并非仅仅从中国的自身利益考量,同时也是站在东南亚各国的根本利益上思考和谋划。CAFTA仲裁中心的建立不仅会从法制的层面对CAFTA的健康发展起到不可替代的强大推动作用,而且也为中国—东盟各国化解和解决各类贸易纠纷提供极大的便利条件,同时亦可节约巨大的法律成本,更重要的是有利于强劲推进中国—东盟各国司法制度、司法体系的融合与发展,意义重大而又深远。

2. 建立CAFTA仲裁中心符合CAFTA框架协议的基本要义,也符合《承认及执行外国仲裁裁决公约》(以下简称《纽约公约》)的精神实质

争端解决机制是任何一个多边经济合作组织得以组成和顺利运作的法律保障,其重要性毋庸置疑。CAFTA自成立之初,各成员国对此都高度重视,进行了长时间的谈判,最后签署了《中国—东盟全面经济合作框架协议争端解决机制协议》(以下简称《争端解决协议》),于2005年7月20日开始实施,为CAFTA争端解决提供了具体的法律框架,它与《框架协议》及之下的其他协议,实质上是程序和实体的关系,共同构成CAFTA的法律基础。

2007年7月1日,《中国—东盟全面经济合作框架协议》之下的《服务贸

易协议》正式实施，该协议对各国法律服务作出具体承诺。CAFTA 的服务贸易协议沿用世界贸易组织（WTO）的《服务贸易总协定》（GATS）的规则，在 WTO 的 GATS 规则体系中，服务部门分类与联合国总产品分类（CPC）相符，法律服务列在第一大类商业服务的专业服务子类之下，仲裁和调解服务是其中的重要内容。中国—东盟自由贸易区是区域经济一体化组织，促进各成员国的法律服务市场开发和法律服务贸易自由化，是 CAFTA 追求的重要目标之一。促进各成员国的法律服务自由竞争，提升法律服务产品质量，完善法律服务体系，是自由贸易区建设和发展的内在要求。根据《争端解决协议》第 4 条到第 13 条的规定，争端解决的方式和程序包括：磋商、调解或调停、仲裁、执行、补偿和中止减让或利益。与 WTO 争端解决机制不同，磋商与调解并非《争端解决协议》的必经程序，采用准司法性的仲裁是解决争端的核心。在上述诸种争端解决方式中，仲裁程序最为体系化、制度化，这也是在贸易和投领域中被各国和各国际性经济组织所普遍采用的模式，具有专业、高效、自主性强的特点。

CAFTA 11 个成员国中有 10 个国家是《纽约公约》的成员国，构成了 CAFTA 仲裁中心设立的国际公法基础。

3. 现行的 CAFTA 争端解决机制需要创新和完善

相对于欧洲共同体的一体化机制和北美自由贸易区的紧密型合作，CAFTA 是一种较松散的区域性经济合作模式，由于历史和现实的原因，各国对程序规则的价值有不同的认识和要求，这一争端解决机制是在充分尊重各国主权和司法独立的基础上经过长时间谈判协调、各方力量妥协的结果。其局限性在所难免。

（1）主体的局限性。《争端解决协议》规定，缔约方有权运用 CAFTA 争端解决机制，即只有各成员国的政府才能作为争端解决机制的主体提起申诉，排除了公司、企业和个人以个体名义提起争端解决程序。这种将主体仅限于国家的立法，虽然秉承了国际法的传统观点，但偏于保守，忽视了一个现实和长远的重大问题，即直接参与并承载了大量区内贸易及投资活动的自然人和法人却被排除在争端解决机制的适格主体之外。东道国与其他成员国的公司、企业或个人发生的争端，虽然带有整体性与普遍性，但更多地表现为个性即私方利益，在贸易与投资争端发生时，私方利益可能会被东道国的违法政策损害，但其所属国政府往往基于政治风险的顾虑而不把争端诉诸于争端解决机构（DSB），最终导致私方投资者的利益遭受实质性的重大损害。事实上，公司、企业或个人之间的争端大多数并非是国家层面的。更多地表现为局部的、个体相互之间的贸易摩擦、冲突等。如果将主体仅限于国家,那么实际存在的绝大多数的商事纠纷就无法得到有效的管辖。这不能不说是CAFTA争端解决机制的一个重大缺陷。

(2)缺少一个主持磋商、调解或调停的中立机构。《争端解决协议》规定,在磋商、调解与调停阶段,由争端双方自我进行。由于缺少一个中立机构来主持,双方的磋商、调解或调停很容易走进死胡同,无法发挥争端解决机制的作用,使其流于形式。

(3)没有常设的管理机构且仲裁庭组成不稳定、非专业性。《争端解决协议》没有规定设立一个常设的仲裁管理机构负责日常的仲裁管理工作,只要申请方提出书面申请即自动成立仲裁庭。仲裁庭的组成凸显临时性,仲裁员由争端双方各推荐1名,仲裁主席则由争端双方达成一致共同选定,如不能达成一致意见则由WTO总干事或国际法院院长指定,虽然体现出选任仲裁员的灵活性,但是仲裁庭的组成缺少稳定性,不利于裁决的连贯性与统一性。

(4)仲裁裁决复核程序的缺失。CAFTA《争端解决协议》没有规定仲裁的复核程序,这就使得一些重大的商事争端在一裁终局机制下加大了风险,如果因仲裁庭组成的不当或明显超越权限,或者裁决赖以成立的理由不清等而使裁决不公正时,受损害方很难采取相应救济措施。

(5)执行程序的欠缺。“民事判决执行难”是中国司法领域长期存在的一个棘手的问题,同样,以国际仲裁方式解决争端,执行也是一个难题。CAFTA争端解决机制中对仲裁庭裁决执行程序的设计,虽然使争端解决机制具有了一定的效力,但其执行方式带有较强的自助性质,缺乏应有的刚性。

综上所述,建立一个CAFTA常设仲裁机构的时机已经成熟,这一问题的研究是目前CAFTA法律领域最具有实质性意义的重大课题之一。

二、CAFTA仲裁中心的职能与组织机构

(一)职能

1. 仲裁中心可以在案件受理后以中立机构的身份主持磋商和调解,化解大量争端。因为CAFTA争端解决机制管辖范围下的纠纷,基本上都与贸易和投资相关,本质上属于私方利益,首推当事人之间的和解。《争端解决协议》中规定的多种解决争端的方法如磋商、调解、调停和仲裁。其追求的核心价值理念是促使争端方和解。西方法律界有一句名言“再胖的诉讼不如瘦的和

解”，仲裁、司法的最高境界并不仅仅是为了分辨是非、追求所谓的“终极真理”，而是化解矛盾、“定分止争”。我们通常所讲的“以事实为依据，以法律为准绳”固然不错，但从私方权益和经济、社会效益的角度来考量，应该加上“以化解为目的”才更加完善。这与当下国际民商法律界通行的“和解”理念完全一致。

2. 仲裁中心可以行使普通商事仲裁的职能，突破现行机制的瓶颈，满足不同主体的需求。CAFTA《争端解决协议》中规定，成员国政府作为主体提起的仲裁亦称为临时仲裁，其本意在于解决成员国之间涉及政策和法律层面的普遍性问题，追求贸易上的平衡性。实际上，自 CAFTA 成立以来，此类问题绝大多数是通过外交途径加以解决的。真正通过临时仲裁解决的案例极为罕见。如果能够创新普通仲裁机制，无疑是一个巨大的突破，对于 CAFTA《争端解决协议》的改革具有里程碑式的重大意义。

3. 仲裁中心可以担负起相对的管理职能。中心负责遴选和管理仲裁员，对仲裁员的资格制定严格的标准，确保其专业性和公正性，同时兼顾各成员国的名额分配。可以考虑按照各成员国的贸易额、投资额比例等确定该国仲裁员的名额，由各成员国向中心推荐，任期四年，期满后再重新确定；中心负责编制和管理仲裁员及专家名册，推荐仲裁员。这种安排既可保持 CAFTA 仲裁程序所要求的灵活性，又兼顾稳定性和专业性，逐步形成一支专业、稳定、高效的仲裁队伍。

4. 仲裁中心可以行使相应的监督职能。对仲裁庭提出相关建议或对裁决的执行“跟随监督”，以弥补监督和执行程序的欠缺。在获得授权或根据复核程序规则行使仲裁裁决复核的职能。

（二）CAFTA 仲裁中心的组织机构

仲裁中心设立理事会，由各成员国推荐常务理事和理事各一名，每届任期四年；再从常务理事中推选一名轮值主席，任期一年；由理事会推荐一名秘书长，全权负责中心的日常管理事务，每届任期四年，可以连任，但不超过两届。秘书长可由理事兼任，也可由理事会聘请专家担任。凡涉及“中心”章程、仲裁规则等重大事项均由理事会集体讨论决定，采取少数服从多数的原则。“中心”下设秘书处、仲裁调解中心、仲裁庭、专家处等职能部门。在秘书长的统一领导和秘书处的统一协调下，按照各自的分工、互相配合、各司其职。具体组织形式为：

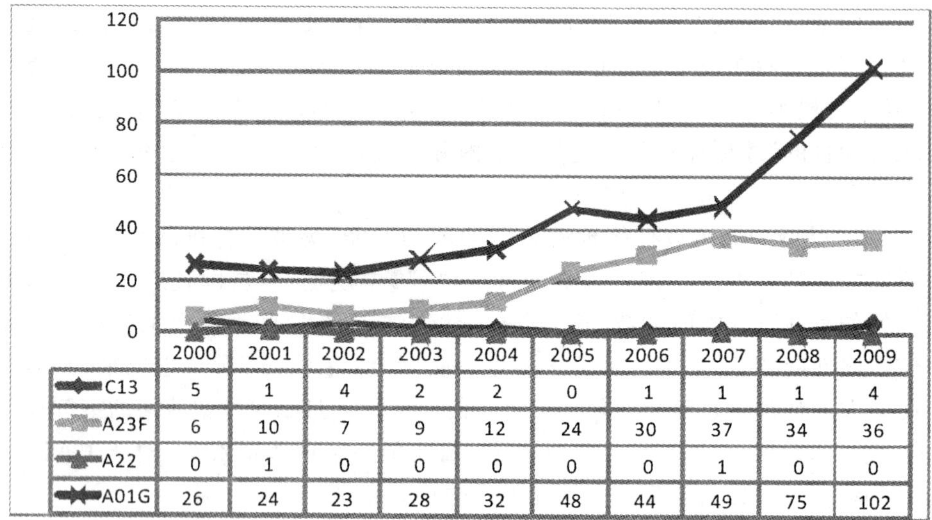

	2000	2001	2002	2003	2004	2005	2006	2007	2008	2009
C13	5	1	4	2	2	0	1	1	1	4
A23F	6	10	7	9	12	24	30	37	34	36
A22	0	1	0	0	0	0	0	1	0	0
A01G	26	24	23	28	32	48	44	49	75	102

三、CAFTA 仲裁中心设驻在中国(海南)的可行性

CAFTA 仲裁中心是 CAFTA 框架内的一个独立的国际性机构,可以设驻在 11 个成员国中的任何一国,综合考虑各成员国的政治、经济、文化等状况,我们认为设驻在中国的有利因素更多,其理由如下:

1. 中国拥有深厚的仲裁资源,多年来积累了丰富的涉外仲裁经验。早在上世纪 50 年代,中国就成立了中国国际贸易仲裁委员会,它是当时中国唯一受理涉外商事争议的仲裁机构。经过 50 年努力现已成为世界重要的国际商事仲裁机构之一,自 1990 年以来受案量一直居于世界其他仲裁机构的前列。1995 年 9 月《中华人民共和国仲裁法》正式施行,1996 年国务院下发文件允许新组建的仲裁委员会受理涉外案件。十年来,中国仲裁事业得以迅猛发展,涉外仲裁案件也逐年增加。目前,中国共有 209 个仲裁机构遍布全国各省、市和自治区,2010 年共受理案件 78923 件,受案标的总额 932 亿元人民币。其中涉港澳台案件和其他涉外案件总额为 1219 件,占受理案件总数的 1.6%。在受理的 78923 件中被法院撤销仲裁裁决和不予执行仲裁裁决的比率均为 0.1%,仲裁质量处于较高水平。2011 年 7 月在中国贵阳市召开了全国仲裁工作年会,主题就是涉外仲裁工作,有 12 家仲裁机构在会上做了主题发言,标志着中国的涉外仲裁工作开始进入了一个良好的发展时期。

2. 中国的经济总量于 2010 年已经跃居世界第二位,GDP 大于东盟 10 国的总和。2010 年,中国和东盟之间的贸易额达到了 2928 亿美元,同比增长

37.5%,中国已成为东盟的第一贸易伙伴和第一大出口目的地,东盟则是中国的第四大贸易伙伴和出口目的地;东盟对华直接投资为63.2亿美元,同比增长35.2%,中国对东盟直接投资25.7亿美元,累计双方之间的投资额已达到108亿美元;中国在东盟的投资企业数量也明显超过东盟各成员国在中国的投资企业数量。因此,作为这一组织之下的仲裁中心,设驻在中国更符合客观实际,也更能够发挥其应有的作用。

3. 海南是中国最大的经济特区,长期以来处于改革开放的最前沿,拥有最开放的政策环境。2009年底开始实施国际旅游岛建设战略,进一步提升了海南改革、开放的形象。这一战略的实施与CAFTA的建成是同步推进的。海南建设国际旅游岛战略的具体目标之一,就是在CAFTA中发挥纽带和桥头堡作用。博鳌亚洲论坛、金砖五国会晤等重大国事活动举办,极大地提高了海南在东南亚地区的知名度。

4. 国家赋予海南享有口岸签证、免签证等最便利、最开放的出入境优惠政策。1988年海南建省伊始,国务院就给予了口岸签证的优惠政策(落地签证),凡是与中国建交国家的人员,均可在海南省办理口岸签证。2010年8月12日,国家进一步批准海南实施26国免签证政策,其中新加坡、文莱、马来西亚、印尼、菲律宾、泰国等6国享有26国团队(2人以上)免签,停留期限为15天;此外,新加坡和文莱还享有个人免签。目前,海南省正在争取国家批准"外国旅游团琼港澳三地自由行"的最新政策。海南的出入境优惠政策对于国际机构开展工作、人员往来具有至关重要的意义。

5. 地缘与交通优势。东南亚国家与中国作有着深厚的历史、文化、经济渊源,近百年来中国移居东南亚各国的华人总数已达1500余万人,其中海南籍的就有300多万人,他们为东南亚地区的开发建设做出了巨大的贡献。海南省处在中国—东南亚的中心位置,是中国离东南亚最近的地方,自然环境与东南亚相似。海南位于南海运输大通道的前端,海口、洋浦、八所、三亚等港口,泊位条件可以承担较大规模的国际航运;海南拥有本土的知名航空企业,美兰机场和凤凰机场都是按照国际标准设计,已开通海口至新加坡、曼谷等航线,海口直飞香港、广州的时间均为50分钟,且每天都有多个航班,中转十分便利。

结　语

CAFTA仲裁中心设想的实现,会是一个相当复杂的过程,将面临诸多

的难题,甚而遭遇阻力,耗费时日。然而,在中国与东南亚各国政府的支持下,在各方面人士的积极努力下,这一目标一定能够实现,"千里之行,始于足下"。若干年后,当回顾这段难忘的历史的时候,我们一定会为之骄傲和自豪。

Proposal on the Establishment of the CAFTA Arbitration Center

Gu Zhaomin Shi Wen

The establishment completion and the development of the China-ASEAN Free Trade Area (CAFTA) boosts a large number of commercial arbitration. Current CAFTA dispute settlement mechanism can't meet the legal needs of plural subjects in the market. Accordingly, this article advocates the establishment of CAFTA arbitration center, and specifically demonstrates its necessity, feasibility, functional role and organization. The aim is to establish a solution platform, which can include coverage China and ASEAN member states, thus making up for the shortcomings of the existing mechanism, and finally adapting to the CAFTA development of the situation urgent need. This article suggests that CAFTA arbitration center should be located in China (Hainan) and gives its main reasons.

When face transnational or exotic Commercial Disputes, most of parties would like to rationally choose relatively neutral , fast and convenient arbitration comparing with the judicial proceedings. Now, the biggest problem is the CAFTA system does not have a relatively uniform and permanent arbitration institution. Hence, most of commercial disputes have to solve by other ways. Establishing a permanent arbitration is not only in accordance with the general direction of the whole economic development in Asia, and also conforms to the overall trend of the world balanced development. The establishment of the arbitration not only play powerful role in promoting an irreplaceable to the healthy development of the CAFTA, but also provides great convenience for the China-ASEAN member countries to defuse and solve all kinds of trade disputes. At the same time, it can also save huge legal costs. Above of all, it can do a favor to promote the integration and development between judicial mechanism, judicial system of China and ASEAN member states, which has significant and far-reaching implications.

The basic meaning of establishing the CAFTA arbitration center in line with the CAFTA framework agreement, and conform to the Convention on the Recognition and enforcement of Foreign Arbitral Awards.

The functions and organization of CAFTA arbitration center.

1. Functions

1)Arbitration center can preside the negotiations and mediation over the identity of a neutral body after case be accepted.

2)Arbitration center can exercise the functions of ordinary commercial arbitration, to break through the bottleneck of the existing mechanisms to meet different needs.

3)Arbitration Centre can perform relative management functions

4)Arbitration Centre can exercise appropriate oversight functions.

2. Organizations of CAFTA arbitration center

The feasibility of CAFTA arbitration center located in China (Hainan)

CAFTA Arbitration Centre is an independent international institution within the CAFTA framework, which can locate in any country of 11 member states. Nevertheless, considering the political, economic, cultural and other conditions of the Member States, there are more favorable factors if the Center locates in China. The reasons is as follows:

1)China has abundant arbitration resources, over the years, has accumulated a wealth of experience in foreign arbitration.

2)China's total economic output in 2010 has been the second largest in the world, GDP is greater than the sum of the other 10 ASEAN countries.

3)Hainan is one of China's largest special economic zone, has long been at the forefront of reform and opening up, has the most privileged open policies.

4)Given by the State Hainan enjoys the most convenient access to Port visa , visa-free, which is the most preferential open-up policies and incentives.

5)Geographical and transportation advantages.

Summary

It is a fairly complex process to make the establishment of CAFTA arbitration center, and will have to face plenty difficulties. Nevertheless, we convince always that with the positive efforts of various sectors and in support of the Governments of China and Southeast Asia countries, this goal will certainly be able to achieve.

中国—东盟自由贸易区法律服务贸易的逐步自由化:越南视角

Nguyen Thanh Tu [*]　林建荣　孙超译

1. 中国—东盟自由贸易区法律服务贸易自由化概述

在贸易全球化和区域化的进程中,法律服务发挥重要甚至是首要的作用,它支持和促进了越来越多的跨境商业交易和投资。在一个法律真空环境中,这样的交易是不可能进行的。某些司法辖区的法律服务的一致性方面仍有很高的要求。这要求全球的律师事务所国际化和区域化。因此,法律服务贸易的自由化是贸易自由化必不可少的一部分,特别是在服务业中。这导致了这样一个事实,即律师和政府贸易谈判代表想把法律服务纳入贸易协议,包括世贸组织《服务贸易总协定》。然而,值得注意的是,提供法律服务取决于法律制度、法律资格、法律文化和法律用语。

根据2007年实行的《东盟宪章》和《东盟经济共同体蓝图》的规定,东南亚国家联盟(东盟)一直在努力创建一个商品、服务、投资、专业人员和资本的自由流动的统一市场。关于服务的自由流通,《东盟经济共同体蓝图》认定:"服务贸易的自由流通是实现东盟经济共同体的重要内容。这个共同体中,没有对于东盟服务服务提供者提供的服务和在受国内法规管制的区域内建立跨国公司的实质性限制";在促进服务的自动流通方面,包括法律服务,到2015年,据述:"为了促进区域内服务的自动流通,东盟还将努力向专业职称的认可方面迈进。"

根据承诺,在东盟框架协议下服务协定(AFAS),包括柬埔寨、印度尼西

* Doctor of Laws; Deputy Director General, Department of International Law, Ministry of Justice of Vietnam (tunt@moj. gov. vn).

亚、泰国、马来西亚、越南的五个东盟成员国，从 2006 年第五个整体计划以来，就已经在法律服务方面做出承诺。考虑到这一切，2008 年，文莱达鲁萨兰国提出了一个题为《东盟自由贸易区渐进法律服务贸易自由化》的提案，旨在引出理念和作为正式讨论东盟自由化的起点。在 2011 年 4 月 13 日至 14 日文莱达鲁萨兰国主办的第六届东盟法律论坛上，代表们和利益相关者第一次有机会仔细商讨这个问题。然而，到 2015 年之前要想真正实现法律服务自由化，需要更多的努力和共识。

另外，东盟已经制定了自由贸易协议关于与其他合作伙伴，包括中国的服务贸易的规章或协议。2002 年 11 月 4 日，东盟成员国和中国签署了全面经济合作框架协议。根据该协议，"缔约国同意迅速谈判，以在 10 年内建立中国—东盟自由贸易区"。

此协议的目标之一是"逐步解放和促进贸易和服务，并创造透明、自由、便利的投资环境"，为了"逐步实现涵盖众多部门的服务贸易自由化"，东盟国家与中国于 2007 年 1 月 14 日就服务贸易签订了一项协议，该协议旨在"超越由东盟成员国和中国在世界贸易组织（WTO）中采用的《服务贸易总协定》。缔约方的具体减让承诺表（第一个协定）作为附件附于 2007 年《服务贸易协议》，只有越南和柬埔寨的法律服务部门推出了承诺表（CPC 861），此承诺与两国在世界贸易组织的承诺相似。然而，十个东盟国家中（老挝除外）的九个成员国和中国是 WTO 成员国。中国—东盟自贸区在法律援助方面的贸易自由应《服务贸易总协定》的协议以及各成员在该领域的具体承诺相符合。例如，中国在加入 WTO 时，承诺开放对外国法律事务所开放服务市场。因此，外国律师事务可在中国以办事处的形式提供法律服务，该办事处可以从事营利性活动。此类办事处不能适用中国法律。但是，他们可以提供与中国法律环境相关的信息。

值得注意的是，在某种程度上，法律服务部门被看作是在服务领域对贸易自由化相当敏感的部门。在任何情况下，开放的法律服务涉及的东道国的市场准入和国民待遇的限制主要有：(1)东道国国家的法律（咨询/代理）；(2)东道国国家法律和/或第三国法律（咨询/代理）；(3)国际法律（咨询/代理）；(4)其他法律文件、认证、咨询和信息服务。目前，这种自由化取决于国家在国际贸易协定下达成的承诺以及特定国家的法律和法规。因此，本文将介绍越南的相关法律、法规和案例研究。然后，本文将继续介绍在中国—东盟自贸区就贸易自由化的一些法律服务方面的初步意见，并以此作为本文的结尾。

2. 越南法律服务贸易的管理

2.1. 越南的国际化承诺

越南在法律服务行业中的第一项国际承诺是在WTO的框架下做出的，该承诺列在具体承诺减让表服务部分中的第二部分第一条A款a项下。该具体承诺减让表由越南申请加入世界贸易组织的工作小组起草。这些承诺在《东盟服务贸易框架》中并未做任何修改，这在2006年的第5个一揽子计划到2010年中的第8个一揽子计划，以及在附属于东盟的具体承诺减让表和与中国在2007年有关服务行业贸易协议中均可以体现。这些承诺具体由2006年《越南律师法》规制，并在越南申请加入世贸组织的国会上的第71号2006/QH11文件上确认。

越南的这些国际承诺包含法律服务(CPC681)但不包括：(1)辩护人或者代表人以委托人的名义参与越南法庭的诉讼程序，和(2)越南法律的法律文件和认证服务。因此，对于模式一和模式二所提供的服务(跨境供应和境外消费)，外国律师事务所有权依据外国的法律提供咨询服务，包括国内法律和/或第三国法律以及国际法律。

就模式三(商业存在)而言，外国律师组织，即以任何商业企业形式(外国律师事务所)在国外建立的执业律师组织，可以在越南建立四种商业存在形式。它们是:(1)外国律师组织分支机构;(2)外国律师组织子公司;(3)一个或多个外国律师组织在越南建立的培养律师的组织;(4)同越南之间的法律伙伴关系而建立的执业律师组织。

正是由于服务贸易的存在，外国律师机构才有了在各法律领域提供咨询服务的权利。然而，只有持有越南法学院或同等机构颁发的学位证明并满足越南国家立法中对于法律职业人员所规定的标准时，他们才可以根据越南法律提供咨询服务。

至于模式四自然人存在的情况中，除在其他相关的部分已有所指的情况(例如涉及“公司内部转让”中受雇于国外律所的律师享有“专家”的资格，)是不受限制的。因而，应该允许他们享有长达三年的准入权，且三年的期限可以根据这些越南公司的经营期而延长。

如上所述，越南在法律服务部分的国际化承诺已被详细地规定下来已，且在2006年律师法中得到更有力的支持。此外，法律服务贸易自由化与法律

从业者的专业资格有关。为了理解法律服务的管理及其贸易自由化，有必要了解基于这样国际化承诺的国家相关规定。

2.2. 2006年的律师法的有关规定与国际化承诺的对比

2.2.1.越南法律实践的规定

2006年的律师法对于本国和外国律师做了两种不同规定。

2.2.1.1.对越南律师

关于律师的资格，越南公民要想成为一个越南律师，必须忠于祖国，遵守宪法和法律，具有良好的道德品质，具有法律本科文凭，并接受法律专业培训，法律执业的试用期届满，具有良好的身体条件(第10条)。一个人要想在越南进行法律执业，应当既满足律师的所有要求，获得司法部授予的法律执业证书，并加入一个省级律师协会(第11条)。

就法律执业的形式而言，一个越南律师可以：(1)通过建立，或者参与建立一个法律执业组织，或雇佣合同为一个法律执业组织工作，或(2)他/她可以以自己的能力独立进行法律执业(第23条)。一个越南律师的法律执业组织可以采取如下形式：(1)以私人企业形式运营的由律师建立的律师办公室；(2)律师事务所，包括至少两名律师和没有资本贡献的成员成立的法律合伙企业；或(3)有限责任律师事务所，包括一个两个或多个成员的有限责任法律事务所和一个独资有限责任律师事务所(第32条至第34条)。

对于法律执业范围，越南律师可以：(1)参与所有诉讼程序，(2)提供法律建议，(3)作为非诉讼业务代表客户执行相关法律工作，和(4)提供其他法律服务(第22条)。

2.2.1.2.对于外国律师和在越南有设立代表处的外国律师组织。

外国律师在越南专业执业的条件是：(1)拥有一个外国机构或者组织颁发的有效的法律执业证书；(2)尊重越南的宪法和法律；(3)被外国律师组织分配到越南执业或已经与外国律师组织或其分支机构达成协议或越南法律执业组织在该外国组织里执业(第74条)。

对于外国律师执业范围，外国律师在越南执业可以提供：外国和国际法律的相关咨询；其他有关外国法的法律服务；如果他/她取得越南的法学学士学位或者满足越南律师的所有要求，可以提供越南法律的咨询。然而，在其组织参与越南的诉讼之前，他/她不能参加诉讼程序(第76条)。

对于在外国建立的外国律师事务所专业实习的条件(外国律师组织)，在外国设立并依法执业的外国律师事务所必须尊重越南的宪法和法律(第

68 条)。

外国法律执业组织在越南执业的有三种形式,即:(1)在越南的外国律师事务所的分支机构;(2) 在越南有 100%的外国资本的有限责任法律公司;(3)合资有限责任律师事务所。

就外国法律组织专业实践范围而言,外国法律公司或者它在越南的分支机构可以提供法律咨询与法律服务,但不能派遣外国律师以抗辩顾问、客户代表、代表一方抗辩的身份参与越南诉讼程序,可以派遣根据越南法律提供咨询的越南律师就外国律所或其分支机构提供过法律咨询服务的案子以抗辩顾问、客户代表、代表一方抗辩的身份参与越南诉讼程序(刑事案件除外,第 70 条)。

2.3. 与越南的承诺对比

一般来说,2006 年的越南的《律师法》对于律师的具体资格要求、形式和法律执业范围、在越南的外国律师机构和外国律师的权利与义务的规定与其对世贸组织、东盟和中国—东盟自由贸易区法律服务部门的承诺似乎是一致的。对于在越南有商业存在的外国法律执业机构的专业执业范围,因为这样的机构可以指派在本机构执业的越南律师参加诉讼,在该机构能为案件提供法律咨询的情况下,作为客户的代理人或作为辩护人,为当事人的合法权益辩护。刑事案件除外。这一规定比越南的承诺更有利和更加自由。然而,与国际承诺相比,2006 年的《律师法》仍有一些顾虑,如外国法律执业机构开展法律业务的形式以及获准加入当地律师协会的国籍要求。

在任何情况下,越南在经过大约五年的实践后,法律服务贸易自由化的进程已经带来了一些益处和机会,阐述如下:

减少外国律所事务所在越南执业的市场准入限制,满足国际经济一体化的高要求;

为越南律师参与国际争端带来机会,这也可以帮助那些律师来提高他们的知识和经验;

促进外国律师事务所律师在越南执业,以便使用和学习它们的知识、经验和人脉。

2.4. 越南的法律服务实践

经过 25 年的“革新开放”(改革进程),越南在经济增长、司法和行政改革等领域获得了巨大成就,法律系统得到改进,并进一步走向国际一体化。在这

种背景下，法律服务和法律行业一直受到鼓励和促进。越南律师的数量和质量一直在增加。2009 年 5 月，成立了越南律师联合会，代表所有的律师和省级律师协会。除了越南律师联合会，63 个省中有 62 个省级律师协会。在 2750 个律师执业机构中，大约有 6250 名律师和 3000 名遗嘱认证的律师。从 2005 年到 2010 年，相关的法律诉讼中，越南律师参与 85000 个刑事案件；53000 个民事案件；3500 个经济案件；1500 个劳动案件；2800 个行政案件。此外，越南律师参加了 145000 多起年法律咨询案件和 50000 件与法律服务相关的其他案件。在此过程中，越南的律师和法律执业机构已经提高了他们的服务质量。它们在某种程度上可以与在越南的外国律师事务所竞争。

外国律师组织在越南有商业存在，这些组织自 1996 年以来就获准在越南执业。直到现在，越南已经有 201 名外国律师和 53 个外国律师的组织。在越南提供法律服务的 53 个外国律师组织中，20 个组织已经建立了 30 个分支机构，其余 33 个已经建立了外国律师事务所（包括 2 个合资律师事务所）。至于在越南执业的东盟外国律师组织，有 3 个外国律师组织（建立 2 个分公司和 2 个外国律师事务所）来自泰国；7 个外国律师组织（建立 6 个分支机构和 4 个外国律师事务所）来自新加坡，1 个外国律师组织（建立一个新加坡和越南合资律师事务所）。

所有在越南的外国律师组织的活动都对创造一个更有利的法律环境做出了贡献——鼓励外国投资，促进商业活动和发展法律服务市场。许多在越南的外国律师组织已经招募了越南的律师，训练他们使其达到国际标准。此外，这些外国律师组织和律师与越南组织和机构合作，给越南律师提供培训、组织有关法律服务方面的研讨会，评论法律规范性文件草案等。他们也参与了起草越南法律和有关国际经济一体化的政策。因此，2011 年 7 月首相批准的“2020 年律师培养协议”决定了需要改进和开放法律服务市场，以及增加与外国律师事务所的合作，尤其是在贸易和商业领域的法律方面的合作。这是为了更好地为越南的综合性国际经济一体化服务。

2.5. 结语

法律服务自由化既是一个国家满足国际承诺的要求，也可以创造一个有竞争力的法律服务市场。令人振奋的是，在中国—东盟自由贸易区和世界贸易组织的背景下，有 5 个东盟成员国和中国已经在法律服务自由化方面做出了一定标准的承诺（新加坡在不久的将来也将加入）。然而，这样的自由化因国家而异——不同法律制度、法律资格、法律文化和语言会有不同程度的自由

化。在中国—东盟自由贸易区真正实现自由化的法律服务还有诸多阻碍,需要加以改进。

在任何情况下,中国—东盟自由贸易区的国家在法律服务方面当前的承诺都是它们开放自身法律服务部门的良好开端,同时也为其他国家树立榜样。为了促进该区域渐进的法律服务自由化,法律服务自由化的标准也应该区域化,并加强法律教育的合作。东盟和中国的律师协会应该向认可东盟的律师资格方向迈进,以及尝试建立一个强大的中国自贸区争端解决机制来发展该地区的法律服务市场。这可能是一个听起来遥不可及的梦想,但没有人可以阻止我们去实现它。

Progressive Liberalisation of Trade in Legal Services in ASEAN-China FTA: Vietnam's Perspective*

Nguyen Thanh Tu**

1. Overview of Liberalisation of Trade in Legal Services in ASEAN-China FTA

In the process of either globalisation or regionalisation of trade, legal services play an important and even pioneering role in supporting and facilitating the increasing number of cross-border commercial transactions and investments. It is impossible to conduct such transactions in a legal vacuum. There remains high demand of a consistent level of legal services across several jurisdictions. This requires law firms in the world to internationalise and regionalise. As a result, the liberalisation of trade in legal services is inevitable part of the liberalisation of trade in general and that in services in particular. ③ This leads to a fact that lawyers and governmental trade negotiators have wanted to incorporate legal services into trade agreements, including the WTO General Agreement on Trade in Services (GATS) of the World

---

* This is a draft paper. It has been prepared strictly in the author's personal capacity. The views expressed herein should not be attributed to the Ministry of Justice of Vietnam or its Department of International Law.

** Nguyen Thanh Tu: Doctor of Laws; Deputy Director General, Department of International Law, Ministry of Justice of Vietnam.

③ Negotiating Proposal for Legal Services, Communication from Australia in the Special Session of the WTO Council for Trade in services, S/CSS/W/67, 27 March 2001.

Trade Organisation. However, it is worth noting that the provision of legal services depends on legal systems, legal qualifications, legal culture, and practicing language. ①

In the Association of South East Asian Nations (ASEAN), it has been striving, as stated in the ASEAN Charter and ASEAN Economic Community Blueprint adopted in 2007, ② to create an ASEAN single market with free movement of goods, services, investment, skilled labour, and freer flow of capital. Regarding the free movement of services, the ASEAN Economic Community Blueprint determines that "free flow of trade in services is one of the important elements in realising ASEAN Economic Community, where there will be substantially no restriction to ASEAN services suppliers in providing services and in establishing companies across national borders within the region, subject to domestic regulations"; and in facilitating the free movement of services, including legal services, by 2015, it is stated that "ASEAN is also working towards recognition of professional qualifications with a view to facilitate their movement within the region". ③ According to Commitments under the ASEAN Framework Agreement on Services (AFAS), five ASEAN Members States, including Cambodia, Indonesia, Thailand, Malaysia, and Vietnam, have scheduled AFAS commitments in legal services since the fifth Package in 2006. ④ Taking into consideration all of this, Brunei Darussalam presented a proposal entitled "The Progressive Liberalisation of Trade in Legal Services in ASEAN" in 2008 which was intended to provoke thought and be a starting point for serious discussion on

---

① Welcoming Remarks by Datin Paduka Hajah Hayati POKSDSP Hj Salleh, Attorney General of Brunei Darussalam at the Opening Ceremony of the 6th ASEAN Law Forum on the Progressive Liberalisation of Trade in Legal Services in ASEAN, Empire Hotel and Country Club, Brunei Darussalam, 13th April 2011 (on file with the author).

② Art. 1.5 ASEAN Charter, para. 9 AEC Blueprint.

③ Paras. 20—21 AEC Blueprint.

④ The latest package of those commitments is the Eighth Package of Commitments under the ASEAN Framework Agreement on Services in 2010. It should be noted that Singapore has been preparing to make some liberal commitments in legal services.

that liberalisation in the ASEAN. ① At the 6th ASEAN Law Forum hosted by Brunei Darussalam on 13—14 April 2011, delegates and relevant stakeholders, for the first time, had an opportunity to deliberate on this issue. However, it requires much more efforts and consensus for the ASEAN to obtain such real liberalisation in legal services by 2015.

In addition, the ASEAN has concluded chapters or agreements on trade in services under its free trade agreements/areas (FTAs) with other partners, including China. On 4 November 2002, ASEAN Member States and China signed a Framework Agreement on Comprehensive Economic Co-Operation in which the Parties agree to negotiate expeditiously in order to establish an ASEAN-China FTA within 10 years. ② One of the objectives of this Agreement is to "progressively liberalise and promote trade in goods and services as well as create a transparent, liberal and facilitative investment regime". ③ In order to "progressively liberalise trade in services with substantial sectoral coverage", ④ ASEAN State Members and China concluded an Agreement on Trade in Services on 14 January 2007 aiming at commitments "beyond those undertaken by the ASEAN Member Countries and China under the World Trade Organisation (WTO) General Agreement on Trade in Services". ⑤ With respect to the Parties' schedules of specific commitments (the first package) annexed to the 2007 Agreement on Trade in Services, only Vietnam and Cambodia introduced commitments in the legal services

---

① "The Progressive Liberalisation of Trade in Legal Services in ASEAN"-Proposal presented by Attorney General's Chambers of Brunei Darussalam at 12th ASEAN Senior Law Officials Meeting, Empire Hotel and Country Club, Brunei Darussalam, 17th Oct. 2008 (on file with the author).

② Article 2 of the Framework Agreement on Comprehensive Economic Co-Operation Between ASEAN and the People's Republic of China, Phnom Penh, 4 November 2002, available at http://www.asean.org/13196.htm.

③ Article 1 of the Framework Agreement, *supra* note 1.

④ Article 4 of the Framework Agreement, *supra* note 1.

⑤ Agreement on Trade in Services of the Framework Agreement on Comprehensive Economic Co-operation between the Association of Southeast Asian Nations, available at http://www.aseansec.org/19346.htm.

sector (CPC 861), which are similar to their commitments in the WTO. However, 9 out of 10 ASEAN Members States (except Laos) and China are WTO Members. The liberalisation of trade in legal services in ASEAN-China FTA should be compatible with the GATS Agreements as well as each WTO Member's specific commitments in this sector. For example, China made specific commitments to open up its legal services market to foreign law firms as part of its accession to WTO. Accordingly, foreign law firms can provide legal services in China in the form of representative offices which offices can engage in profit-making activities. Such representative offices cannot practice Chinese law. However, they can provide information on the impact of the Chinese legal environment. ①

It should be noted that the legal services sector has been regarded, to some extent, a highly sensitive sector in the process of the liberalisation of trade in services. In any case, the liberalisation of legal services relates to limitations on market access and national treatment of practising in a host country: (i) host country law (advisory/representation); (ii) home country law and/or third country law (advisory/representation); (iii) international law (advisory/representation); and(iv) other legal documentation, certification, advisory, and information services. At the moment, such liberalisation depends on national commitments under international trade agreements as well as specific national laws and regulations. Therefore, this paper continues by presenting Vietnam's relevant laws and regulations as a case study. After that, some preliminary remarks on liberalisation of trade in legal services in ASEAN-China FTA are made to conclude the paper.

---

① Report of the Working P*arty on* the Accession of China (Schedule of Specific Commitments on Services-List of Article II MFN Exemptions), WT/ACC/CHN/49/Add. 2, 1 October 2001. See also Andrew Godwin, "The Professional 'Tug of War': The Regulation of Foreign Lawyers in China, Business Scope Issues and Some Suggestions for Reform", 33 *Melb. U. L. Rev.* 132 (2009).

2. Regulation of Trade in Legal Services in Vietnam

2.1. Vietnam's International Commitments

The first international commitments of Vietnam in the legal services sector were in the framework of the WTO. They were listed in PartII. 1. A (a) of the Schedule of Specific Commitments in Services drafted by the Working Party on the Accession of Vietnam in October 2006. ① These commitments were used without changes in Vietnam's Commitments under ASEAN Framework Agreement on Services (AFAS), which can be found in the 5th Package in 2006 to the 8th Package in 2010, as well as in Vietnam's Schedule of Specific Commitments annexed to the ASEAN and China Agreement on Trade in Services in January 2007. Those commitments of Vietnam are regulated in detail in the Law on Lawyers of 2006② and confirmed in Resolution No. 71/2006/QH11 of the National Assembly on Ratification of Protocol on Vietnam's Accession to WTO. ③

Although those international commitments of Vietnam are in legal services (CPC 681), they do not include: (i) participation in litigation proceedings in the capacity of defenders or representatives of their clients before the courts of Vietnam and (ii) legal documentation and certification services of the laws of Vietnam. ④ Consequently, for Mode 1 and Mode 2 of services supply (cross-border supply and consumption abroad), foreign law firms shall have the right to provide advisory services on foreign law, including home country law and/or third country law as well as international law.

---

① WT/ACC/VNM/48/Add. 2.

② Law No. 65/2006/QH11 dated 29 June 2006.

③ Resolution No. 71/2006/QH11 dated 29 November 2006.

④ According to CPC 86130, legal documentation and certification services include "the provision of advice and the execution of various tasks necessary for the drawing up or certification of documents". It means that drawing up of wills, marriage contracts, commercial contracts, business charters etc. regarding Vietnamese law and notary activities are excluded from the scope of the commitments.

Regarding Mode 3 (commercial presence), foreign lawyers' organizations,[①] i. e. organisations of practicing lawyers established in any commercial corporate form (foreign law firms) in foreign countries, can establish their commercial presence in Vietnam in four forms. They are: (i) branches of foreign lawyers' organisations; (ii) subsidiaries of foreign lawyers' organisations; (iii) foreign law firms (in Vietnam), i. e. organisations of practicing lawyers established in Vietnam by one or more foreign lawyers' organisations under Vietnamese regulations; and (iv) partnership between foreign lawyers' organisations and Vietnam's law partnerships.

With such commercial presence, foreign lawyers' organisations have the right to provide advisory services in all law fields. However, they can provide advisory services on Vietnamese laws only when these services are supplied by a lawyer who holds a law degree awarded by a Vietnamese law school (or equivalence) and satisfies criteria regulated under national legislation for Vietnamese law practitioners.

With respect to Mode 4 (presence of natural persons), it is unbound, except as indicated in the horizontal section, e. g. regarding "intra-corporate transferees", lawyers working for a foreign law firms in foreign countries can be qualified as "specialist"; therefore, they shall be granted entry and stay permit for an initial period of three years which may be extended subject to the term of operation of those firms in Vietnam.

As noted above, Vietnam's international commitments in the legal services sector have been regulated in detail and even more favourably in the Law on Lawyers of 2006.[②] In addition, trade liberalisation in legal services relates to professional qualifications of law practitioners. In order to understand regulations in legal services and their trade liberalisation, it is therefore necessary to understand national relevant regulations on the basis of such international commitments.

---

① A "foreign lawyers organisation" is an organisation of practicing lawyers established in any commercial corporate form in foreign countries (including firms, companies, corporations, etc.) by one or more foreign lawyers or law firms.

② Law No. 65/2006/QH11 dated 29 June 2006.

2.2. Relevant Provisions in the Law on Lawyers of 2006 and Comparison with the Commitments

2.2.1. Regulations for Law Practicing in Vietnam

The Law on Lawyers of 2006 provides two different regulations for Vietnamese and foreign lawyers.

2.2.1.1. For Vietnamese Lawyers

Regarding qualifications of a lawyer, in order to become a Vietnamese lawyer, it is required that that Vietnamese citizen is loyal to the Fatherland, observes the Constitution and law, has good moral qualities, possesses a law bachelor diploma, has been trained in legal profession, have gone through the probation of legal profession, and has good health for law practice (Art. 10). In order to practice law in Vietnam, that person shall both meet all the qualifications of a lawyer and obtain a law practice certificate granted by the Ministry of Justice and join a provincial bar association (Art. 11).

With respect to forms of law practice, a Vietnamese lawyer may practice law in either (i) a law-practicing organisation by establishing, or joining in the establishment of, a law-practicing organisation or working for the law-practicing organisation under an employment contract, or (ii) his/her own capacity, i. e. practicing law individually (Art. 23). A law-practicing organizations of Vietnamese lawyer(s) can be under the form of: (i) lawyer's office set up by a lawyer, organized and operated in the form of a private enterprise; (ii) a law firm, including law partnership set up by at least two lawyers and not have capital-contributing members; or (iii) a limited liability law firm, including a limited liability law firm of two or more members and a limited liability law firm of one member (Art. 32～34).

For law practicing scope, Vietnamese lawyers can: (i) participate in all litigation proceedings, (ii) provide legal advices, (iii) act as a non-litigation representative for clients to perform law-related works, and(iv) provide other legal services (Art. 22).

2.2.1.2. For Foreign Lawyers and Foreign Lawyers' Organizations Having Commercial Presence in Vietnam

Conditions for professional practice by foreign lawyers in Vietnam are: (i) having a valid law practice certificate granted by a competent foreign agency or organization; (ii) respecting the Constitution and law of Vietnam; (iii) having been assigned by a foreign lawyers' organisation to practice in Vietnam or have agreed with a foreign lawyers' organisation or its branch in Vietnam or a Vietnamese law practising organisation to work in that organisation (Art. 74).

With respect to the scope of practice by foreign lawyers, a foreign lawyer practicing in Vietnam may provide: consultancy on foreign and international law; other legal services concerning foreign law; consultancy on Vietnamese law if he/she obtains a bachelor of law degree of Vietnam and meets all the requirements as for a Vietnamese lawyer. However, he/she cannot participate in litigation proceedings before the bodies conducting litigation proceedings of Vietnam (Art. 76).

Regarding conditions for professional practice by foreign law firms established in foreign countries (foreign lawyers' organisations), it is required that foreign law firms which have been set up and lawfully practicing law in foreign countries, respect the Constitution and law of Vietnam may practice law in Vietnam (Art. 68).

For forms of foreign law-practicing organisations practicing law in Vietnam, they can operate in Vietnam under three forms, namely: (i) branches in Vietnam of foreign law firms; (ii) limited liability law firms in Vietnam with 100% foreign capital; and (iii) joint-venture limited liability law firms.

With respect to scope of professional practice by foreign law-practicing organisations, a foreign law firm or its branch practicing law in Vietnam may provide legal consultancy and/or other legal services; may not assign its foreign lawyers to participate litigation proceedings in the capacity of defence counsel or as the representative of clients or as the person who defends legitimate rights and interests of parties before the Vietnamese bodies conducting litigation proceedings; may assign Vietnamese lawyers who are practicing in that organization to provide consultancy on Vietnamese law, participate litigation proceedings in the capacity of the representative of clients or as the person who defends legitimate rights and interests of parties before a Viet-

namese court in respect of the cases where that foreign law firm or its branch has provided legal consultancy, except for a criminal case (Art. 70).

2.3. Comparison with Vietnam's Commitments

In general, the regulations of the Law on Lawyers of 2006 in terms of specifications and conditions, forms and scope of law practice, rights and obligations of foreign lawyers' organizations and foreign lawyers in Vietnam are compatible with Vietnam's commitments to the WTO, ASEAN and ASEAN-China FTA in the legal services sector. Regarding the scope of professional practice in by foreign law-practicing organizations with commercial presence in Vietnam, because such an organization may assign Vietnamese lawyers who are practicing in that organization to participate litigation proceedings in the capacity of the representative of clients or as the person who defends legitimate rights and interests of parties before a Vietnamese court in respect of the cases where that organization has provided legal consultancy, except for a criminal case, this regulation is more favourable and liberal than Vietnam's commitments. However, there remain some concerns relating to the Law of Lawyers of 2006 in comparison with the international commitments such as forms of foreign law-practicing organizations practicing law in Vietnam and nationality requirement for being admitted to local bars.

In any case, the process of trade liberalisation in legal services in Vietnam after approximately five years has brought some benefits and opportunities as follows:

—Reducing market access restrictions for foreign law firms practicing law in Vietnam, satisfying high requirements of international economic integration;

—Bringing opportunities for Vietnamese lawyers to participate in international disputes; this may help those lawyers to improve their knowledge and experience;

—Facilitating foreign law firms practicing law in Vietnam in order to use and learn their knowledge, experience and connection.

2.4. Legal Services in Vietnam in Practice

After 25 years of "doi moi" (the reform process), Vietnam gained achievements in the fields of economic growth, judicial and administrative reforms, legal system improvement and international integration. In that context, legal services and legal profession have been encouraged and facilitated. The number and quality of Vietnamese lawyers have been increased. In May 2009, Vietnam Bar Federation was founded to represent all lawyers and provincial bar associations. In addition to the Vietnam Bar Federation, there are 62 provincial bar associations in 63 provinces in Vietnam with approximately 6,250 lawyers and 3000 probate lawyers in 2750 law practicing organizations. ① From 2005 to 2010, relating to legal proceedings, Vietnamese lawyers participated in 85,000 criminal cases; 53,000 civil cases; 3,500 economic cases; 1,500 labour cases; 2,800 administrative cases. In addition, Vietnamese lawyers participated in more than 145,000 legal consultancy cases and 50,000 other legal services-related cases. ② In this process, Vietnamese lawyers and law practicing organizations have increased the quality of their services. They, to some extent may compete with foreign law firm in Vietnam.

Regarding foreign lawyers' organizations having their commercial presence in Vietnam, such organisations have been permitted to practice in Vietnam since 1996. Until now, there are 201 foreign lawyers and 53 foreign lawyers' organizations in Vietnam. Out of 53 foreign lawyers organizations practicing legal services in Vietnam, 20 organisations have established 30 branches and 33 organisations have established foreign law firms (including 2 joint-ventured law firms). For ASEAN foreign lawyers organizations practicing in Vietnam, there are 3 foreign lawyers organizations (establishing 2 branches and 2 foreign law firms) from Thailand; 7 organizations (establishing 6 branches and 4 foreign law firms) from Singapore; and 1 organisation

① The Strategy for the Development of Lawyers to 2020 approved by the Prime Minister in Decision No. 1072/QD-TTg dated 05 July 2011.

② Ibid.

(establishing a joint-venture law firm with Singapore and Vietnamese law firms).

All activities of foreign lawyers' organizations in Vietnam have contributed to create a more favourable legal environment, encourage foreign investment, promote business activities and develop the legal services market in Vietnam. Many foreign lawyers' organizations in Vietnam have recruited Vietnamese lawyers, trained them to meet international standards. Furthermore, these foreign lawyers' organizations and lawyers have cooperated with Vietnamese organisations and agencies to providetraining activities for Vietnamese lawyers, organize relevant workshop and seminars in legal services, make comments on draft legal normative documents ... They also have participated in drafting Vietnamese laws and policies relating to international economic integration. As a result, the Strategy for the Development of Lawyers to 2020 approved by the Prime Minister in July 2011 determines the need to improve and liberalise the legal services markets as well as to increase cooperation with foreign law firms, especially in the field of trade and commercial law. ① This is to serve well the comprehensive international economic integration of Vietnam.

2.5. Preliminary Remarks

Liberalisation of legal services is a requirement to both meet international commitments of a country and to create a competitive market of legal services. It is encouraging, in the context of the ASEAN-China FTA and the WTO, to have five ASEAN members plus China already making some level of commitments for the liberalisation in legal services (and Singapore in the near future). However, such liberalisation is still different from country to country the differences in legal systems, legal qualifications, legal culture, and languages. It is generally still quite restrictive and in need of being improved upon in order to achieve real liberalisation of legal services in the ASEAN-China FTA.

In any case, current commitments in legal services of some countries in

---

① Ibid.

the ASEAN-China FTA are good starting points for them to open up their legal services sector and create incentives for other countries to follow the former. In order to facilitate the progressive liberalisation of legal services in the region, it should regionalise the level of commitments in liberalisation in legal services, strengthen cooperation in legal education and among bar associations in ASEAN and China, work towards recognition of lawyers qualifications in ASEAN as well as try to establish a strong-China FTA dispute settlement mechanism to develop the legal services market in the region. This may be a sweat dream, but no one can prevent us to do it.

中国—东盟自贸区仲裁中心的机遇及建设

刘想树*

内容摘要　在当前形势下,设立中国—东盟自贸区仲裁中心的可能性及机遇已经具备。该仲裁中心应在服务自贸区发展的目标下明确其定位,并广泛选聘高素质仲裁员,加强制度创新,强化其裁决的执行力。

随着中国—东盟自贸区于 2010 年 1 月 1 日如期建成,一个拥有 19 亿消费者,GDP 总量逾 7 万亿美元的经济区已经展现在我们面前。按人口算,这将是世界上最大的自由贸易区;从经济规模上看,是仅次于欧盟和北美自由贸易区的全球第三大自由贸易区;更为引人注目的时,这是发展中国家组成的最大的自由贸易区。

中国—东盟自贸区建成时虽恰逢国际金融危机持续发酵的不利外部经济环境,但在区内各国政府及企业的共同努力下,区域贸易总量稳步增长,区内经济活动日渐活跃。事实证明,自贸区在促进各国经济发展,实现各国共同受益方面发挥着不可替代的积极作用。

当然,我们也应注意到,中国—东盟自贸区在构建一体化的贸易、投资及服务平台的同时,区内企业及个人在经济交往过程中产生的纠纷也将不可避免的增加。在此情况下,设立专门的中国—东盟自贸区仲裁中心,通过仲裁等多元化纠纷解决机制公正高效地解决纠纷就显得十分必要。下面,笔者就中国—东盟自贸区仲裁中心的建设与发展问题谈几点感想。

一、中国—东盟自贸区仲裁中心的机遇

从世界范围来看,以仲裁为代表的替代性纠纷解决机制(ADR)方兴未

---

* 刘想树,西南政法大学副校长,教授、博士生导师,中国—东盟法律研究中心理事。

艾,仲裁在中国—东盟自贸区经贸纠纷的解决中理应发挥重要作用,并且,我们也有理由对中国—东盟自贸区仲裁中心的建设与发展寄予厚望。

首先,中国与东盟各国间不断发展的国家间关系是中国—东盟自贸区仲裁中心建设的政治基础。2003 年 10 月,在中国与东盟第六次领导人会议上,双方将关系提升至"面向和平与繁荣的战略伙伴关系"的高度。在各国高层的共同努力和培育下,中国与东盟的各种对话机制已建立并逐步完善,包括首脑级的非正式会晤,外交、经济、财政部长级会议,财政、央行副部长级会议、高管会议等政府机制。在这些政府间对话机制中,包括中国—东盟自贸区发展在内的经济问题占有重要位置。可以说,正是各国领导层这种对促进自贸区发展,实现各国经济互利共赢的共识,为中国—东盟自贸区仲裁中心的建设和发展奠定了坚实的政治基础。

其次,中国与东盟日益密切的经济往来是中国—东盟自贸区仲裁中心发展的经济支撑。自上个世纪 90 年代以来特别是中国—东盟自贸区建成后,中国与东盟各国的贸易总量稳步增长。根据中国海关总署 2011 年 8 月的统计数据,东盟已超过日本,成为继欧盟、美国之后中国的第三大贸易伙伴。在传统货物贸易的带动下,中国与东盟间投资及服务贸易亦呈良性发展态势。众所周知,仲裁业务的开展和兴旺,必须建基于健康活跃的经济环境之上。而中国与东盟间已经呈现的、并将持续发展的"多赢式"经济互动无疑可以构成中国—东盟自贸区仲裁中心发展的重要支撑。

最后,中国与东盟间文化交流与理解是中国—东盟自贸区仲裁中心壮大的社会土壤。仲裁作为一种纠纷解决方式,其制度架构和实际运作受文化传统及民众心理的影响较为显著。从历史上看,中国与东盟各国间的文化交流源远流长且从未中断。当下,在西方文化借全球化之风盛行于世的同时,中国与东盟的本土文化依然保持了相对的独立性和旺盛的生命力。在中国与东盟政治互信和经济互利的背景下,本地区的文化交流也在不同层次的多元平台上顺利开展。这种"互相尊重,求同存异"的文化交流态势,对于构筑共通的对仲裁机制的理解与认知,并由此形成有利于仲裁壮大的社会沃土,意义重大。

二、中国—东盟自贸区仲裁中心的定位

我们在这里探讨的中国—东盟自贸区仲裁中心,所提供的是旨在促进自贸区经济发展的经贸纠纷解决服务。总体而言,中国—东盟自贸区框架内的经贸纠纷大致包括三种类型:国家间经贸争端、一方为国家另一方为私主体的

经贸争议、双方均为私主体的经贸纠纷。中国—东盟自贸区仲裁中心的定位就是该仲裁中心主要解决何种类型的经贸争议问题。

根据 2004 年 11 月在万象签订的《中华人民共和国与东南亚国家联盟全面经济合作框架协议争端解决机制协议》(以下简称《争端解决机制协议》),中国与东盟各国约定通过磋商、调解、调停或仲裁方式解决自贸区框架内国家间的经贸争端。根据《争端解决机制协议》,其安排的仲裁机制属于临时仲裁范畴。因此,这类经贸争端目前不必纳入中国—东盟自贸区仲裁中心的受案范围。当然,至于今后是否有必要将其纳入,理论界及实务界可以根据情势的发展再作进一步的探讨。

关于双方均为私主体的经贸纠纷,根据当前国际商事仲裁的实践,一般由当事人基于意思自治约定仲裁机构。并且,本地区内有多家较有影响力的国际商事仲裁机构,如中国国际经济贸易仲裁委员会、香港国际仲裁中心、新加坡国际仲裁中心等。因此,这类经贸纠纷是否可由中国—东盟自贸区仲裁中心解决,应视乎当事人意愿而定,不宜做统一要求。

一方为国家另一方为私主体的经贸争议(这类争议通常发生在投资领域),因涉及国家而有其特殊性。从争议解决机构的公信力和公正性考虑,由超脱于自贸区各国之外并具有相对独立性的中国—东盟自贸区仲裁中心解决颇为合适。

三、中国—东盟自贸区仲裁中心建设中应注意的几个问题

要想建设一个富有实效的中国—东盟自贸区仲裁中心,将会面临一系列需要解决的问题。笔者仅就当下的初步思考,就以下几点略陈己见以供探讨。

(一)应广泛选聘高素质仲裁员

"仲裁的好坏取决于仲裁员"是国际仲裁界的经典格言。在很大程度上,仲裁员是仲裁吸引力之所在,因此,能否选聘到高素质的仲裁员,形成富有口碑的仲裁员队伍,对于中国—东盟自贸区仲裁中心的运转具有重要意义。

笔者以为,仲裁员的高素质主要体现在两个方面:一是业务素质;一是职业操守。

仲裁员所处理的经贸争议往往具有专业性强、复杂程度高的特点,这就要求其不仅具有扎实的法律功底,还应有丰富的经贸领域的实践经验。因此,在选聘仲裁员时,应以服务自贸区发展为目标,将仲裁中心定位和地区人才状况

相联系,具体选聘标准可综合考虑教育背景、专业经历、仲裁经验、行业评价等因素。

仲裁员职业操守的核心是对其独立性和公正性的坚持。当我们将仲裁中心定位在主要解决一方为国家一方为私主体时,即使我们从制度设计可要求仲裁员不得参与其本国作为直接当事方案件,也很难完全排除某一仲裁员与其所裁决案件涉及的国家存在不同类型不同程度的利益纠葛的情况。在此背景下,仲裁员能否坚持其职业操守,恪守独立性和公正性就显得十分关键。

(二)应积极探索仲裁与调解相结合的新型争议解决方案

从当下争议解决机制的发展趋势来看,不同争议解决方式的互通与融合是潮流所向。从应然的角度看,吸收各种争议解决方式优点,组合形成更有效的新型争议解决方案也颇具探索价值。

在中国国内,在仲裁程序中有机融入调解机制的实践已有多年,并形成了很多可资借鉴的经验。

从功能上看,仲裁中调解有利于维持争议方的商业合作关系。选择争端解决方式是当事人商业战略的一部分,仲裁中调解更多的着眼于纠纷的解决,以及争议方将来商业合作关系的维持等,在一定程度上说效率高于公平。

实践中我们发现,往往是在仲裁中占据有利地位的当事方愿意尝试和对方和解的可能,因为通过其有限的经济上的让步可以有效地保持和对方未来的合作关系,增加了远期利益。而在仲裁中处于相对不利地位的当事人基于降低风险减少损失的考虑,也乐于接受调解。

从效果上看,由于仲裁中调解最大限度地发挥当事人解决争议的主动性。对于一个充分体现了自治原则并基于争议各方合意形成的包含调解内容的裁决,获得自动履行的可能性也大大增加。

我以为在中国以及世界范围内进行的在仲裁中融入调解机制的尝试和取得的经验完全可以应用到中国—东盟自贸区仲裁中心的实践中。当然,由于中国—东盟自贸区仲裁中心所处理的案件可能包括一方主体为国家的情况,既有的在仲裁中调解的经验有必要结合仲裁中心受理的案件的特点不断加以改进和完善。

(三)应强化仲裁中心裁决的执行力

中国—东盟自贸区仲裁中心一旦设立并运行,其裁决能否顺利执行,不仅直接影响仲裁当事方的权益,还事关仲裁中心的公信力和权威性,甚至可能影

响到中国—东盟自贸区的发展。有鉴于此，通过制度性安排消除障碍，强化仲裁中心裁决的执行力实属必要。

具体而言，对于中国—东盟自贸区仲裁中心针对各当事方均为私主体的案件所做出的裁决，可以研究是否能通过区域性的安排，在《纽约公约》的基础上进一步限制各国拒绝承认和执行裁决的理由，简化相关程序，提高执行效率和执行成功率。

由于中国—东盟自贸区仲裁中心将可能受理一方主体为国家的案件，对于此类裁决，在强化其执行力的制度设计方面，ICSID的经验可资借鉴。可考虑通过自贸区各国的协议，规定中国—东盟自贸区仲裁中心裁决一经做出，即对各方产生约束力。任一当事方应承认中国—东盟自贸区仲裁中心做出的裁决具有约束力并自觉执行该裁决。若任何一方不履行裁决，对私主体而言，国家当事方可向自贸区内任一国家的主管法院提出强制执行该项裁决的申请。收到申请的国家的法院则应无条件执行该项裁决，并且不得以裁决违反本国公共秩序为由拒绝承认与执行。若国家当事人不自动执行中国—东盟自贸区仲裁中心的裁决，或因国家享有豁免权而不得强制执行该裁决，该项裁决所涉及的私主体的母国则可因此行使对本国私主体的外交保护，或诉诸《争端解决机制协议》以求公平解决。

当然，中国—东盟自贸区仲裁中心所涉及的问题十分广泛，甚至其是否有设立的必要，都是可以争论的。笔者以为，针对这些问题的探讨应该是开放性的，只要是以促进中国—东盟自贸区发展，服务中国—东盟关系大局为目的，任何建构性或解构性的意见都应当允许表达，并应当被认真对待。也只有如此，中国与东盟的合作才会更有成效，中国与东盟的关系才会更加紧密。

Opportunities for the Establishment and Construction of the Arbitration Center of CAFTA

Liu Xiangshu*

Abstract: Under the present situation, it is possible and feasible to construct the Arbitration Center of CAFTA. The key to successfully establish the Arbitration Center is to get clear orientations of running the center, hire arbitrators with high quality, promote systematic innovations, and strengthen the enforcement of arbitral awards.

We should note that, the China-ASEAN Free Trade Area provides a integrated platform for the trade, investment and services, trade disputes between local enterprises and individuals, even the countries inevitably increased in the process of economic exchanges. In this case, it is very necessary to establish the China-ASEAN Free Trade Area Arbitration Centre, and provide a fair and effective mechanism to solve disputes through arbitrations.

The possibility and feasibility of establishing the Arbitration Center of CAFTA have been fulfilled under the present situation. From a global perspective, the arbitration, as one of an alternative dispute resolution mechanism (ADR), is in the ascendant, playing an important role in resolving trade disputes through arbitration in China-ASEAN Free Trade Area. We have high hope for the construction and development of China-ASEAN Free Trade arbitration Centre.

First, the continuous development of inter-State relations between Chi-

* Vice president professor of Southwest University of Polifical Science and Law, consultatiue member of China-ASEAN Legal Research Center.

na and ASEAN countries is the political foundation of China -ASEAN Free Trade Area Arbitration Centre building. Secondly, the increasingly closer economic ties between China and ASEAN are supporting role of the economic development of China-ASEAN Free Trade Area Arbitration Centre. Finally, cultural communications and understanding between China and ASEAN are the social base for the expansion of China-ASEAN Free Trade Area Arbitration Center.

We consider that the Arbitration Center of the China-ASEAN Free Trade Area aims at promoting the FTA economic development through provision of service to resolve economic and trade disputes. Overall, within the framework of China-ASEAN Free Trade Area, the economic and trade disputes generally include three types: the economic and trade disputes between countries, the economic and trade dispute between a private body as one party and the member country as the other party, the economic and trade disputes of between two private sides. And the orientation of the China-ASEAN Free Trade Area Arbitration Centre is mainly dedicated to solving the economic and trade disputes of those 3 types.

In order to build a highly efficiently function Arbitration Centre of the ASEAN Free Trade Area, we are facing a series of problems to be solved. There are three major problems should be paid more attention to:

(1)Hire arbitrators with high qualification of disputes settlement;

(2)Explore new approaches to resolve trade disputes like arbitration and mediation system;

(3)Strengthen and enhance the implementation and enforcement of the arbitration award of CAFTA.

To establish the China-ASEAN Free Trade Area Arbitration Centre is very complicated, it is extremely rich in content, involving the fields of sovereignty, territory, politics, economy and society, moreover, it could be argued whether the center should be established or not. I think that the member states should be open while addressing issues related to promote the development of the China-ASEAN Free Trade Area as long as the serve the purpose of the overall relations and situations between China-ASEAN, any constructive or deconstructive comments should be allowed to express, and

should be taken seriously. Then the cooperation between China and ASEAN will be more effective, and the relationship between China and ASEAN will be strengthened.

略论区域贸易协定战略实施中的统筹安排

张晓君[*]　刘彬[**]

内容摘要　当代众多区域贸易协定必然会给国际贸易法治秩序带来较大混乱，如何对区域贸易协定加以统筹安排是各国面临的重要课题。目前，欧美在区域贸易协定的战略协调方面已有实践，在协定的"排序"和实体条款设计方面初见成效，具有参考价值。我国在积极推动自由贸易区实践的同时，亦应结合中国与东盟自由贸易区等成功范例，制订系统的自由贸易区战略，以避免不同自由贸易区彼此间的制度冲突，从而提高自由贸易区的利用效率，更好地促进我国外贸事业发展和其他外交目标的实现。

关键词　区域贸易协定；统筹安排；排序；欧美经验；中国实践

目前，WTO多哈回合仍然陷于停滞状态，2008年以来的国际金融危机以及新近的欧债危机更让全球贸易自由化进程雪上加霜。在这种形势下，各国纷纷加快各自的区域经济一体化进程，其典型代表便是区域贸易协定(RTA)。据WTO官方资料统计，截至2012年1月15日，已通报到GATT/WTO的RTA大约有511个，其中现行有效的已达319个。③ 如此众多的RTAs必然会给国际贸易法治秩序带来较大的混乱，对各国自身利益也有深刻影响，因此如何统筹安排RTAs是各国面临的重要课题。

* 张晓君，西南政法大学国际法学院教授、博士生导师，中国—东盟法律研究中心秘书长。

** 刘彬，西南政法大学国际法学院副教授。

③　Http://www.wto.org/english/tratop_e/region_e/region_e.htm，访问日期：2012年3月2日。

一、区域贸易协定统筹安排的意义

在冷战后,全球合作已经从过去的若干“高级合作者”(top cooperators)互为伙伴的格局逐渐转变为多样化、异质化的伙伴关系格局。国际贸易领域自然也不例外,并且国家间在贸易领域的合作远多于其他领域。[①] 因此,一国对外缔结 RTA 活动必然出现协定数量众多、伙伴关系多样的局面,各个 RTA 的交错作用使国家需要统筹安排相关进程,以避免利益冲撞和实现综合效用最大化。这种统筹安排是一国根据本国利益自主进行的,但并非主体的单向控制性活动。因为 RTA 的制度特点和实际效果以及其他国家的政策反应将会反过来影响一国的政策选择,因此这种统筹安排是一个互动与沟通的过程。

从当代“新区域主义”的总体发展态势来看,目前各国的 RTA 实践中 FTA(自由贸易区)占据了压倒性数量优势,由此将导致以下若干突出问题:

首先,多个 FTA 的生效时间、过渡期、优惠安排的内容、伙伴国的比较优势各不相同,可能会使贸易转移[②]多次、重复地发生,不仅本身会减少世界福利,而且会在资源重新配置过程中引起由于先前资源的专用性而带来的损失。[③] 原产地规则的重复或不一致导致经济低效则是 FTA 制度冲突中的另一个重要问题。欧盟、美国、日本等发达成员目前实行不同的 FTA 原产地规则,而与上述多个大国都存在 FTA 关系的中小国家由于要同时实行多种原产地制度,更加深了其经济不利地位及其对外谈判其他 FTA 的难度,也给它们的海关监管工作大大增加了复杂性。以不少拉美国家为例,各国国内的利益集团已经根据现有的原产地制度形成了固定的商业运作模式和既得经济利益,要想改变现状非常困难,这也就给它们与其他国家缔结新的 FTA 制造了

---

① Antoni Estevadeordal and Kati Suominen, Sequencing Regional Trade Integration and Cooperation Agreements: Describing a Dataset for A New Research Agenda, available at http://idbdocs. iadb. org/wsdocs/getdocument. aspx? docnum = 811019, 访问日期:2012 年 5 月 16 日。

② “贸易转移”和“贸易创造”是研究 FTA 经济效应的一对常用术语,前者指成员间关税互惠削减导致成员与非成员之间贸易减少,产生对非成员的不利结果;后者指成员间关税互惠削减产生的成员彼此间贸易增加及经济福利的创造。

③ 李荣林、宫占奎、孟夏:《中国与东盟自由贸易区研究》,天津大学出版社 2007 年版,第 302 页。

明显障碍，不利于世界贸易进一步自由化。

其次，从各国众多 FTA 的条文内容来看，在实体法律制度上出现了以 WTO 法为典范的明显趋同化，包括货物的国民待遇、市场准入的手续与措施、贸易救济措施、卫生和植物卫生措施、服务贸易条款等多个方面。但是，各国 FTA 在实体条文制度的设计上仍然颇多差异之处，即便同一国家对外缔结的 FTA，同类条款的具体内容彼此间也有很大差异，这就给国际贸易法治秩序带来了相当大的管理混乱，对于 WTO 多边主义贸易秩序也是一种冲击。

因此，FTA 的战略协调将成为区域贸易协定统筹工作的重心，而大国的有关实践将发挥重要的示范作用。

二、欧美的 FTA 实践启示

在全球范围内，欧美是 FTA 实践的先行者，能够为其他国家包括我国在内提供很多启示。

(一)宏观战略层面的统筹协调

国内有学者对欧美国家的 FTA 战略协调作了研究，指出其关税政策的协调主要包括：在缔约对象的选择上，优先选择重要贸易伙伴以减少贸易转移，或选择 FTA 的轴心国家以充分利用其桥梁作用；FTA 中立即免税的商品范围不断扩大，削减关税的过渡期逐步缩短，以尽快用新协定的贸易创造纠正先前协定的贸易转移。① 以上措施的确值得其他国家认真借鉴。国外也有学者指出，美国等大国还积极探索与 RTA 伙伴建立“局部性关税同盟”(sectoral customs union)的可能性，从而尽可能对第三国实行同一关税；坚持不对 RTA 伙伴取消美国反倾销等贸易救济措施的使用。② 以上措施主要着眼于减少 RTA 对第三方的“贸易转移”损害。

此外，对伙伴国家及自身的经济利益影响也是欧美大国在主导区域一体化时的重要考量因素。以过去美国主导下的 FTAA(美洲自由贸易区)进程

---

① 李荣林、宫占奎、孟夏：《中国与东盟自由贸易区研究》，天津大学出版社 2007 年版，第 302～308、319～324 页。

② Matthew Schaefer, Ensuring That Regional Trade Agreements Complement the WTO System: US Unilateralism A Supplement to WTO Initiatives? *Journal of International Economic Law*, Vol. 10, 2007, pp. 601～602.

为例,据分析,拉美和加勒比海地区的众多小国可以考虑以两种方式加入现有的NAFTA(北美自由贸易区):一是单个国家逐个加入,二是这些小国之间已经组建了不少RTA,可以集团式加入NAFTA。逐个加入有利于一些特定国家短期内在经济上迅速获益,并获得国内改革的动力,但代价则是其他小国将会受损;集团式加入有利于整个美洲地区均衡和稳步的经济一体化,对美国的经济福利也更有利,但缺点是该地区一些特定国家就难以获得特殊利益。[①]因此对于主导国家美国来说,这就构成一个微妙的政策权衡过程。尽管FTAA由于各种复杂障碍至今难以成功,但区域贸易协定统筹安排之重要性于其中可见一斑。

以上协调是就经济意义而言的,但是欧美等大国的FTA战略不可能仅限于经济考量,美国有时甚至更看重政治因素。双边FTA合作进程中各种复杂因素使得"排序"(sequencing)概念应运而生,即分析并确认FTA建设进程中若干特定要素在特定时段发挥的作用,推动合作进程朝着有利于自身政治经济目标的方向发展。[②] FTA缔结中的"排序"问题对于缺乏区域主导国家、一体化合作深度不足的亚洲国家似乎更为突出。中国也无法回避类似于FTAA这样的"大区域"内的宏观"排序"考量,例如与东盟国家的FTA缔结活动已有较为明显的体现。

(二)实体条款方面的统筹协调

目前,欧美对外FTA在实体条款方面呈现出一定程度上的共性。例如欧美注意原产地规则的统一和简化,推行"泛欧模式"和"NAFTA模式",并实行各种累积制度,对非敏感产业逐步放松原产地规则要求。[③] 欧盟近年来还有一系列关于RTA原产地规则的改革动向。而美国在FTA实体条款的统筹协调方面更为突出,这主要体现在其已经拥有了较为成型的FTA范式。首先,美国早就形成了"NAFTA范式",各个FTA除传统的货物贸易与服务贸易之外,还模仿NAFTA规定了劳工标准、环境保护、政府采购、知识产权

---

① Frank J. Garcia, NAFTA and the Creation of the FTAA: A Critique of Piecemeal Accession, *Virginia Journal of International Law*, Vol. 35, 1995, p. 585.

② 蔡鹏鸿:《东亚双边自由贸易区的国际政治经济学分析》,载《当代亚太》2005年第3期。

③ 马建军、付松:《基于美欧经验的自由贸易区发展战略》,载《国际经济合作》2007年第5期。

和投资内容，并且设置分散的争端解决机制。其次，美国后来又形成了“超WTO范式”，在知识产权等领域要求对方承担超出WTO水平的义务，此外又大量涉足WTO尚未形成有效成果的“新领域”，例如电子商务、透明度、反腐败和贸易能力建设等贸易便利化措施方面。①

客观而论，欧美重视FTA中的贸易便利化措施对于减轻FTA贸易转移确有一定作用。有经济学者通过大量的经验性数据证明，贸易便利化方面更为出色的RTA将产生较大的贸易创造和较小的贸易转移，对单纯的关税减让有替代作用，更有利于全球贸易走向自由化。② 为换取发展水平落后的FTA对象国在市场准入、知识产权、环境保护和劳工标准等方面的让步，欧美近年来在FTA中几乎都加入了贸易便利化等政策支持措施，对发展中国家制度和能力的建设提供支持和援助。有学者认为这些内容不如放到WTO多边框架中讨论更好。③ 但是，贸易便利化议题目前在多哈回合中已经被搁置，因此在双边FTA中加强此类制度建设亦不失为一种可行选择。当然，欧美以上述种种议题为条件作出贸易便利化等制度支持承诺，对于发展中国家的综合利弊仍是需要深入研究的。

欧美FTA在实体条款方面还有一个普遍特征，那就是在农业自由化方面步伐保守，这与它们在WTO中的立场如出一辙，其根本原因在于农业问题在欧美内部政治中的敏感性。而许多发展中国家在农业出口方面拥有一定优势，希望欧美能够充分开放农业市场。因此，欧美这一做法有利于保障其私利，而对发展中国家的利益则构成重大制约。

三、我国区域贸易协定战略的相关展望

目前，我国也正在积极推行自由贸易区战略，并取得了迅速进展。④ 但在

---

① 陈咏梅：《美式FTA范式探略》，载《现代法学》2012年第5期。

② Hongshik Lee and Innwon Park, In Search of Optimised Regional Trade Agreements and Applications to East Asia, *The World Economy*, Vol. 30, Iss. 5, 2007, pp. 783～806.

③ Bernard Hoekman, Designing North-South Trade Agreements to Promote Economic Development, presented at the International Trade Roundtable 2005, *the WTO at 10 Years: the Regional Challenge to Multilateralism*, Brussels, 2005, p. 27.

④ 中国自由贸易区服务网，http://fta.mofcom.gov.cn/index.shtml，访问日期：2012年6月10日。

新区域主义大潮中，中国仍然是一个后来者，自由贸易协定缔结活动方兴未艾，这表明中国目前还远未像欧盟那样因对外FTA过多而达到一个利益上的临界点。但随着中国对外FTA的逐步增加，各种FTA的统筹安排问题难以回避。

应看到，中国在这方面已有较好范例，例如与东盟国家的FTA缔结活动。从中国角度而言，与东盟十国缔结FTA可以实现经济上获益、减少贸易摩擦，政治上强化信任，进而加强中国在亚太政治经济格局中的影响力和谈判地位，自不待言。但从东盟十国角度而言，事实上十国的发展水平也存在较大差异，在FTA倡议提出之际，它们的反应也各不相同。例如东盟6个老成员中新加坡对此最为积极，泰国、文莱较为积极，印尼则相对谨慎；4个新成员则更关注差别待遇和广泛的经济技术合作事项。[①] 中国最终没有选择与东盟国家分批次地缔结FTA，而是选择与东盟十国缔结整体性FTA，同时又在框架协议中针对东盟新老成员分别实行不同的自由化时间表。而后，鉴于新加坡在东盟国家中情况特殊，贸易自由化要求更高，中国又单独与新加坡缔结了双边FTA。纵观此次与东盟国家的协定缔结活动，中国充分考虑了区域经济的整体发展、政治关系的平衡推进，同时还做到了具体对象具体对待，是一次成功的“排序”实践。

但目前，我国区域贸易协定实践似尚存一些不足，须从宏观战略层面认真审视并加以改进，以求综合效益最大化之效果。

(一)我国区域贸易协定实践的主要不足

1.协定缔结活动缺乏系统性思路

从我国目前对FTA对象国的选择思路来看，除经贸利益因素之外，总体上具有明显的重视周边国家、发展中国家和资源市场的倾向。有学者指出：跟美日等发达国家以及智利、墨西哥等部分发展中国家相比，中国目前仍然缺乏系统的整体的自由贸易区战略，表现在对具体目标、选择标准等重要问题没有明确，缺少系统完整的战略规划，不能给贸易伙伴国以明确的信号和意图。[②] 在笔者看来，中国目前对外FTA在对外贸易量的覆盖度上与智利、墨西哥等

---

① 参见李荣林、宫占奎、孟夏:《中国与东盟自由贸易区研究》，天津大学出版社2007年版，第168～173页。

② 辛文琦:《我国自由贸易区建设有待突破的几个瓶颈》，载《现代财经》2010年第8期。

国家相比，也显得不够。[①] 因此，不同协定的统筹安排与“排序”问题在我国的自由贸易区战略中也应提上议事日程，以避免不同自由贸易区彼此间的制度冲突，并提高自由贸易区的利用效率，更好地促进我国外贸事业发展和其他外交目标的实现。

2. 协定实体条款存在一定混乱

中国对外各个 FTA 的实体条款存在差异，给贸易管理带来相当不便，与 WTO 规则的关系也有待理清。例如在贸易救济措施条款领域，中国在与巴基斯坦、智利、东盟的 FTA 中，都没有规定全球性保障措施可以对另一方排除适用。但在 2008 年与新西兰的 FTA 则规定：如果原产于另一方的货物的进口并未造成损害，则可将其排除在全球性保障措施之外。2008 年中国与新加坡 FTA 仿效了中国与新西兰 FTA 的以上规定。但 2009 年中国与秘鲁 FTA 以及 2010 年中国与哥斯达黎加 FTA 关于全球性保障措施的条款又发生了变化，没有重复以上规定。如此一来，这不但对于中国商务部增加了进出口监管工作的复杂性，也存在着违反 WTO 非歧视原则的潜在可能性。

在其他类型的实体法律制度方面，中国对外各个 FTA 也存在一定程度的不足，增加政府监管成本或未能有效达到经济目标。例如，一些研究原产地规则的学者批评说，中国对外 FTA 优惠性原产地规则的认定标准过于笼统，特定产品缺乏专门规定，[②]程序性规则不足，[③]以及原产地规则作用单一，仅仅确认产品身份并防止贸易偏移，对本国产业政策方面的保护和引导作用不够，[④]等等。

---

① 在拉美国家中，智利是区域贸易协定的积极参与者，从 FTA 中获得了大量的国际市场准入机会。智利政府希望潜在的贸易伙伴中的 90%都能够被双边或诸边贸易协定所覆盖，其 FTA 对象国的选择范围包括欧盟、欧洲自由贸易区、加拿大、美国、墨西哥、澳大利亚、新西兰、中国、日本、韩国、新加坡等，可见其选择面很广且覆盖了主要贸易伙伴。以上参见孟夏：《亚太区域贸易安排研究》，南开大学出版社 2005 年版，第 188 页。

② 李婧：《中国 FTA 实践的原产地规则评析》，载《福建论坛》(人文社会科学版)2010 年第 9 期。

③ 易在成：《优惠原产地规则与 WTO 多边贸易体制的冲突与协调》，载《河北法学》2006 年第 4 期。

④ 孟国碧：《论优惠性货物原产地规则的双刃剑效应》，载《河北法学》2009 年第 4 期。

(二)相关建议与对策

为此,本文提出以下几点建议:

1. 进一步加强同周边发展中国家或重要资源生产国的FTA谈判或可行性研究,特别是与中亚五国、印度以及海湾国家等贸易伙伴要加快步伐,通过经贸关系的加强来巩固政治联系,确保中国拥有良好发展的周边环境和资源供给来源。例如可考虑利用上海合作组织的现有平台,与中亚五国(甚至包括俄罗斯)商讨优惠贸易关系的可能性。在已建成的FTA(例如中国与巴基斯坦FTA或中国与东盟FTA)中,可考虑适度加快关税壁垒削减进程和部门覆盖度,或在关税壁垒已充分削减的情况下,加快非关税壁垒自由化进程,力争将贸易创造功能最大化。

2. 在欧美等主要贸易伙伴由于种种原因暂时不可能与我国缔结FTA的现状下,我国可考虑与一些重要的FTA"轴心"国家(例如墨西哥、韩国、日本等)缔结FTA,以利用这些国家在FTA网络中的"轴心"地位,从而更顺利地进入其他国家的市场。[①] 与"轴心"国家缔结FTA除利用其特殊地位获取经济利益之外,还可望在一定程度上缓解中国目前面临的严峻的贸易摩擦形势。例如墨西哥是目前对中国发起贸易救济措施较多的发展中国家,如中墨之间能缔结FTA,那么可望争取墨西哥方面在FTA中承诺对贸易救济措施进行节制使用。

3. 在西方发达国家对与我国缔结FTA总体上持消极态度的现状下,我国可以考虑有意识地选择一些发达国家进行重点突破,再由小及大进行逐步扩展。鉴于欧盟是关税同盟,无法各个突破,那么那些不是欧盟成员国但发展水平较高的欧洲国家(例如瑞士、挪威、冰岛等"欧洲自由贸易区"成员国等),我国不妨重点考虑。[②] 若能在一两个国家上取得突破,即可利用欧洲自由贸易区与欧盟之间的FTA关系,将我国产品更顺利地间接打入欧盟市场。此外,北美自由贸易区中的加拿大似乎也可考虑,这将有助于我国产品更好地进入美国市场(前文所述与墨西哥缔结FTA亦可收类似之效果)。

---

① 这方面令人鼓舞的是,中国已经与新加坡、智利等"轴心"国家缔结了FTA。而中日韩自由贸易区的构想也得到了三国官方的确认,参见新华网:《第四次中日韩领导人会议宣言》,at http://news.xinhuanet.com/world/2011-05/22/c_121444999_2.htm,访问日期:2012年1月30日。但必须看到,中日政治关系现状是一个较大制约因素。

② 目前冰岛、挪威等国已经进入我国FTA谈判的议程。

4. 在与发展中国家的双边 FTA 中加强贸易投资便利化措施的规定。如前所述，欧美发达国家常常以贸易投资便利化措施为诱饵，换取发展中国家在知识产权、环境保护、劳工标准等方面的让步，这固然值得我国警惕。但在我国与发展中国家的 FTA 中，本着互利互助的精神，加强贸易投资便利化的规定有助于降低交易成本，从而实现更大的贸易创造并减少贸易转移。目前从我国与发展中国家之间的 FTA 条文来看，这方面的规定还比较笼统，不利于对外释放明确的政策信息，有待细化。比较典型的例子是中国与东盟 FTA 框架协议第二部分"其他经济合作领域"，尽管列举了很多潜在的合作事项，但形成较正式制度安排的却不多，说明我国目前在贸易投资便利化方面的实际重视程度仍然不足。

5. 加强优惠性原产地规则的研究，改变目前 FTA 原产地条文较为粗糙笼统的现状。宜根据中国现实的产业状况与贸易伙伴的特点，在产业宏观导向上善用双边累积、对角累积以及完全累积等多种累积规则，在产品微观环节上灵活运用 CTC、VC、TP 等不同标准，以更好地促进我国产业与区域经济的发展。同时，仍需顾及 FTA 原产地规则在宏观模式上的相对稳定性和一致性，以避免 FTA 之间制度冲突带来的不利影响。目前，中国与东盟自由贸易区协定以及两个 CEPA、ECFA 的原产地规则尤其需要重点设计，因为这四个自由贸易协定与中国存在"近水楼台"的关系，对中国南部沿海省份的出口推动和产业导向意义更为重大。

6. 在 FTA 实体条文制度方面，我国须尽快考虑出台自己的 FTA 范本。目前美国依仗其强势地位，在对外 FTA 谈判中广泛推行"NAFTA 范式"与"超 WTO 范式"，以此保障美国的经济和政治利益并贯彻其社会文化理念，而广大发展中国家则面临着利益得失不均衡的风险。作为最大的发展中国家，中国如果不拥有自己的 FTA 范本，势必在全球 FTA 浪潮中失去主动权。中国 FTA 范本可考虑在一定程度上吸收美式 FTA 的合理成分，例如将投资内容纳入 FTA，贸易与投资领域分别设置争端解决机制（这些已被中国现有 FTA 所采用）；在贸易救济措施等领域应尽量统一规定，减少商务部门监管负担；此外可在 FTA 中广泛纳入贸易能力建设、电子商务、透明度、企业交流、次区域开发、金融合作等内容，以推进经贸合作深度；在农业自由化方面应根据国情谨慎处理，量力而行，不宜在实体法律条款中作出硬性义务规定；而对于知识产权、竞争政策、环境保护等欧美热衷的领域，现阶段作为发展中国家，中国尚不宜盲目接受过高程度的义务。

On the Issue of Comprehensive Arrangement in the Implementation of the Regional Trade Agreement Strategy

Zhang Xiaojun* Liu Bin**

Abstract: Nowadays, the proliferation of the regional trade agreements will surely bring great confusion for the legal order of international trade, establishing an overall arrangement in the implementation of the regional trade agreement system is an urgent request for the countries in China-ASEAN area. Currently, EU and USA already have made some instructive practices on the strategic co-ordination of regional trade agreements, and this has produced initial effects and has reference values on sequencing of agreements and designing of substantive provisions. While China is actively engaging in the practice of free trade areas, we should also adopt systematic strategies of free trade areas in view of successful examples like CAFTA, to avoid the institutional conflicts among different free trade areas and improve the efficiency in the use of free trade areas, therefore, promote the development of China's foreign trade and utilize it for China's foreign policy goals.

Keywords: Regional trade agreements; Total arrangement; Sequencing; EU and USA experience; China's practice.

---

* Zhang Xiaojun, Dean of International Law School of Southuest University of Politices and Law, Dr. & Prof. of law, the secretary-general of China-ASEAN Law Research Center.

** Liu Bin, associale professor of International Law School of Southwest University of politics and Law, Pr. of Law. http//www. wto. rog/english/tratop_e/region_e. htm, last visited on Mar. 2, 2012.

For the time being, with the Doha round of world trade talks at a standstill, the global trade liberalization could not have come at a worse time under the situation of the global financial crisis since 2008 and of recent European debt crisis. In this case, countries work on accelerating regional economic integration, the typical strategy is the creation of regional trade agreement (RTA). As more than 3193RTAs have been implemented and over 511 RTAs have been signed, undoubtedly, so many RTAs raise confusions and conflicts in the implementation of international trade law, moreover, these will have an impact on self-interest of the states concerned. As a result, the major challenge facing all countries today is how to make a comprehensive arrangement in the implementation of the regional trade agreement. From the perspective of *New Regionalism*, the main trend solving international trade conflicts worldwide is overwhelmingly adopting of the FTA strategy in the practice of RTA, which has caused notable problem as follow:

Firstly, different FTA has its own certain time of taking effect, transition period, the contents of the preferential trade arrangement, moreover, the comparative advantages of the partner countries inside the treaty are variance. So many differences, not only may decrease the global welfare through repeated trade diversion, but also may damage the dedicated nature of resources through the redistribution of the resources.

Secondly, in the aspect of the contents from different FTAs' provisions, there is an assimilation tendency in the legislation of FTA by taking the provisions of WTO as an example, which includes national treatment, market access administration, trade remedies, sanitary and phytosanitary measures, and the provision of service trade and so on.

European and North American countries have been pioneers in the practice of FTA, their achievements offering us inspiration for implementing an overall arrangement strategies of the regional trade agreement.

(1)Strategic planning and overall coordination macro level.

(2)United arrangement on substantial provisions.

Presently, China has actively promoting the strategy of the free trade area, and has made rapidly progress. But facing the huge tide of the New

Regionalism, China is still a beginner , with dynamic activities of FTAs, which indicate China has not reach the roof of surplus by abusing FTAs as the Euro does. However, with the rapid growth of the FTAs have signed, the problem of the united arrangement should be fully addressed. So far China successfully using the FTA strategy within CAFTA to promote the profit, and reduce the trade attritions and so on, however, the practice has also gotten some insufficiency to improve.

(1)The lack of systematical thoughts while concluding treaties.

From the aspect of choosing a target country of FTA, not only should take account of the economic and trade interest factor, but also think of the overall economical trends of neighborhood, and the orientation of the resources in developing countries.

(2)There are some anarchy in the substantial provisions of the treaties.

The substantial provisionsof China's FTAs are diverse, which has caused conflict both in trade regulation and in relationship between FTAs and the WTO rules.

In this essay, we address a few advices as below:

a. Further strengthen the FTA negotiations or feasibility researches between the adjacent developing countries or the important resources producing countries, especially, the China-Asia 5, China-India, and China-Gulf states, through the economy and trade relationships to strengthen the association of the politics, and ensure a yearn developing adjacent environment and the origin of resource supplement.

b. As for many reasons that we cannot conclude FTA treaties between Euro or the U. S. , we'd better strengthen the relationship between some FTA "axle" countries, such as Mexico, Korea, Japan and so on,in order to hold the chance to conclude FTAs with them, which helps entering into their markets freely.

c. As the fact that many developed countries held the passive attitudes to conclude FTAs with us, we'd consciously select some of them as a breakthrough in order to break the blocks gradually.

d. Strengthen the measures of facilitating investment trade in the bilateral FTAs between China and the developing countries.

e. Strengthen the research on preference of the place of originin order to change the fact that the provisions of the place of origin in FTAs now are rough and ambiguity.

f. It's time for us to consider working out our own FTA sample copy in order to improve the substantial provision system.

中国—东盟自贸区争端解决机制专论

DISPUTE SETTLEMENT MECHANISM FOR CAFTA

中国—东盟自由贸易区（CAFTA）争端解决机制的现状、挑战与前瞻

曾文革[*]　包李梅[**]

内容提要　中国—东盟自贸区的构建中，经济合作领域广泛，合作方式多样，随着合作的不断深入和扩大，经济争端的产生是不可避免的，一个完善的争端解决机制对于自贸区发展的保障作用是无可替代的。《中国—东盟关于争端解决机制的协议》应运而生，为CAFTA争端解决机制的建立提供了法律上的依据。本文在分析CAFTA争端解决机制现状的基础上，提出今后发展中可能出现的挑战，并对机制的发展进行了前瞻性的分析。

关键词　中国—东盟自由贸易区；争端解决机制；未来发展

2010年中国—东盟自由贸易区正式启动，双边经贸关系也更上一个新的台阶，从当前相互贸易的数额来看，中国与东盟国家已经互为贸易大国。随着经济合作上地逐步深入，彼此在货物贸易、相互投资和服务贸易等领域均有很大程度的发展。自贸区范围内也签署了诸多多边或者双边协议，对具体领域内的合作内容进行了规范，以此实现自贸区内公平、透明和便利的市场环境。《中国—东盟全面经济合作框架协议》（以下简称《框架协议》），作为自贸区法律框架中的灵魂性文件，确定了中国与东盟经济合作的宗旨、目的、领域和方式，随后签署的《货物贸易协议》、《服务贸易协定》、《投资协定》以及《争端解决机制协议》，有机结合共同构建了自贸区的法律框架。其中CAFTA争端解决机制的创建，是保障经济领域合作的重要机制，如果缺少了一个完善的争端解决机制，就无法及时、有效地对出现的纠纷进行解决，久而久之，自贸区内的权利义务得不到权威机制的保障，便会使整个自贸区的发展蒙上阴影。作为

* 曾文革，重庆大学法学院教授、博士生导师。中国—东盟法律研究中心研究员。

** 包李梅，重庆大学法学院经济法专业研究生。

CAFTA 的“安全卫士”,该机制的重要意义不言而喻。但是 CAFTA 争端解决机制从创建至今,通过该机制解决的案件寥寥无几,因此有必要深入地对该机制进行分析,挖掘其还存在的不足之处,探讨其发展趋势,以期最大化地发挥其解决纠纷的效能。

一、CAFTA 争端解决机制的现状

(一)CAFTA 争端解决机制概况

中国—东盟自贸区的顺利建成,意味着双边经济合作的逐渐深入和合作领域的慢慢扩展,[①]虽然在当前的双边合作的大部分领域中,均有或多或少的多边、双边协议对缔约国的行为进行约束,并确定彼此的权利义务,但是经济争端的发生总是不可避免的。而且 CAFTA 是国家与区域经济组织构成的区域经济组织,有着其自身独有的特殊性。自贸区的成员内,还有两个非 WTO 成员,即越南和老挝,因此具有普遍适用性的 WTO 争端解决机制在自贸区范围内的适用还存在一定的局限性。在这一特殊的背景下,有必要在面临争端时,促使中国与东盟国家通过谈判建立科学、合理并适合双方发展的解决机制。《框架协议》第 11 条的规定:“各缔约方应在本协议生效一年内,为实施本协议建立适当的正式的争端解决程序与机制。”《中国与东盟关于争端解决机制的协议》应运而生,为自贸区争端解决机制的建立提供了法律上的依据。因此它是落实《框架协议》的重要步骤和措施。《争端解决机制协议》的签署,为自贸区争端解决机制的建立提供了法律依据,立足现实基础,履行其为自贸区的构建和完善保驾护航的宗旨,最终推动实现贸易自由化。

该协议主要包括四个部分的内容。[②] 其一是关于适用范围的内容,将《框架协议》项下发生的争端均纳入了争端解决机制的调整范围,也赋予当事方自由选择其他解决方式的权利,对该机制的适用是自愿的。比如协议第 2 条第 5 款规定:“本协定不妨碍缔约方依据其均是缔约方的其他条约,诉诸该条约

---

① 唐彬、郭凯:《中国—东盟自由贸易区的发展和未来展望》,载《国际经贸》2008 年第 1 期。

② 金霞:《从比较法的角度看中国—东盟自由贸易区争端解决机制》,载《经济问题探索》2011 年第 3 期。

项下争端解决程序的权利”。[①] 其二，是关于争端解决方式的问题，该协议确定了磋商、调解或调停、仲裁四种方式，其中前三种均是协商性的解决方式，是建立在争端双方沟通和交流的基础上，适用这些方式也是由争端方自愿选择的，这些方式的适用一方面是鼓励成员国以和平、和缓的方式解决之间的争端，另一方面在程序上规范较为灵活，提高了解决的效率。仲裁则是在磋商等方式不能解决问题之后，才由起诉方请求启动的程序。协议对仲裁程序的规范也表达得非常详细，具体对仲裁程序中的仲裁庭、仲裁程序、期限、地点选择、第三方问题等均有规定。其三是关于执行程序的问题，因为磋商、调解或调停所达成的协议不具有执行力，对当事方不具有约束力，因此这里所说的执行，主要是指的对仲裁报告的执行，协议规定了仲裁裁决执行的程序、期限等，也设置了补偿和中止减让或利益这一临时性执行措施。其四是有关于该机制的其他问题，包括语言、费用、修订等内容。

(二)CAFTA 争端解决机制的特点

1. 争端解决方式的灵活性

CATFA 争端解决机制规定了多种争端解决方式，非司法解决方式包括磋商、调解或调停，这些方式主要以双方的合意协商为主，是较为缓和、平和的争端解决机制；司法解决方式有仲裁，仲裁庭所作的裁决有约束力、执行力，相比上述方式，呈现出一种刚性的特点。不同的方式有助于争端方通过协商选择合适的、高效率的、低成本的方式解决争端。无论是非司法方式还是司法方式，均呈现出极大的灵活性，其中非司法方式可以随时开始、随时结束，仲裁方式对仲裁地点、仲裁人员的选择等方面也具有较大的灵活性。CATFA 争端解决机制这样的设置，为缔约国之间争端的解决提供了极大的便利，更有利于合作关系的继续保持和推进。

2. 争端解决方式的和平性

多种多样的争端解决方式中，磋商、调解或调停均是更偏重和平解决的方式。虽然并未规定这些方式为必经程序，但是从协议的相关规定可以看出，整个争端解决机制更倾向于促使当事方采纳和平的方式解决争端，比如双方当事方可以在同意的条件下，在最终报告散发前，任意的终止仲裁庭程序，甚至在仲裁裁决作出之前的任何阶段，仲裁庭应做一定的努力促使争端当事方友

---

① Agreement on Dispute Settlement Mechanism of the Framework Between ASEAN and PRC, at http://59.77.27.55/Article/ShowArticle.asp? ArticleID=534.

好解决争端,有义务建议双方对友好方式的采纳和适用。

3. 争端解决当事方的平等性

争端解决机制的申述主体限于国家,各当事方在地位上是平等,机制平等地照顾自贸区内各成员国的要求。此外,还规定了第三方界入程序的权利使得缔约方享有充分合理的机会争取和维护自己的利益,并赋予缔约方提供证据并在仲裁庭为自己辩护的权利。所有的这些均是基于平等性考虑作出的约定,这些规定是该协议所创设的争端解决机制对当事方平等性的尊重和保护的一种体现。例如协议第 6 条第 4 款便作了这样的规定:“每一争端当事方的书面陈述应可使其他争端当事方获得,且每一争端当事方有权在争端的其他当事方向仲裁庭陈述意见时在场。”

4. 向发展中国家的偏向性

从中国和东盟国家的经济发展程度来看,自贸区内缔约国更多是属于发展中国家,在历史背景上有着相似的地方,虽然其中一些国家在世界经济局势的改变大潮中抓住了机遇,实现了本国经济的飞跃,经济发展水平达到了发达国家水平。但是不能从根本上改变中国—东盟之间南南合作的性质。基于这一现状特点,倾向自贸区内大多数国家的利益,便是倾向发展中国家的利益,因此这一争端解决机制的创设更多是偏向发展中国家的。

5. 争端解决机制的完备性

该协议的签署,为中国—东盟自贸区创建了一个较为成熟的争端解决机制。协议内容一共有 18 条,对适用范围、解决方式、执行等问题均做了全面、具体、详细的规定,使《框架协议》项下所有权利义务的争端得以在本争端解决机制下寻求解决。自贸区的构建以及顺利建成之后,不可避免地会出现这样那样的经济争端,因此一个完备的争端解决机制也是自贸区不可或缺的一个部分,是自贸区的支柱。它可以为自贸区的顺利运行树立一个保护的屏障,实现为协议下缔约方经济争端定分止争。

6. 申诉主体的明确性

中国—东盟争端解决机制是自贸区自身包涵的内容之一,协议对争端解决机制的申诉主体进行了明确,只有一国政府才能作为争端解决机制的主体提起申诉,而不包括个人。这一有别于 WTO 争端解决机制的规定,是出于政治安全的考虑,虽然经贸领域的合作可以为双方创造巨大的经济利益,挖掘市场潜力,但是双方在政治领域上还存在一定的敏感、不安定因素。协议将申诉主体限定在国家这一主体上,主要是为了避免因个人申诉的原因导致一些政治上的问题,否则政治上的不安定,最终会影响双方经济上的长期合作。

二、CAFTA 争端解决机制面临的挑战

协议的签署为自贸区创建了一个较为完备的争端解决机制，协议内容涉及方方面面，确定了多种争端解决方式，该机制提倡缔约国之间和平友好地解决争端。协议这一定位的确定对于当前 CAFTA 的发展而言是非常适用的。因为双边在经济上的合作还处于一个起步阶段，中国与东盟国家之间也还存在一定程度上的政治敏感地带，虽然实现区域经济一体化和贸易自由化是创建自贸区的最初宗旨和最终目的，但基于当前现实，对双边政治上和平友好关系的维持和发展也是重中之重。只有首先保证了双边政治关系的友好和平，方能可持续地发展经济合作。但是随着中国与东盟国家政治友好关系地逐渐巩固，以及经济合作程度的逐渐深入，当前的 CAFTA 争端解决机制也会迎来新的挑战。

（一）主体范围问题

《争端解决机制协议》在序言中便指明了争端解决机制的主体为国家，即只有成员国国家政府才能作为机制的主体提起请求，私人、企业等均不享有向 CAFTA 争端解决机制提起请求的权利。这样的规定一方面是基于政治上的安全考虑，因为中国和东盟国家之间还存在一定的不稳定因素，[①]如果将私人主体纳入 CAFTA 争端解决机制的主体范围，对私人起诉往往不能全面管理，从而出现引发双边政治敏感的可能性，一旦导致政治上的不安定，最终也还会阻碍贸易合作和经济发展。另一方面，也基于对个人利益的保护，因为在个人利益与他国利益发生一定程度的冲突时，私人所属的国家会基于大局考虑，搁置个人利益以维持国与国之间的和平交往和经济合作。但是在自贸区内的合作，往往不是国家与国家之间进行的经济上合作，而是具体到企业、私人之间的往来，个人与个人利益、个人与国家利益之间不可避免地会产生一定的冲突，不能以逃避的态度置之不顾。这一机制将国家作为唯一主体，与企业是主要主体的实践之间存在脱节。自贸区内的争端解决机制未将私人、企业纳入主体范围，一旦他们在经济合作中出现争端，只能寻求 ICSID（国际投资争端解决中心）或者其他国际仲裁组织予以解决，这就增加了自贸区内争端解决的

---

① 尤安山：《中国—东盟自由贸易区建设——理论、实践、前景》，上海社会科学院出版社 2008 年版。

时间和金钱耗费。而且将争端留待其他争端解决机制予以解决,鉴于相互间宗旨、精神、模式等的差异,其他机制未必能合理有效地解决争端,也不能全面地维护争端各当事方权利。

(二)仲裁程序问题

有关自贸区争端解决机制的机构问题,协议仅仅创设了联络点,在各成员国内设立联络点,由其负责协议内所有事项的联系事务,仲裁庭的设立也是临时组建的。根据协议第7条的规定:"仲裁庭应包括三名仲裁员,由起诉方在被诉方收到设立仲裁庭请求之日起20日内指定一名仲裁员,由被诉方在收到设立仲裁庭请求之日起30日内指定一名仲裁员,第三名则由双方当事人在协商的基础上共同指定。"仲裁庭的设立是随着当事方确定仲裁员而设立,随着争端的解决而解散,虽然这样的设置方便争端方在需要的时候聘请仲裁员,比较灵活、快捷,也节约了人力物力。但是这一协议所创建的争端解决机制是自贸区内唯一的官方正式争端解决机制,缺乏常设机构在法律程序上也显得不正式。而且根据上述规定,仲裁庭的仲裁员是根据当事方自己指定,协议要求仲裁员公正公平地履行仲裁职能,仲裁员自身也要具备相关方面的专业知识,但是有关回避的内容,协议只对仲裁主席设置了国籍上的回避。此外,协议也对当事方不能协商指定仲裁员的情况作了规范,即根据具体情况请求WTO总干事或者国际法院院长进行指定。这两点笔者都认为存在可完善之处。随着双边合作的深入,会出现越来越多的纠纷,出现的纠纷所涉及的领域也会逐渐扩展,仲裁作为争端解决的重要方式,其完善对自贸区的发展有着重大的意义。

(三)仲裁裁决执行问题

争端的解决方法主要包括是政治、协商或者司法的方式。[①] 协议确定自贸区争端解决机制内的争端解决方法主要是调解解决方式和仲裁解决方式,其中调解解决方式有磋商、调解两种方式。我们所讲的CAFTA争端解决机制的执行是指在仲裁解决方式下对仲裁裁决的执行。仲裁庭作出的仲裁裁决,是对当事方具有法律约束力的裁决。CAFTA争端解决机制仲裁相较于一般的涉外仲裁,有其特殊性,争端解决机制的主体范围限定为国家政府,起诉方和被诉方均是国家政府,因此仲裁裁决对具体的国家行为也具有约束力。

---

① 陈安:《国际经济法学》,北京大学出版社2001年版,第497页。

仲裁裁决在国内的执行具体是以法律法规完善的方式还是以政策的形式实现，都是需要加以考虑的问题。因此本文中有关仲裁裁决的问题是对具体的仲裁裁决在国内的执行的问题。而且仲裁裁决虽然是对国家的约束，但是最终会在国内涉及相关企业、私人，如何让国内企业、个人及时地应对因纠纷仲裁裁决所产生的影响，也是我国在发展中国与东盟经济往来中不可忽略的一个问题。虽然当前在自贸区争端解决机制中我国并没有作为被诉方有需要执行的仲裁裁决，但是随着双边贸易的深入和自贸区的发展，往往难以避免会涉入纠纷，也不可避免地会适用仲裁的方式解决纠纷，因此在国内预先考虑建立产业预警机制等，对我国在双边经济合作中的发展也是及其有利的，也是必需的。

（四）惩罚机制问题

惩罚机制的缺失首先表现在仲裁程序中各当事方不遵守期间限制或者不履行相关义务时缺乏惩罚机制，这对于程序的顺利进行创造了钻空子的可能，一些当事方会一味的拖延，造成仲裁程序的实质瘫痪。协议对仲裁裁决的执行规定由当事方协商确定，首先由被诉方通知起诉方有关执行的具体意向，然后在限定或者协商的时间内执行完毕。但是对其惩罚措施只设置了补偿和中止减让或利益这一临时措施，“起诉方可以寻求对于仲裁庭认定有违反《框架协议》或者造成丧失或损害情形的部门相同的部门中止减让或利益，如果不可行或者无效，则寻求中止其他部门项下的减让或利益”，然而针对具体的程度和力度方面，协议却没有相应地做准确的规范。这一点需要在一定程度上借鉴WTO和北美自贸区的争端解决机制的相关规定：“其惩罚水平应与利益损害相当”。

（五）上诉机制问题

纵观争端协议内容，仲裁是“一裁终局”的，未作上诉程序的设定。[①] 上诉机制的缺失意味着当事方在仲裁过程中一旦出现程序上、或实体上的不当时，便失去了维护自己权益的程序和可能性，尤其是在在诉讼过程中，出现仲裁庭组成不当、明显超越权限等情况。因为如果是实体上的不合法或者不合理，当事方还可以通过达成新的仲裁协议，或者其他方式继续解决彼此的纠纷。但是如果是因为程序上的不当，又通过仲裁程序达成了一个具有法律效力的仲

① 肖小文：《CAFTA争端解决机制的法律探讨》，载《学术论坛》2011年第3期。

裁,在这种情况下,对于当事方中处于不利地位的一方,上诉机制的缺失便使其失去了通过上诉获得申诉的权利。虽然制度设计时未纳入上诉机制,是旨在提升机制的运行效率,促使当事方采纳其他协商方式解决争端,但是上诉机制的缺失最终会导致某些当事方的合法权益找不到合法的程序而得不到维护。

三、CAFTA 争端解决机制的前瞻

从 CAFTA 争端解决机制的现状来看,该机制具备较大的灵活性和自主性。其建立是对自由贸易区运作的一个保障,《争端解决机制协议》与《框架协议》实质上就是程序法与实体法的关系。只有这一争端解决机制的存在,才能有效、合法、合理地解决自由贸易区在实践中出现的纠纷,通过一系列的程序和措施,保障自贸区内各缔约方的权利得到行使,督促其履行自己的义务,使自贸区内呈现一种繁荣有序的景象,实现自由贸易区的顺利构建和健康发展。中国—东盟自贸区的进程充满风雨,CAFTA 争端解决机制从创设至今也是质疑诸多,而且不断发展的经济合作对其提出了一些新的挑战,针对新的挑战我们也要不断地推动机制的完善和发展,只有 CAFTA 争端解决机制的与时俱进,才能最大限度地发挥其对自贸区运作的保障功能,对其未来发展我们还是有理由充满信心的。

(一)在争端解决机制外创设商事仲裁机制

自贸区经贸的发展和合作的深入是一个必然趋势。因为自贸区的顺利建成,中国与东盟将发展成为一个统一的市场,双边经济上的往来也会随着增多,不可避免地会发生纠纷,自贸区内唯一的官方争端解决机制却将最主要的主体——企业、个人划出了主体范围,使其产生纠纷时要寻求其他争端解决机制,这无疑增加了争端解决的难度。但是具体的扩大主体范围的方式,并不必然地通过双边协议将原来《争端解决机制协议》中有关主体的范围进行扩大。因为一旦将私人主体纳入 CAFTA 争端解决机制的主体范围,这对于自贸区成员国在区域内维护本国经济主权也有不利之处。从目前中国和东盟国家在政治关系来看,一些不恰当的私人起诉,还是有可能引发政治上的矛盾,进而

影响双边在经济领域的合作。[①] 因此有必要建立单独的中国—东盟商事纠纷解决机制，专门解决自贸区内私人主体之间的商事纠纷。

(二)完善仲裁程序

首先是常设机构的创设，协议对争端解决机制的机构只是在各国创设联络点，由其负责所有联系事务，但是创设常设机构是必须的。仲裁庭不限定地点的组建，对于处理成员国之间跨国纠纷是有利的，方便当事方自行安排各自方便的地点解决纠纷。但是争端解决机制还是需要创设一常设机构，负责争端解决机制的日常事务，包括档案的管理、调解和调停的主持、仲裁员名单管理，还可以考虑将上诉机构设置在此。常设争端解决机制相比这样临时性的机构，有其无可替代的优点，常设争端机制可以有一套科学的运作流程和不断地累积经验。而且当前协议中有关 WTO 总干事和国际法院院长指定仲裁员的制度，显得不合理，这一职责也可以考虑将其纳入这一常设机构中行使。

其次是有关仲裁人员组成的完善，协议第 7 条中确定在当事方未能就第三名仲裁员达成共识的情况下，由 WTO 总干事或者国际法院院长进行指定，但是从 WTO 或者国际法院的相关规则中，并未找到这一权利的法律依据。[②] 也就是说，无论是 WTO 总干事还是国际法院的院长，均没有这一国际法上的依据行使这一职责。因此有必要对这一规定作一定的修正，这一权利应该由自贸区内部机构行使，可以由秘书处在仲裁专家名单中抽签。这一不足之处，从另一侧面也体现了设立创设常设机构的必要性。此外，协议第 7 条规定仲裁主席不能属于争端当事方国民或者在当事方常住或在当事方从业，这也存在一定的缺陷，因为这一禁止性条件不应只放置在仲裁主席，而未对其他仲裁员作此限定。再加上仲裁员是由当事方分别自己指定一位，这样难免会出现这样的局面，自己指定的仲裁员只从自己的立场出发争取自己的利益，使得仲裁难以公平公正的裁决，成员国对仲裁的信任度也会逐渐降低，最终会导致整个争端机制的威信降低。因此，这一禁止性条件，可以考虑同样适用于其他仲裁员。

---

① 沈四宝：《论中国—东盟商事争议解决机制的构想和建议》，此文为第四届“中国—东盟法律合作与发展高层论坛”发言稿(2010 年 11 月)。

② 龚柏华：《区域贸易安排争端解决机制比较研究》，载《上海对外贸易学院学报》2005 年第 8 期。

(三)完善仲裁裁决在国内的执行

CAFTA争端解决的解决方式中的磋商、调解和调停等属协商性的方式,该方式下具体的程序和执行,均是由双边协商进行的。而仲裁是由仲裁员基于公平公正对案件进行调查后作出了一个判断,仲裁裁决的执行是具有强制性的。而且自贸区争端解决机制内仲裁也具有特殊性,其主体是国家,仲裁并不能和民事仲裁裁决一样,通过国内法院的承认进而执行。目前为止,我国还未有通过这一争端解决机制进行的案件处理,上诉无论是协商性的还是程序性的执行方案,其执行主体是国家,需要国家采用一定的方式进行执行,对其进行执行之后必然地会对国内相关产业产生一定的影响。因此一方面要在如何执行仲裁裁决以减少对国内产业的影响进行考虑,因为仲裁裁决的执行均有期限的规定,可以先使用相应的政策,实现对仲裁裁决的执行,然后采用法律的方式对原有的制度、规范进行修改和完善,以稳定国内相关产业。此外,还要在国内创建相应的预警机制,一旦国内产业的某些指标超出自贸区某些协议的规范时,政府便开始督促该行业进行渐进式的改进和完善。

(四)完善惩罚机制

《争端解决机制协议》对未在规定时间内执行仲裁裁决的情况下,赋予起诉方实施补偿、中止减让或利益措施的权利,即可以由双方协商达成补偿调整协议,或者在补偿协议无法在限定时间内达成的情况下,由起诉方寻求对于仲裁庭认定有违反《框架协议》或者造成损失的部门相同的部门中止减让或利益。当前协议的缺陷是未对具体的补偿水平等做出规定,可以借鉴WTO或者北美自贸区的相关规范,对这一惩罚措施进行具体水平方面的限定,即要求惩罚水平应于利益丧失或者损害水平相当。此外,在被诉方认为惩罚水平存在不合理之处时,赋予其提起仲裁的权利,这样方能有效地防止一些滥用惩罚权的情况。

(五)创建上诉机制

自贸区争端解决机制对上诉机制的缺失,对维护当事方的权利方面存在极大的漏洞。仲裁是争端解决机制常用且重要的一种争端解决方式,通过具体的仲裁程序,达成仲裁裁决并据此执行。但是对于一些因程序不合法原因导致的仲裁裁决不合法,缺乏上诉机制处理此类情况。因为如果是实体法的

不当适用，还可以由当事方在此达成仲裁裁决重新仲裁。北美自贸区的争端解决机制中设置了相应的特别异动程序，作为上诉机制解决程序性违法案件。[①] 因此有必要借鉴北美自由贸易区的这一制度措施，创设上诉机制，具体的机构设置，可以将其放置在上述建议的常设机构中。

结　论

《中国—东盟关于争端解决机制协定》的签署，为自贸区争端解决机制的创建提供了法律上的依据。从协议的内容来看，其主体限定国家、强调磋商等和平型解决方式、争端解决的灵活性等，使CAFTA争端解决机制呈现政治性和司法性并存。[②] 但是从主体限定和偏向和平性解决方式等内容可以看出，该机制从一定程度上讲，政治性更强。[③] 该机制的创建，并没有简单地复制WTO争端解决机制或者是北美自贸区争端解决机制这些业已顺利运行的机制，[④]而是在充分考虑自贸区贸易合作、经济实力以及各缔约国的政治、文化和历史因素，综合形成的一个颇具儒家思想的争端解决机制，提倡争端的和平解决。政府间通过长久磋商最后选定这一政治偏向性的争端解决机制，CAFTA争端解决机制的这一定位也是从有利于双方关系的正常化出发的。事实上，带有较强自主性和灵活性的争端解决机制，在当前未能快速实现争端解决机制司法化的条件下，对双方争端的有效解决和自贸区的发展起了实质意义上的推动作用。随着自贸区的顺利建成，以及双边经济合作的逐渐深入，争端不可避免地会出现，当前争端的解决更多是依赖协商性解决方式，这些争端解决方式的程序设置的比较灵活，从另一方面看，则略显随意，尤其是对其执行，执行力度让人堪忧。这些都需要从争端解决机制的外部和内部诸多方面加以改善。此外，纵观WTO争端解决机制和北美自由贸易区争端解决机制、欧洲法院等区域争端解决机制，其发展的路线均是逐渐从政治性向司法性发展的

---

① 陈伟贤：《建立完善东盟自由贸易区争端解决机制》，载《经营管理者》2011年第5期。

② 衣淑玲：《CAFTA争端解决机制的完善与发展趋势》，载《西南政法大学学报》2006年第8期。

③ 孙志煜：《CAFTA争端解决机制条约化之路——NAFTA、CAFTA争端解决机制的比较视角》，载《武汉大学学报》(哲学社会科学版)2010年第5期。

④ 张彬：《国际区域经济一体化比较研究》，人民出版社2010年版。

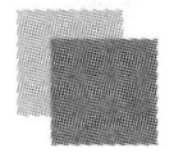

一个过程,[①]因此司法化是否是CAFTA争端解决机制发展的一个趋势,值得进一步思考。

① 樊安、李春玲:《构建更具司法性的中国—东盟自由贸易区争端解决机制》,载《学术探索》2011年第2期。

China-ASEAN Free Trade Area(CAFTA) Dispute Settlement Mechanism's Current Situation, Challenges and Prospect

Zeng Wenge　Bao Limei

Abstract: In the process of China-ASEAN Free Trade Area's construction, the cooperation between china and ASEAN countries turns to be closer. The cooperation field is becoming wider, and more complex. Dispute between contracting parties is unavoidable in the process of cooperation. For the development of the Free Trade Area, a dispute settlement mechanism will play an irreplaceable security role. 〈Agreement on Dispute Settlement Mechanism of the Framework between ASEAN and PRC〉 emerges as the time required, and it provides a legal basis for the CAFTA dispute settlement mechanism. The paper based on the analysis of the CAFTA dispute settlement mechanism's current situation, puts forward its challenges, and presents the prospective analysis of CAFTA dispute mechanism.

Key words: China-ASEAN Free Trade Area(CAFTA); dispute settlement mechanism

The bilateral economic and trade relations come to a new stage when China-ASEAN Free Trade Area launched officially in 2010. China and ASEAN countries have been each other's largest trading nation. There is a deepening economic cooperation between China and ASEAN countries, the cooperation field is becoming wider, and more complex. The cooperation can be founded every field, including trade in goods, trade in service, and mutual investment. Even "Framework agreement on comprehensive economic cooperation between the people's republic of China and the Association of

South East Asian Nations" is the soul of the legal framework of trade document, a dispute settlement mechanism will play an irreplaceable security role, because of the unavoidable dispute in the process of cooperation. 〈Agreement on Dispute Settlement Mechanism of the Framework between ASEAN and PRC〉 emerges as the time required, and it provides a legal basis for the CAFTA dispute settlement mechanism. The paper based on the analysis of the CAFTA dispute settlement mechanism's current situation, puts forward its challenges, and presents the prospective analysis of CAFTA dispute mechanism.

The first part is about the current situation of the CAFTA dispute mechanism. The history of 〈Agreement on Dispute Settlement Mechanism of the Framework between ASEAN and PRC〉 is introduced in brief. Then the content about it is expounded into four parts. First is about the sphere of application, second is the dispute resolution, third is enforcement process, the last is other problems of the mechanism. We can draw the characteristics of the CAFTA dispute mechanism through its content. Then the author summarized these features in six key words: flexibility, peace, equality, bias, completeness, clarity.

CAFTA dispute settlement mechanism is coming across new challenge, because it is a protocol mechanism more than a dispute settlement mechanism. A deepening economic cooperation will put forward new requirements, the author pointed out five challenges. First is the problem of the extension of subject, so far the subject of CAFTA dispute settlement mechanism is country, but the economic cooperation is happened personally or between person and company, there exist a gap which reducing the function of the mechanism. Second is the problem of the arbitration procedure, the Institutional settings and staffing shall be improved. Third is the enforcement of arbitration award problem, implementation requires more specific because the subject of the mechanism is country. Forth is about punishment mechanism, if the defendant country does not enforce the arbitration, there is no punishment mechanism which can supervise the implementation. Fifth is about the appellate mechanism, the arbitration of CAFTA dispute settlement mechanism is "final cut", when there is some injustice in procedures or enti-

ty, this "final cut" will increase the difficulty of safeguarding the rights and interests.

The last part shows the new challenges of CAFTA dispute settlement mechanism, which requires some improvement. In order to maximize its protection function, the most important way is making the CAFTA dispute settlement mechanism to keep pace with the times. We still have confidence for its development in the future. Based on the content stated in last three parts, the author also summarized four improvements. Firstly, there can be a commercial arbitration mechanism parallel with CAFTA dispute settlement mechanism, in order to expand the scope of subject, especially the personal subjects and companies. Second, to improve the arbitration proceeding, lay the keynote on structural establishment and staff. Third is about perfecting the arbitration enforcement in the domestic implementation, attaching importance to amending of the municipal law. The last is the creation of the punishment mechanism and appellate mechanism, which are all key link of the mechanism.

The creation of CAFTA dispute settlement mechanism, is not a simple copy from the WTO dispute settlement mechanism or NAFTA dispute settlement mechanism. But in consideration of the FTA trade cooperation, economic strength and political relationship, cultural and historical factors, they integrated a dispute settlement mechanism, which advocates peaceful settlement. Similar to the WTO dispute settlement mechanism and the North American Free Trade Area of dispute settlement mechanism, its development route is from a process of political orientation to judicial development gradually. Therefore, the judicial tendency is a worthy consideration trend for the development of the CAFTA dispute settlement mechanism.

条约争端:WTO 和中国东盟自由贸易区争端解决机制

Vilawan Mangklatanakul* 宁红燕 译

简介:在过去的几年中,全球化对国际贸易和投资产生了重大影响。跨境交易变得频繁,跨国公司延伸到世界各地,但是增长的过程中也产生了各种争端,因此争端解决机制在一定程度上对保证法律确定性尤为重要。法律确定性反过来又能提供稳定和可预测性的贸易体系。

本文将讨论一些争端解决机制,这些解决机制能够有效地适用在国际贸易和投资领域不同类型的条约争端中。具体地说,笔者将着重谈到 WTO 争端解决机制和中国—东盟自由贸易协定的争端解决机制。

随着投资者影响力增大,各国越来越倾向于推动自己的政策和获取利益,涉及贸易争端解决的所有成员都不容忽视。为了从这样复杂的关系中获取最大利益,我们需要了解私人部门和国家怎样通过不同的机制相互作用。

一、争端类型

争端类型大致可分为两大类:国家与国家之间的争端,投资者与国家之间的争端。

传统上,随着国际公法与国际私法的分离,条约争端更多地涉及国家与国家之间的争端。根据定义,只有缔约国有权谈判并制定条约。因此,根据该条约规定,有权提出主张的成员必须是该条约的缔约国,这主要涉及 WTO 争端解决机制和中国东盟自由贸易协定争端解决机制。

随着跨国公司越来越多的参与和他们对商界影响力的增大,对那些本有权提出主张的组织进行限制则显得不合理。国家为维护其公民的利益,在某些特定情形下允许个人投资者加入谈判席位,个人投资者与国家意见相左情

---

* 作者是泰国条法司国际法发展部主任。

形的条款在条约中也有体现。这主要是中国—东盟自由贸易协定争端解决机制的条约争端。

二、国家与国家之间的争端

(一)WTO 争端解决机制

《WTO 协议》成立了世界贸易组织，并规定 WTO 的职能主要是执行《关于争端解决规则与程序的谅解》(以下简称《争端解决谅解》)这一多边贸易协议。

WTO 争端解决机制是在关贸总协定争端机制的基础上产生和发展的，其中最重要的是乌拉圭回合通过的《争端解决谅解》协议。该协议是为 WTO 这个多边贸易体制提供保障和可预见性的中心环节，是 WTO 规则实际有效执行的根本保证，反映了 WTO 争端解决机制的主要价值并体现了其重要性。这些原则可以从《争端解决谅解》第 3 条体现："WTO 争端解决机制用来保护其成员'涵盖协议'下的权利和义务的平衡，并依照国际法解释的习惯规则对现有条款进行解释。"它也指出，WTO 的基本功能就是及时解决争端并保障成员国之间权利和义务。

无论争端解决的结果如何，成员国一致同意，《WTO 协议》中规定成员国的权利和义务不能增加或者减少。《争端解决谅解》明确规定，成员国有权针对《WTO 协定》第 9 条规定寻求有权解释。

争端解决的目的是寻求一个积极解决争端的方式，该方式能够被各成员普遍接受，并符合《WTO 协定》精神。因此，尽管《争端解决谅解》针对违反行为规定解决措施，但是它也明确指出，"争端解决机制首要目标是发现不符合'涵盖协议'措施、被作为最终手段的报复性措施并将其及时改正"。

(二)范围和适用

《争端解决谅解》在"涵盖协定"的附录 1 有所体现，在附录 2 中规定了特殊以及其他规则和程序，在 1947 年《关贸总协定》第 22 条及第 23 条有关争端解决原则的条款中也被确认。

1947 年《关税与贸易总协定》第 23 条规定："如一缔约方认为由于(a)另一缔约方未能实施其对于本协定所承担的义务，或(b)另一缔约方实施某种措施(不论该措施是否与本协定的规定有抵触)；或(c)存在着任何其他情况，

它根据本协定直接或间接可享受利益正在丧失或受到损害,或者使本协定规定的目标的实现受到损害,则缔约方为了使问题能得到满意的调整,可以向其认为有关的缔约方提出书面请求或建议。有关缔约方对提出的请求或建议应给予积极的考虑。”

此外,《争端解决谅解》第 4 条规定,每一成员承诺对另一成员提出的有关在前者领土内采取的、影响任何使用协定运用的措施的交涉给予积极考虑,并提供充分的磋商机会。因此,《争端解决谅解》并不局限于《WTO 协定》中所规定的违反行为,像“任何影响‘涵盖协定’的表示以及措施”的非违反争端也被纳入。这标志着《争端解决谅解》在适用范围上比《WTO 协定》更广。

虽然《争端解决谅解》只适用于国家与国家间的争端,但遭受另一缔约国侵害的私人部门可向本国请求以国家名义提起主张。因此,理解这些侵害的具体内容以及如何利用《争端解决谅解》维护自身利益对于私营部门尤为重要。

根据第 2.1 条,争端解决机构的建立是为了执行《争端解决谅解》的相关规定,促进“涵盖规定”的磋商和争端解决。争端解决机构有权设立专家组,有权以“反向协商一致原则”通过专家组和上诉机构的报告,监督建议或裁决的执行,并授权成员国中止减让或中止其应承担的其他义务。

(三)争端解决机制程序

1. 磋商:磋商是争端解决的必经程序

《争端解决谅解》规定,一成员向另一成员提出磋商要求后,被要求方应在接到请求后的 10 天内做出答复。如同意举行磋商,则磋商应在接到请求后 30 天内开始。如果被要求方在接到请求后 10 天内没有做出反应,或在 30 天内或相互同意的其他时间内未进行磋商,则要求进行磋商的成员可以直接向争端解决机构要求成立专家组。

为提高磋商有效性,每一成员承诺对另一成员提出的有关在前者领土内采取的、影响任何使用协定运用措施的交涉给予积极考虑,并提供充分的磋商机会。所有此类磋商请求应由请求磋商的成员通知争端解决机构及有关理事会和委员会,提交书面磋商请求,说明理由,并指出相关法律依据。

2. 成立专家组:磋商未果,投诉方可向争端解决机构请求成立专家组

当一方提出要求进行协商的 30 天内,必须开始协商,如果 60 天后争端仍未得以解决,一方便可申请成立专家小组。争端解决机构在接到申请后的第二次会议上必须做出决定,即同意或不同意成立专家小组。只有争端解决机

构全体反对，专家小组才不能成立。专家组的设立比争端解决机构的设立要复杂，专家组的成员可以是政府官员，也可以是非政府人士，这些成员均以个人身份工作，不代表任何政府或组织，WTO 成员不得对他们做出指示或施加影响。专家组成员是独立的，且不得为争端国家的公民。

通常情况下，专家组首先听取争端各方陈述和答辩意见。然后，专家组将报告初稿的事实和理由发给争端各方。在专家组规定的时间内，争端各方应提交书面意见。待收到各方的书面意见后，专家组应在调查、取证的基础上完成一份中期报告，并向争端各方散发，再听取争端各方的意见和评议。为使程序更加有效，专家组进行审查的期限，自专家组组成和职权范围议定之日起最终报告提交争端各方之日止，一般不超过 6～8 个月。根据《争端解决谅解》第 16 条规定，尽管有上诉机构，专家组意见仍然要做出。

3. 上诉机构审理：当事方对专家组报告不服，可以提起上诉

上诉机构是一个由 7 人组成的常设机构，通常由其中的 3 个人共同审理上诉案件。上诉机构成员由争端解决机构任命，任期四年，可连任一次。上诉机构的审议，自争端一方提起上诉之日起到上诉机构散发其报告之日为止，一般不超过 60 天。争端解决机构应在上诉机构报告散发后的 30 天内通过该报告，除非争端解决机构经过协商一致决定不予通过。

4. 补偿和中止减让：争端一方胜诉，则进入执行监督程序

如果上诉一方的抱怨的确合理，上诉审理机构也作出裁决立即停止侵害。为了保证裁决的执行，争端解决机构要起到监督作用。如果败诉方未能执行争端解决机构的建议或裁决，则胜诉方可以要求争端解决机构授权中止减让或中止其应承担的其他义务。但是，这样的补偿和中止制度被认为是合理期限内未履行义务所采取的“临时性措施”。

三、中国—东盟自由贸易区

《中国—东盟自由贸易区全面经济合作框架协议》第 11 条第 1 款规定了争端解决机制。此条约规定了正式解决争端程序以保证未来中国—东盟自由贸易经济合作的正常运行。各缔约方应在协议生效 1 年内，为实施协议建立适当的正式的争端解决程序与机制。

(一)范围和适用

《中国—东盟自由贸易区争端解决机制协议》仅限于国家之间。缔约国间

关于货物、投资和服务的争端解决方式在《争端解决机制协议》的第 21 条、第 13 条、第 30 条中都有规定。

《争端解决机制协议》第 2 条全面规定了该协议的适用范围。根据该条的规定,《争端解决机制协议》适用于《框架协议》下发生的争议。由于《框架协议》包括其附件,各缔约方也可以继续根据《框架协议》缔约更多的协定,因此《框架协议》的内容除目前已经达成的协议之外,还包括将来依据其缔结的所有法律文件。由于缔约方之间的争议可能同时涉及多个条约的规定,因此需要确定具体适用的争端解决程序。如果争议当事人已经选择根据该协议解决争议,除非当事人一致同意采用一种以上的争端解决机制,否则当事人就不得再选择其他争端解决机制来解决争端。

(二)磋商

只要缔约方根据《框架协议》直接或间接享有的利益遭到损害,或者《框架协议》任何目的的实现受到阻碍,则缔约方可以对另一缔约方提出磋商。与 WTO《争端解决谅解》不同,《框架协议》下的《争端解决机制协议》不包括非违反争端。磋商是解决争端有效方式,但是如果一成员不要求磋商或者提出磋商要求后另一方在 30 天内没有答复,那么根据第 6 条规定,要求方可以提出仲裁程序。一般情况下,如果争端在 60 日未解决,当事人可以书面申请仲裁庭审理。

(三)仲裁庭

《争端解决机制协议》第 7 条第 6 款规定,仲裁员不能是争端任何一方国家成员,一般采取不公开的方式审理争议。根据第 7 条第 6 款规定,如果双方在规定时间内都未能指定仲裁员,那么适用独任仲裁员制度。但是,仲裁员不能是争议当事人方的国民。由于中国—东盟自由经济区国家关系紧密,因此有必要核查仲裁员是否与当事人一方有关系。

(四)多方投诉

《争端解决机制协议》规定下的这种活动的特点是一方败诉会影响到其他人。因此,也可能会有不止一个申诉方。在此情形下,第 4 条第 6 款规定,一方无论何时认为自己在正在进行的磋商中享有实体利益,都可以递交书面申请要求加入磋商。如果一方认为自己对既存利益有异议,那么也可加入磋商。

关于首席仲裁员的任命,如果双方都要求自己选定,根据第 6 条第 3 款规

定，仲裁庭实行独任仲裁形式，其中仲裁员为双方共同选定人员。但是，当事人双方的权益都应考虑在内。如果适用独任仲裁形式，双方当事人的权利义务不应增加或减少。虽然这种形式看似合理，有时却很难解决争端。另外，如果采用多位仲裁员形式，双方共同指定一人为首席仲裁员，尽最大能力解决争端。

对仲裁庭审议的争端享有实质利益并且已经将其利益书面通知争端当事方和其他缔约方的第三方，应享有向仲裁庭提交书面陈述的机会。而且这些书面陈述也应提交争端当事方，并反映在仲裁报告中。另外，如果第三方认为争议所涉措施造成其在《框架协议》项下的利益丧失或减损，则该第三方可诉诸《框架协议》项下的正常争端解决程序。

（五）执行、中止减让或利益和补偿

根据第 13 条规定，如果建议和裁决未在合理期限内执行，当事方可采取相应的临时措施，如中止减让或利益和补偿。中止减让或利益应限于未正确执行仲裁庭建议的争端方所享有的减让或利益。补偿是自愿的，而且如果给予，应与《框架协议》一致。

（六）投资者和国家

经济全球化过程中出现了跨国经济一体化，这样的集成是成功的，跨国的生产方式在一定程度上具有相同性。随着跨国公司在经济、政治领域的影响越来越大，国际贸易规则需要注意这些跨国公司的需求。因此，主权国家有权按照自己的意愿制定规则，他们往往想要限制这种大范围的资本流动行为（外国直接投资）。

有些国家尤其是发展中国家极力吸引外国直接投资，这其中是有原委的。外国直接投资不仅为国内市场引入资本，同样它们也创造就业机会、增加收入和税收。它们也可以带来新的技术，促进某些特殊领域的发展。同时，外国直接投资增加竞争，为当地企业提供激励措施来提高它们的标准。当然，主权国家必须确保它们有足够的权利控制政策以保护公民福利。反过来，跨国公司外国投资者也需要获得相应待遇，政府不得任意征收或侵犯它们的权利。简而言之，国家在极力吸引外国直接投资的同时也想限制其权力，因此跨国公司要遵守东道国政府政策。要确保外国投资者和主权国家的关系关键在于平衡两者之间利益，这往往以国际标准为依据，但至少要在以条约为基础的标准范围内。

(七)最主要成员

每当谈到外国投资者或者投资问题,我们都会想到三个主要因素:母国、东道国、投资者。

正如本文前面所提到的,一般说来,主权国家被认为是国际法传统意义上的最主要成员。如果是这样的话,投资过程中产生的法律问题将由投资者母国以国家名义与被投资国通过外交途径解决,并不须投资者积极参与。投资者母国为维护本国国民利益将代替投资者提出主张,主张一般都是东道国实施违背国际法原则的行为侵害到母国利益。

但是,随着对外直接投资逐渐成为令人满意的经济实体,许多资本输出国因投资者发言权不断扩大而接受更多义务。投资条约中常常可见赋予投资者争端解决权利的条款,这意味着外国投资者在投资协议中享有国际发言权,可以使用国际争端解决程序来对抗东道国或者代替东道国履行义务的代理商或实体,进而保护投资协议中的投资者。尽管条约赋予投资者权利提出主张对抗东道国,事实上并没有明确东道国的义务。一方面,东道国仅仅对于母国负有义务,母国才是两国投资协议的缔约方。另一方面,根据两国投资协议规定,投资者在投资协议之外的权利上有权向东道国提出主张。从后者看,外国投资者可能已经被授予对抗国家的权利能力。这一观点将在《中国—东盟自由贸易协定》和《投资协议》的法律问题中谈到。

此外,必须指出要了解国际投资规则下缔约国间的关系就不能忽略投资者的作用,非政府组织和政府组织一样都要考虑在内。毫无疑问,跨国公司常常游说本国政府,成功率多大难以查明。这些组织对经济、政治产生越来越大的影响,甚至会决定一国国家政策。因此,不可对其小觑。

(八)法律问题

正如上文提到的国家和投资者关系的维系关键在于平衡他们之间的利益。为了从外国直接投资获得最大收益,发展中国家须采取例如经营要求、有利于投资者转移科学技术到东道国国内劳动力市场的积极措施吸引投资者。一方必须认识到双方利益所在并集中在可能的灵活性上以实现共同目标。联合国贸易和发展会议的宗旨是促进国际贸易,特别是加速发展中国家的经济和贸易发展进程,制定国际贸易和有关经济发展问题的原则和政策。贸发会议的主要目标是帮助发展中国家增强国家能力,最大限度地获取贸易和投机机会,加速发展进程,并协助它们应付全球化带来的挑战和在公平的基础上融

入世界经济。

法律问题可以分为三类:有关来源的问题、有关标准的问题、有关解决的问题。

1. 有关来源的问题

让每一个人对现行法律形式和内容满意是极其困难的,更不用说国际投资方面的法律。一般看来,国际投资方面的法律与国际条约都是混合型的法律。双边和区域条约的重要性已经日益超过国际法。投资条约有时会用来重申缔约国都可以接受的外国投资者国际最低利益标准,这些标准被广泛用于商业行为,最终形成国际惯例,像最惠国待遇标准和国民待遇标准。但是,不同的标准在给予前通常要仔细核查其是否涉及敏感政策领域。

我们还应认识到,随着跨国公司在全球范围影响的不断扩大,政府间组织和非政府组织开始推行软法和行为准则。上文简要谈过,这些文书并不具备法律效力,但是它们为今后立法奠定了基础。因此,法律工作者最好的方法就是放眼未来,对不断出现的文件采取一种宽容的态度。

2. 有关标准的问题

国际投资法有关实体标准改变需要考虑主要政策问题,这些问题往往是国际投资协议中的核心点,像保护投资者以及他们的投资资金,发展落实国家政策的相关经济措施,限制投资者行为,赋予母国、东道国法律义务。许可制度,设立权,待遇标准,公平待遇,充分保护,知识产权和透明度原则,这些规定在国际投资协议中都有所体现。可能还涉及确定经营要求,转移科学技术,赋予跨国公司更多社会责任以保护本地企业发展的相关政策。

3. 有关解决的问题

目前,有待解决的核心问题是如何解决投资者和东道国之间的争端,程序中会采用《国际投资法》相关规定,因此投资者必须首先认识到行为是否符合东道国的法律规范。此外,如果用尽国内救济,投资者应考虑如何利用国际争端解决机制维护个人利益。如果有效解决机制可以适用,投资者权利将有保障。因此,可预测性水平增加,从而减少风险投资,使得东道国吸引更多外资。

尽管有国内争端解决方式可以使用,但投资者常会选择国际层面的救济像特设国际仲裁或其他国际制度体系。解决国际争端最重要的仲裁机构是国际投资解决中心(ICSID),其所规定的程序要求较为独特。

四、《中国—东盟投资协议》

为确定投资者和东道国双方权利义务,中国与东盟国家签署的《中国东盟全面经济合作框架协议》第 5 条与第 8 条规定建立自由、便利、透明和竞争原则。虽然中国东盟自由贸易区对争端解决机制在《框架协议》第 11 条第 1 款有规定,《投资协议》自身对投资者和东道国也规定了争端解决机制。

(一)范围和适用

《投资协议》适用与缔约国有关在其领土范围内的投资者以及投资,广义上的投资是指投资者根据另一方国家相关法、法规、政策在其领土之内投入的资产。可是《协议》条款对投资行为的规定并不详尽,所以,投资方应该考虑东道国国内相关法律法规以及政策,以保证他们的投资符合法律规定。

为达到解决争端目的,有限的条款对投资者对国家的争端解决机制进行规定,《投资协议》第 14 条的争端解决机制适用于一个缔约方与另一个缔约方的投资者之间产生的,涉及因前一缔约方违反该协议第 4 条(国民待遇)、第 5 条(最惠国待遇)、第 7 条(投资待遇)、第 8 条(征收)、第 9 条(损失补偿)、第 10 条(转移和利润回扣),通过对某一投资的管理、经营、运营、销售或其他处置等行为给投资者造成损失或损害的投资争端。需要强调的是只有实际损失被加以考虑,非违反争端不在范围之内。

(二)程序

与《关贸总协定》的纠纷解决机制类似,在适用第 14 条第 4 款前要先经过磋商和谈判。对于上述投资争端,在当事方磋商未果时,投资者可以用尽东道国当地救济或提交仲裁。在国际仲裁方面,《投资协议》给予了投资者更多地选择:(a)提交解决投资争端国际中心(ICSID);或(b)根据联合国贸易法委员会规则进行仲裁;或(c)由争端当事方同意的其他仲裁机构或根据其他仲裁规则仲裁。

此外,即使投资者已将争端提交缔约方国内法院,如果投资者在最终裁决做出前从国内法院撤回申请,投资者仍可提交国际争端解决机构。然而,对于印尼、菲律宾、泰国、越南,一旦投资者将争端提交给投资东道国有管辖权的法院和行政法庭,或者依第十四条启动国际投资仲裁程序,则选定的程序是终局的。

(三)提交仲裁机构

如果投资者不选择提交争端主管国国内法院,应根据《协议》第 14 条第 6 款规定提交调解或仲裁:(a)将争端提交调解或仲裁发生在争端所涉投资者知道,或者在合理情况下应当知道对本协议义务的违反对其或其投资造成损失之后的 3 年内;以及(b)争端所涉投资者在提交请求 90 日前以书面方式将欲将此争端提交调解或仲裁的意愿通知争端所涉缔约方。

争端所涉缔约国收到通知后,可要求争端所涉投资者在提交争端前完成其国内法规规定的国内行政复议程序。当投资者提出争端缔约方采取或执行税收措施已违背第 8 条(征收),应争端缔约方请求,争端缔约方和非争端缔约方应举行磋商,以决定争议中的税收措施是否等效于征收或国有化。任何依照本协议设立的仲裁庭应根据本款认真考虑双方的决定。

如缔约方未能启动此类磋商,也未能在自收到磋商请求的 180 天内,决定此类税收措施是否等效于征收或国有化,则不应阻止争端所涉投资者根据本条款将其要求提交仲裁。

结　论

若想全面了解东盟法律文件精神,首先是要理解"东盟模式"。保罗·戴维森将"东盟模式"描述为:"为大国领导人和部长提供一个聚首并交换对地区安全和经济议题的意见的途径,而不是通过谈判解决法律中存在的强制性问题。"但是,这种情形只是过去式,现如今各成员国更多地是讨论经济合作计划、签订双边、多边条约这些法律实体问题。如果在金钱利益上出现模棱两可之处,成员国采取友好有效措施解决争端,东盟须加强法制建设达到解决争端的更高水平。因此,条约争端不再局限于传统意义上的缔约国国内政策,交流合作才是解决自由贸易区和对外直接投资争端的关键。

Treaty Disputes: Dispute Settlement Mechanisms under the WTO and China-ASEAN FTA

Vilawan Mangklatanakul *

Introduction

Over the past years, globalization has had a significant impact on international trade and investment. Cross border transactions are now common and multinational companies spread out all over the world. With such growth emerge conflicts with multinational characteristics that need to be addressed. Dispute settlement mechanism is thus important to ensure a degree of legal certainty which in turn provides stability and predictability to the trading system as a whole.

In this paper, I will discuss a few examples of dispute settlement mechanisms available in different types of treaty disputes relating to international trade and investment. Specifically, I will examine dispute settlement processes under WTO's Understanding on Rules and Procedures governing the Settlement of Disputes (DSU) and the China-ASEAN Free Trade Agreement (CAFTA).

With investors becoming more influential and states increasingly pushing their policies and interests, the benefits of all players involved in trade and dispute settlement cannot be neglected. In order to benefit from such a

* Vilawan Mangklatanakul: Director, International Law Development Divisson Department of Treaties and Legal Affairs Ministry of Foreign Affairs.

relationship, We need to carefully examine how the private sector and the states may interact through these different mechanisms.

Types of disputes

One may broadly divide different types of disputes into two main categories: State to State and Investor to State disputes.

Traditionally, with the separations between public and private international law, treaty dispute is associated more with State to State disputes. By definition, those who are able to negotiate a treaty are the contracting states. Thus, it comes as no surprise that those who also have the right to bring a claim under the treaty would be a state who is a party to the treaty. I will consider these types of treaty disputes in relation to dispute settlement mechanisms under the WTO and CAFTA.

With the increasing involvement of multinational companies and their growing influence in the commercial world, such limitation on those who will explicitly have the right to bring a claim is clearly not sufficient. Since states have to take into account the interests of its citizens, it is thus a natural progression for treaties to be negotiated and international instrument to be established in such a way that allow individual investors to have standing in certain circumstances. Provisions allowing measures for investors to bring claims against states are often, therefore, negotiated into an agreement. I will consider this type of treaty dispute in relation to dispute settlement mechanism under CAFTA.

State to State Disputes

The WTO

The Agreement Establishing the World Trade Organizations ("WTO Agreement") provides that one of the principle functions of the WTO is the administration of the Understanding on Rules and Procedures governing the Settlement of Disputes (DSU).

Built on the past GATT practices with several fundamental changes in the operation of the system, the DSU states that the dispute settlement system is "a central element in providing security and predictability to the multilateral trading system"①. This sets out the general philosophy of WTO dispute settlement mechanism and reflects its importance. These principles can be discerned from Article 3 of the DSU as follows:

—The dispute settlement mechanism of the WTO serves to preserve the rights and obligations of the Members under the covered agreements, and to clarify the existing provision of those agreements in accordance with customary rules of interpretation of public international law. It is also noted that prompt settlement of disputes is essential to the functioning of the WTO and the maintenance of a proper balance between the rights and the obligations of WTO members.

—The Members agreed that the results of the dispute settlement process cannot add to or diminish the rights and obligation provided in the WTO's Agreements. It is explicitly noted in the DSU that the Members have the rights to seek authoritative interpretation of provisions pursuant to Article IX of the WTO Agreement, which itself provides that it is the exclusive means for interpreting the WTO Agreement.

—Throughout the provisions in the Article, the aim of dispute settlement is highlighted to be to secure a positive solution to a dispute and that a solution that is acceptable to the parties and consistent with the WTO's agreements is clearly to be preferred. Therefore, while the DSU provides for measures against non-compliance, it explicitly states that "the first objective of the dispute settlement mechanism is usually to secure the withdrawal of the measures concerned if these are found to be inconsistent with the provisions of any of the covered agreements" and retaliatory measures are to be regarded as the last resort.

Scope and Application

The DSU is to be applied to "covered agreements" which are listed in its

---

① Article 3.2 of the DSU.

Appendix 1, with special or additional rules and procedures contained in the covered agreements identified in Appendix 2. The principles for the management of disputes applied under Articles of XXII and XXIII of GATT 1947 are also affirmed.

Article XXIII of the GATT 1947 states that:

"If any contracting party should consider that any benefit accruing to it directly or indirectly under this Agreement is being nullified or impaired or that the attainment of any objective of the Agreement is being impeded as the result of

(a) the failure of another contracting party to carry out its obligations under this Agreement, or

(b) the application by another contracting party of any measure, whether or not it conflicts with the provisions of this Agreement, or

(c) the existence of any other situation,

the contracting party may, with a view to the satisfactory adjustment of the matter, make written representations or proposals to the other contracting party or parties which it considers to be concerned. Any contracting party thus approached shall give sympathetic consideration to the representations or proposals made to it."

Additionally, Article 4.2 of the DSU states that each member shall also undertake sympathetic consideration to and afford adequate opportunity for consultation regarding "any representations made by another member concerning measures affecting the operation of any covered agreement taken within the territory of the former".

Thus, the DSU is not confined to cases where there is a violation of the WTO Agreement. Non-violation dispute is clearly allowed, with "any representations" and "measures affecting the operation of any covered agreement" signifying a wide scope for its application.

While the DSU only applies to State to State disputes, private sectors who have suffered from measures from another contracting state could convince their own state to bring a claim. It is therefore very important for players in the private sector to understand what these violations are and how they can be used in order to rely on the DSU to their benefit.

In accordance with Article 2. 1, the Dispute Settlement Body (DSB) is established to administer the DSU, as well as the consultation and dispute settlement provisions of the covered agreements.

Thus, the DSB will have the authority to establish panels, adopt panel and Appellate Body reports, maintain surveillance of implementation of rulings and recommendations and authorize suspension of concessions and other obligations under the covered agreements.

The DSU Procedure

There are 4 major phrases of WTO dispute settlement. These are consultations, panel establishment, appellate body process and implementation and suspension of concession phrase.

1)Consultations: The parties must first attempt to resolve their differences through consultations.

The DSU sets out the rules regarding the consultations①-of which there are no rules beyond that consultations are to be entered into in good faith and are to be held within 30 days of a request. Despite the loose structure of consultations, significant numbers of cases end at this stage (either through settlements or abandonment of a case). Consultations are without prejudice and are confidential unless the parties agreed otherwise. Through the consultation process, it is hoped that the parties will reach a satisfactory solution without having to resort to the "legalistic approach".

This stage of the process encourages disputes to be solved amicably and in good faith. However, such encouragement can be seen throughout the whole process of the DSU. At anytime during process, the parties may agree to use "good offices, conciliation and mediation" as alternatives. These shall be confidential, without prejudice, may begin and be terminated at any time. They can even continue alongside the panel process.

2)Panel Process: If consultation fails, the complaining party may demand that a panel of independent experts be established to rule on the dispute.

---

① Article 4 of the DSU.

If consultations fail to resolve a dispute within the 60 day time frame specified under Article 4, a complainant may insist on the establishment of a panel. And if the complaining party so requested, a panel shall be established at the DSB meeting following that at which the request first appears on the DSB's agenda. The DSB is then required to establish a panel unless there is a consensus in the DSB not to establish a panel.

The establishment of a panel has much more structure than earlier consultation process. Panel members are chosen with a view to ensure the independence of the member and thus a diverse background and a wide spectrum of experience is required. However, citizens of the members whose governments are parties to the dispute shall not be allowed to serve on the panel unless otherwise agreed by the parties to the dispute.

There are fixed time period for panel reviews and all meetings are held in closed session. All documents submitted are treated as confidential. Disputing parties and any third parties can only be present through the panel's invitation. After the hearings and deliberations, the panel will prepare a report detailing its conclusions. Under the DSU, the time limits suggest that the panel report should normally be issued within 6 to 8 months of the establishment of the panel. And unless there is an appeal, the panel report will be adopted in accordance with Article 16 of the DSU.

3) Appellate Body: An appeal by any party to the dispute to the Appellate Body is possible.

The DSU creates a standing Appellate Body with 7 members, appointed for 4 year terms and representative of WTO membership and only 1 reappointment is permitted.

The Appellate Body hears appeal of panel reports and is required to issue its report within 60 (or at most 90) days from the date of the appeal. Its review is, however, limited to issues of law and legal interpretation developed by the panel. Its report is adopted automatically by the DSB within 30 days.

4) Implementation and Suspension of Concession: If the complaining party succeeds, the DSB is charged with monitoring the implementation of its recommendations.

Typically, if the complaint is found to be justified, the panel/appellate body report typically recommends that the violation is to be ceased. After the adoption of the report, the DSB monitors whether the recommendations are implemented. If not, the possibility of negotiated compensation or authorization to withdraw concessions then arises. The party whose complaint is found to be justified is entitled to seek compensation from the non-complying member or request DSB authority to suspend concessions previously made to that member ("retaliation"). Such suspension of concessions is to be authorized automatically in the absence of implementation or compensation, unless there's a consensus in the DSB to the contrary.

However, such compensation and suspension of concessions are viewed as "temporary measures" to be used when a report is not implemented at a reasonable time.

China-ASEAN FTA

Dispute settlement mechanism exists within the CAFTA itself. Agreement on dispute settlement is established in accordance with Paragraph 1 of Article 11 of the Framework Agreement on Comprehensive Economic Co-operation between the Association of South East Asian Nations and the People's Republic of China ("Framework Agreement"). This provides for the establishment of appropriate formal dispute settlement procedures and mechanism for the purposes of the Framework Agreement within 1 year after the date of entry into force of the Framework Agreement.

The Agreement on Dispute Settlement Mechanism between the Association of Southeast Asian Nations and the People's Republic of China ("DSM Agreement") was therefore established in 2005.

Scope and Application

The CAFTA DSM Agreement only applies to states. Disputes between contracting parties under the Agreements on goods, investment and services, will come under the Agreement on Dispute Settlement, in accordance with Articles 21, 13 and 30 of these Agreements respectively.

The Agreement applies to disputes arising under the Framework Agreement including the Annexes. Also, since all future legal instruments are included in any reference to the Framework Agreement according to Article 2 (1), disputes between the parties arising under the Agreements on goods, investment and services are covered.

It should be noted that once a forum has been selected by the complaining party during the dispute settlement proceedings, that forum shall be used to the exclusion of any other for such dispute, unless the parties to the dispute expressly agree to the use of more than one dispute settlement forum in respect of that particular dispute.

Process

The whole process is triggered by a request for consultation which is based on a complaint from a party with respect to "any matter affecting the implementation or application of the Framework Agreement whereby: (a) any benefit accruing to the complaining party directly or indirectly under the Framework Agreement is being nullified or impaired; or (b) the attainment of any objective of the Framework Agreement is being impeded" as a result of the failure of the party complained against to carry out its obligations under the Framework Agreement.

Explicitly, unlike the scope of WTO's DSU, Article 4. 1 states in its footnote that non-violation disputes are not permitted. Coupled with the limitation stated in the basis of the complaint, consultations will be allowed where the benefit being nullifies or impaired is actual benefit, not just reasonably expected.

The consultation is a chance for the party complained against to address the complaint properly. However, if the party chose not to do so, and the request for consultation is not answered within 30 days, the requesting party may proceed directly to request for the appointment of an arbitral tribunal under Article 6.

Throughout the whole dispute settlement process, the parties to the dispute may agree to conciliation or mediation at any time. They may also agree to begin and terminate such alternatives at anytime. Thus, conciliation

and mediation may occur and, are most likely to occur, alongside dispute settlement process.

Generally, if consultations are not successful in settling the dispute within 60 days after the date of receipt of the request for consultations, the complaining party may make a written request to the party complained against to appoint an arbitral tribunal under Article 6.

Arbitral tribunal

While Article 7(6) of the Agreement states that the chair of the tribunal cannot be a national of any party to the dispute, the matter is silent when apply to members of the tribunal. Article 7(2) also provides that sole arbitrator may be appointed if any party to the dispute fails to appoint an arbitrator within the period provided. However, there is no indication that such sole arbitrator cannot be a national of any party to the dispute[①]. In any case, it remains to be seen whether sole arbitrator is appropriate in a situation where the parties are in close relation as the present case in CAFTA.

Multi-party complaint

Having regards to the characteristics of activities under these Agreements, the alleged failure of a party may affect more than one party to the Agreements. Thus, it is possible for there to be more than one complaining party. In this case, Article 4(6) provides that whenever a party (other than those to a dispute) considers that it has a substantial interest in consultations being held pursuant to the Article, such party may notify the parties to a dispute in writing of its desire to be joined in the consultations . If the party complained against agrees that the claim of substantial interest is well-founded, the party may be joined in the consultation. If such an agreement cannot be obtained, then the requesting party may request for separate consultations under the Article.

At the appointment of arbitral tribunal stage, if there are more than one

---

① Unless that sole arbitrator is seen as the chair of the tribunal itself, then Article 7(6) applies.

complaining party requesting the appointment, Article 6(3) provides that a single arbitral tribunal may, whenever feasible, be appointed by the parties concerned. However, the parties' respective rights need to be taken into account. If a single arbitral tribunal is appointed, it shall be organized in such manner that the rights which the parties would have enjoyed had separate arbitral tribunals examined the same matter are in no way impaired. While this seems to be a reasonable position, such organization may be difficult to achieve in some cases.

Moreover, if more than one arbitral tribunal is appointed, in this situation, to examine the same matter, the same arbitrator shall be appointed by the parties concerned to serve on each of the separate arbitral tribunals and the timetable for the proceedings harmonized to the greatest extent possible.

If there is a third party having a substantial interest in a dispute already before an arbitral tribunal who have notified its interest in writing to the parties to such a dispute and the remaining Parties, that third party shall have an opportunity to make written submission to the tribunal. These written submissions will be given to the parties to the dispute and may be reflected in the report of the arbitral tribunal. Such third party also has a choice to recourse to normal dispute settlement procedures under theAgreement if the third party considers that the measure nullifies or impairs benefits accruing to it under the Framework Agreement.

Implementation, Compensation and Suspension of Concessions or Benefits

If recommendations and ruling are not implemented within a reasonable period of time, compensation and suspension of concession or benefits may be used as temporary measures, by virtue of Article 13. Any suspension of concessions or benefit shall be restricted to those accruing under the Framework Agreement to the Party which has failed to bring the measure found to be inconsistent with the Framework Agreement into compliance with the recommendations of the arbitral tribunal.

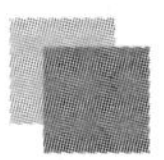

Investor to State

From the process of economic globalization arose transnational economic integration. For such integration to be successful, transnational mode of production needs to have a degree of uniformity across geographical boundaries. With multinational enterprises gaining increasing economic and therefore political influences, it may be said that international business regulation needs to therefore take notice of what these enterprises demand. Thus, it follows that sovereign states, though still have the right to regulate as they think fit, may want to limit such power in exchange of inducing a wider source of capital-namely foreign direct investments (FDIs).

There are many reasons why sovereign states, especially developing countries, may want to attract FDIs. Not only that FDIs increase capital in their domestic market overall, they could help create jobs, increase incomes and thus tax revenues. They could also bring in new technologies and contribute to the development of particular sectors where FDIs are common. They could increase competition and provide incentives for local businesses to improve their standards. Having said that, sovereign states also need to ensure they retain enough power to control their policies and (hopefully in cases of democratic states) protect their citizens' welfares. Multinational enterprises, in turn, need to be assured that they will be treated fairly as foreign investors-that their investments cannot be arbitrarily taken or their rights blindly infringed. In short, while FDIs are desirable and sovereign states seem to be prepared to limit their power in order to attract them, foreign investors still need to respect the policy space of the host government. The key for the relationship between foreign investors and sovereign states to work in such environment thus lies in balancing these interests, possibly through an acceptance of international standards of treatment, at least at treaty based standards.

The principal players

When one considers a scenario involving foreign investors and investment, one may see a set of three main actors: the home state, the host state

and the investors.

As I have mentioned briefly earlier in this paper, with sovereign states traditionally seen as the principal players of international law, generally, only the home state and the host state will have legal standing. By this, I mean legal issues arising out of this scenario would typically be dealt with through diplomatic channel where the home state will make direct representations to the host state without the active participation of the investors themselves[①]. The investor's claim would be taken up by its home state in order to protect the interests of its own citizen. The basis for such claim would be that the host state, by its action towards the foreign investor, has committed a breach of international law (which may be in the form of a treaty) against the home state.

However, with FDIs being desirable in a growing economy, many capital-importing countries are prepared to accept further obligation in international law by extending such *locus standi* to the investors. It has now become increasingly common for an investment treaty to contain a clause provided for a direct, treaty based dispute settlement rights to investors[②]. This means foreign investors can now enjoy a level of international *locus standi* before international tribunal, using international dispute settlement procedure against the host state and/or even its agents and entities in relation to the host state's obligation to protect investor in investment agreements. While this scenario seems to give foreign investor the right to bring claim against the host state, it does not actually clarify the nature of the host state's obligations. On the one hand, the host state still only owes its obligations to the home state-with whom the host state sees as a contracting party to their investment agreement. On the other hand, it may be argued, that, by the investment agreement between the two states, the investor holds the right of

① Even though it is the property/rights of the investors that were alleged to have been infringed/breached by the host state, in this scenario, the private investors would NOT be recognized as a subject of international law.

② To name but a few: bilateral investment agreements between Thailand and Argentina, Thailand and Belgo-Luxemburg and Thailand and Bulgaria.

action against the host state which are new and independent of any rights held by the home's state under that investment agreement. From the latter view, foreign investors may have been granted treaty-based rights of action against the state. This particular issue will further be discussed below when the legal issues typically involved in an investment agreement and the CAFTA itself are considered.

Before moving on to do so, it is worth pointing out that just as one cannot ignore investors while examining the relationship between the parties in international investment rules, the roles of non-governmental organization (NGOs) as well as intergovernmental organization (IGOs) also need to be taken into account. There can be little doubt that multinational enterprises lobby their governments (and in some cases, others' too), albeit their success rates difficult to pinpoint. These NGOs and IGOs, with their ideologies, whether it be promoting the rights to industrial development or demanding more corporate social responsibilities, have political influences which are gaining more weight on the economic and political world and thus on a state's national policies①. Their influences are a part of the voices of the "civil society" that non-economic standards may be pushed forwards-both on the investors and the states. Thus, to ignore these players as a formative influence in international legal instrument would mean the full picture may be missed. NGOs and IGOs' power are therefore not to be underestimated.

The legal issues

As briefly mentioned above, the key for the relationship between state and investors to work lies in the balancing act between their interests. In order to benefit fully from FDIs, a developing host country may need positive measures to increase the investors' contribution such as performance require-

---

① Typically, these organizations find gaps in the law/regulations and contest such regulatory order by placing these issues on the political agenda, demanding that their ideologies be heard and applied. While these demands or, in some cases, the resulting instrument may be non-binding in a strict legal sense, they help to create a climate and laying down the setting for the possibility that binding obligations may follow.

ments or incentives for investors to transfer technologies and skills to the host country's domestic workforce. A degree of regulation is needed to implement such policies. Controls over foreign investors and the manner in which their investments may be developed will therefore need to be imposed. Thus, it is hardly surprising to find that the host states' desired policy goals will be in conflict with their obligations to protect foreign investors and their investments. One must recognize the need for both sides' interests to exist and focus on the possible flexibility to develop a common goal in order to preserve the right for the host state to regulate for legitimate purposes as well as the its commitment to protect investors and their investment.

According to UNCTAD, "flexibility ... relates to a particular set of objectives, those that concerned the promotion of the development of developing countries parties to IIAs, without losing sight of the need for stability, predictability and transparency for investors" and "... particular conditions prevailing in developing countries and to the realities of the economic asymmetries between those countries and developedcountries" need to be recognized①. In order to achieve the objectives while recognizing the prevailing conditions as noted by UNCTAD, one need to look at the legal issues underlying a typical investment agreement and consider whether they, together in a particular case, could provide "stability, predictability and transparency" for investors while giving developing countries enough room for their "policy space".

I propose that these legal issues may be divided broadly into three categories: issues concerning sources, issues concerning standards and issues concerning settlement.

a) Issues concerning sources

It is notoriously difficult for anyone to agree on the precise content and form of customary law-let alone in the context of international investment. Generally, a kind of norm may be seen emerging from a mixture of binding and non-binding instruments as well as international treaties. Bilateral and

---

① UNCTAD, *International Investment Agreements: Flexibility for Development* (United Nations, New York and Geneva, 2000) at 15.

regional treaties have increasingly becoming more significant as a source of international law in this area. These investment treaties may be used to restate international minimum standards of treatment of foreign investors as accepted by the contracting parties. Standards which have long been widely used in commercial conduct may gained the status of customary international law via these treaties, such as the most-favoured-nation (MFN) standard and national treatment (NT) standard. However, giving different standards treaty status in such a way is very likely to involved sensitive policy area which needs to be examined in a case-by-case basis.

It should also be recognized that, in relations to the increasing influences multinational enterprises, NGOs and IGOs seem to be acquiring, soft law or code of conducts pushed forward by such organizations/institutions cannot be ignored. As briefly mentioned before, these instruments may not have a binding legal effect but they could very well set the stage for binding instruments to come later. It is thus always a good idea for practitioners to keep their eyes open for new trend to come in their areas.

b)Issues concerning standards

Major policy issues need to be considered when developing substantive standards in international investment law. These issues are at the "core" of a given international investment agreement. Among other things, one must look at the protection of investor and their investments, the development of economic related measures designed to implement national policies, limitation to investors' actions and measures and obligations of host and home states. These are likely to involved various consideration of provisions which are to be in an international investment agreement such as provisions setting down scope and definition involved, admissions, rights of establishment, standard of treatment, fair and equitable treatment, full protection, property rights, transparency. They may also involve setting down performance requirements, transfer of technology and corporate social responsibility to confer further benefit of the FDI to the host state and leave more space for national policy.

c)Issues concerning settlement

Central to this grouping of issues is how settlement of dispute between

investor and host countries is to be dealt with. International investment law obviously needs to be enforced. Thus, one must consider how this is to be done under national legal systems. In additions, if domestic remedies fail or are not preferred, one must also see further how international dispute settlement mechanism should be applied under the circumstances of individual cases. If effective dispute settlement mechanisms are available, investors' rights are more likely to be reinforced. Thus, the level of predictability will be increased, resulting in the reduction of investment risks, making the host country more attractive to investors.

While there may be domestic systems of settlement available, investors may prefer an internationalized approach such as an ad hoc international arbitration or a more institutional system. The most important arbitral institution with regards to investment disputes is the International Centre for Settlement of Investment Disputes (ICSID), with specific procedural requirements for the use of the system laid out in the ICSID Convention.

China-ASEAN Investment Agreement

To understand their rights and obligations, Investors and states under CAFTA would want to refer to the specific Agreement on Investment of the Framework Agreementon Comprehensive Economic Co-operation between the Association of Southeast Asian Nations and the People's Republic of China (the "Investment Agreement"), established by virtue of Articles 5 and 8 of the Framework Agreement in order to "promote investments and create a liberal, facilitative, transparent and competitive investment regime"[①].

While dispute settlement mechanism exists within the ACFTA itself in accordance with Para 1 of Article 11 of the Framework Agreement, the Investment Agreement has its own provisions[②] for such mechanism which allows for disputes a foreign investor and a contracting state. For disputes between contracting states, Article 13 provides that the DSM Agreement shall apply.

---

① Preamble of the Investment Agreement.

② Specifically Article 13 and 14.

Scope and Application

The whole Investment Agreement apply to measures adopted or maintain by a contracting state relating to investors or another party and investment of investor of another party in its territory. ① Investment is defined broadly to be "every kind of asset invested by the investors of a Party in accordance with the relevant laws, regulations and policies of another Party in the territory of the latter". ② While examples are given to clarify the types of activities which will be seen as an investment for the purpose of the Agreement, they are not exhaustive. Thus, one must also consider the relevant laws, regulations and policies of the host state in order to make sure they/their investments are covered by the Agreement.

For dispute settlement purpose, in particular, the relevant provisions giving basis to investor to state dispute mechanism only apply to limited numbers of Articles. These are Article 4 (National Treatment), Article 5 (Most-Favoured Nation Treatment), Article 7 (Treatment of Investment), Article 8 (Expropriation), Article 9 (Compensation for Losses) and Article 10 (Transfer and Repatriation of Profits). The mechanism provided for under Article 14 will only apply to investment disputes between a party and an investor of another party concerning an alleged breach of an obligation of the former party which fall under these Articles and causes loss or damage to the investor in relation to its investment with respect to the management, conduct, operation, or sale or other disposition of an investment. Thus, it seems only actual loss will be considered. Also, like the DSM Agreement, non-violation dispute will not be considered.

Additionally, there is a link between the dispute settlement mechanism for investor to state dispute in the area of services relating to an investment under the Investment Agreement. In accordance with Article 3(5) of the Investment Agreement, the mechanism under Article 14 may be applied to any measures affecting the supply of a service by a service supplier of a Party

---

① Article 3 of the Investment Agreement.

② Article 1(d) of the Investment Agreement.

through commercial presence in the territory of another party but ONLY to the extent that they relate to an investment and an obligation under the Investment Agreement. It should be noted that the same standards will apply i. e. that non-violation dispute will not be considered and only actual loss will be taken into account.

Process

Similar to the DSM Agreement, consultation and negotiations need to be requested before an investor can submit to use the mechanism under Article 14 (4). Only if the disputes cannot be resolved through consultation and negotiations after 6 months from the date of such written request that the investor may submit its claim.

Unless the parties to the disputes agreed otherwise, investor has the choice to submit its claim (a) to the courts or administrative tribunals of the disputing Party, provided such courts or administrative tribunals have jurisdiction; or (b) under the ICSID if both the disputing Party and the non-disputing party are parties to the ICSID Convention; or (c) under ICSID Additional Facility Rules if either of the disputing party or non-disputing Party is a party to the ICSID Convention or (d) to arbitration under the rules of the United Nations Commission on International Trade Law; or (e) if the disputing parties agree, to any other arbitration institution or under any other arbitration rules.

Once the dispute has been submitted to a competent domestic court, the investor may still submit it to international dispute settlement provided that the investor has withdrawn the case from the domestic court before a final judgment is reached. However, in the case of Indonesia, Philippines, Thailand and Viet Nam, once the investor has submitted the dispute to one of the courts/tribunals/arbitral institutions under Article 14 (4), the choice of procedure is final. This is likely to stop the dispute being prolong since there is only one chance for a court or an arbitral tribunal to consider the case whereas allowing investor to change its mind and withdraw the case may encourage tactical choice being made by an investor.

Submission of dispute to arbitral institutions

If investor chooses not to submit the dispute to a competent domestic court, the submission has to be in accordance with Article 14(6). The requirements are that (a) the submission of the dispute must take place within 3 years of the time at which the disputing investor became aware, or should reasonably have become aware, of a breach of an obligation under the Investment Agreement causing loss or damage to the investor or its investment AND (b) the investor must provide a written notice, which shall be submitted at least 90 days before the claim is submitted, to the disputing Party of his/her intent to submit the dispute to such conciliation or arbitration.

The disputing Party, upon receipt of such notice, may require the investor to go through any applicable domestic administrative review procedure specified by its domestic laws and regulations before the submission of the dispute to the arbitral tribunals. In addition, the notice has to comply with sub-paragraphs (i), (ii) and (iii) of Article 14 (6) (b) as well[①].

Separate process for disputes arising from alleged breach of Article 8 (Expropriation) in the case involving taxation measures

Investors cannot directly request the disputing state for a consultation in this case. If an investor is claiming that the disputing Party is in breach of Article 8 (Expropriation) by the adoption or enforcement of a taxation measure, the disputing Party (the host state) and the non-disputing Party (the home state) shall, upon request of the disputing party, hold consultations with a view to

---

① (i) nominating a forum within sub-paragraphs 4(b)-4 (e) as the forum for dispute settlement and, in case of sub-paragraph (b) nominate whether conciliation or arbitration is being sought; (ii) waive the right to initiate or continue any proceedings, excluding proceedings for interim measures of protection referred to in Paragraph 7, before any of the other dispute settlement forum referred to in Paragraph 4 in relation to the matter under dispute; and (iii) briefly summarize the alleged breach of the disputing Party under this Agreement, including the Articles alleged to have been breached, and the loss or damaged allegedly caused to the investor or its investment.

determine whether such taxation measure has had such effect. A tribunal may also be established to give serious consideration to the question.

If both Parties fail to initiate consultations or to determine the question above within one hundred and eighty days from the date of receipt of the request for consultation, the investor shall then be able to submit its claim to arbitration in accordance with Article 14 in the same process as having been discussed.

Conclusion

It had been said that one must understand the ASEAN way in order to fully see the full picture of what an ASEAN document really contains①. Paul Davidson described the ASEAN way as "involves processes including intensive informal and discreet discussions behind the scenes to work out the general consensus which then acts as the starting point around which the unanimous decision is finally accepted in more formal meetings, rather than across-the-table negotiations involving bargaining and give-and-take that results in deals enforceable in a court of law". ② While this may have been the case in the past, legal certainties are now being embraced with more enthusiasm as ASEAN engages in more economic co-operation schemes, bilateral or multilateral investment treaties among member states or with their partners outside South East Asia. Ambiguity costs money and there must be an efficient process to settle dispute amicably and fairly when they arise. Thus, ASEAN has to become more legalistic as a higher degree of legal certainty is needed. Treaty disputes will therefore no longer be confined to areas traditionally known to primarily involve contracting states and their national policies. Communication and co-operation are the keys to reap the full potentials of an FTA and FDIs.

---

① Alyssa B. Greenwald, The ASEAN-China Free Trade Area (ACFTA): A Legal Response to China's Economic Rise? *Duke Journal of Comparative & International Law*, Vol. 16:193, 202 (2006).

② Paul J. Davidson, The ASEAN way and Role of Law in ASEAN Economic Cooperation, 8 *S.Y.B.I.L* 165, 167 (2004).

中国的条约争端解决机制及实践*

马新民**

内容摘要 条约争端是属于法律性质而非事实问题的争端,是缔约方围绕着条约的解释和适用而产生的分歧或争议,既涉及缔约方实体权利和义务问题,也涉及程序性问题。中国尚未参加或对外缔结关于条约争端解决的专门性条约,有关条约争端的规定散见于中国缔结的双边条约或参加的国际条约有关争端解决的条款中。中国的条约争端解决机制基本形成了以谈判协商为核心,以仲裁为补充,并辅之以调停与和解等第三方介入的争端解决机制。

关于"中国的条约争端解决机制及实践",本文着重分析三个问题:一是什么是条约争端,二是中国参加或缔结的条约是如何规定解决条约争端的,三是中国解决条约争端有何特点、其基本精神是什么。

一、条约争端和解决办法

条约争端是国际争端的主要形式之一。它属于法律性质而非事实问题的争端,是缔约方围绕着条约的解释和适用而产生的分歧或争议,既涉及缔约方实体权利和义务问题,也涉及程序性问题。根据中国的实践,这类争端不仅包括以条约或协定等为名称的文件引起的争议,还包括不以条约或协定为名称、但旨在确定缔约方权利和义务的其他形式的文件引起的争议。条约作为当代国际法最主要的依据,不仅是国家交往与合作的保障,而且是现代国际秩序重要组成部分,因此,条约争端能否得到妥善处理,不仅关系到国际法的有效实

* 本文是系 2011 年 9 月在吉隆坡举行的"中国—东盟法律合作与发展高端法律论坛"上的发言。

** 马新民,中国外交部条法司参赞。

施，直接影响国家间关系的状况，更重要的是决定国际秩序的稳定和发展。

中国一贯重视处理条约争端问题，始终遵循《联合国宪章》确立的和平解决国际争端国际法基本原则，承认谈判、协商、调查、调停、和解等外交途径以及仲裁和司法机构等法律途径，是处理包括条约争端在内的各种国际争端的通常办法。原则上，除调查这种主要涉及事实问题的争端解决方法外，其他办法都应适用于条约争端解决。

二、中国的条约关于条约争端解决办法的规定

中国在条约争端解决机制方面的国际缔约实践起步较晚，但发展较快。中国的条约争端解决机制是与中国融入国际社会的历史进程密不可分的。

1949 年中华人民共和国成立后的很长一段时间内，谈判和协商基本是解决条约争端的唯一方法。自 1971 年恢复联合国合法席位，特别是 1978 年改革开放以来，中国广泛参与国际立法活动，迄已参加 300 多项国际公约、对外缔结了两万多项双边条约。这些条约基本都以不同形式规定了解决条约争端的方法。除继续采用谈判和协商办法外，仲裁、任择性的斡旋、调停与和解等第三方介入的解决办法也被采用，目前中国的条约争端机制已逐步形成多种争端解决办法并存的局面。

总体看，中国尚未参加或对外缔结关于条约争端解决的专门性条约，有关条约争端的规定散见于中国缔结的双边条约或参加的国际条约有关争端解决的条款中。大体有以下三种模式：

一是规定通过谈判和协商解决有关条约争端。中国对外缔结的政治和外交类双边条约，包括引渡、司法协助、互免签证、领事等涉及主权的条约，以及民航、交通、海运、税收类技术性双边条约，一般都把谈判和协商作为解决相关条约争端的唯一方式。

二是规定可通过谈判和协商、仲裁解决有关条约争端。中国对外缔结的投资保护、贸易、商业、经济、科技、文化等非政治类双边条约，以及中国参加的部分经贸、科技、交通运输、航空、航海、环境、卫生、文化等技术性国际公约，一般都规定缔约方应首先通过谈判和协商解决有关争端，如不能解决，经协商或应缔约一方请求，应提交仲裁解决。但中国在参加人权、反恐、打击跨国有组织犯罪等国际条约中，都对其中有关将争端提交仲裁的规定作出保留，不接受通过仲裁解决此类条约争端。

三是规定可通过谈判和协商、仲裁以及调停或和解等第三方介入解决有

关条约争端。如有些条约规定缔约方可同时选择谈判和协商、调停、和解、仲裁、司法解决或其选择的其他和平方式。也有一些条约规定缔约方应首先采取谈判和协商,与此同时允许自愿选择调解或调停等第三方介入解决办法,如上述办法无法解决,可约定选择仲裁或争端解决机构程序,如WTO争端解决程序、中国--东盟自由贸易区《争端解决机制协议》、双边自贸区协定大体属于此类。

三、中国的条约争端解决机制的特点及基本精神

从中国的条约争端解决缔约实践可以看出,中国的条约争端解决机制有以下特点:

一是谈判和协商是解决条约争端的优先和主要方式。中国对外缔结的双边条约大多把谈判和协商作为解决条约争端的唯一和优先的方法,很多条约甚至把谈判和协商作为缔约方解决有关争端的一项义务。中国参加的国际公约一般也把谈判和协商作为解决争端的首要方式。

二是自愿仲裁是解决条约争端的重要补充。中国在对外缔结和参加的非政治、外交、安全类条约中广泛采用或接受通过非强制性仲裁解决有关条约争端的办法。但这种仲裁通常是自愿的、非首选的,通常只有在谈判和协商无法解决争端的情况下,经缔结方协商同意或经缔约一方请求才得使用。谈判和协商是首要和前提,仲裁只是必要补充。

三是谨慎采用调停与和解等第三方介入的争端解决办法。调停、和解等办法涉及非缔约方介入条约争端,中国一般较少在条约争端解决中采用这种办法。目前只有双边自由贸易协定和个别经贸类国际条约采纳了这种争端解决办法。

四是不接受国际司法机构的强制管辖权。中国不接受国际法院的强制管辖权,也从未与任何国家签订将争端提交国际法院的特别协议。中国对外缔结的双边条约从未同意将有关争端诉诸国际法院,对参加的国际公约规定的强制性司法解决争端条款都毫无例外地作出保留。对有关经贸、科技、航空、环境、交通运输、文化等技术性的国际公约所规定的须经缔约方同意提交国际法院解决争端的任择性条款,中国虽未作保留,但从未同意向国际法院提交过任何争端案件。中国尚没有将争端提交国际司法机构的先例。

需要指出的是,中国一直重视国际司法机构在维护国际和平与正义方面的重要作用,积极支持国际司法机构的工作,有多位中国籍法官在国际法院、

国际海洋法法庭、南斯拉夫问题国际刑事法庭等国际司法机构任职，为有关国际司法机构的发展做出了重要贡献。

简而言之，中国的条约争端解决机制基本形成了以谈判协商为核心，以仲裁为补充，并辅之以调停与和解等第三方介入的争端解决机制。这一机制是一个以平等自愿为前提、以国际法为依据、以友好协商为核心、以互利共赢为目标的和平解决争端机制，体现了“合意”这一条约法的精神，符合中国的国情和国际通行做法，已被实践证明是可行、有效的。

中国的条约争端解决机制是中国独立自主和平外交政策的具体体现和必然要求。中国坚持走和平发展道路，高度重视维护国家主权，反对外来干涉，也从不干涉他国内政。中国始终相信当事方的“合意”是解决分歧的根本，一贯致力于同当事方进行友好协商，避免任何无利害关系的第三方卷入争议中。对待条约争端，中国一贯主张根据公认的国际法，通过当事国之间的直接对话协商加以解决。

同时，中国的条约争端解决机制也与中国传统文化精髓一脉相承。中国几千年来崇尚“和为贵”，非迫不得已不愿对簿公堂，讲求用非对抗性方式而不是通过诉讼方式解决矛盾分歧。

无数的事实证明，通过谈判和协商解决条约争端的利用率高，有效性强，已被证明是解决条约争端的“快行道”和理想选择。

2011 年是中国与东盟建立对话伙伴关系 20 周年。20 年来，中国—东盟关系取得了长足发展，互利合作不断深化，如期建成了惠及区内十几亿人民的中国—东盟自贸区。中国法律界愿进一步加强与东盟各国同事的合作与交流，丰富双边关系内涵，为中国—东盟睦邻友好关系奠定坚实的法律基础！

The Mechanism and Practices of Dispute Settlement under the Treaties in China

Ma Xinmin

This paper focuses on the following three questions: firstly, What is the dispute under the treaties? secondly, What are the rules created in the treaties China has attended to cope with the disputes? thirdly, What are the criteria and traits China coping with the disputes under the treaties?

The dispute under treaties is a kind of dispute related to the interpretation and application of the treaties. According to the practice of China, such disputes include controversy led by documents in the name or not in the name of treaty or agreements.

China has attached great importance to the disputes under the treaty, and always follows the basic international legal principle the peaceful settlement of international disputes—stipulated and established in the Charter of the United Nations, admits the diplomatic means such as negotiations, consultations, investigation, mediation, reconciliation and others, as well as the legal means including arbitration and judicial institutions, which are the common ways to cope with the disputes including the treaty related dispute. In principle, Except designed only for the fact finding, all the means are applicable to the disputes under the treaties.

Although China's attendance to the establishment of the mechanism of treaty disputes settlement starts late, it develops fast. And the treaty-related dispute settlement mechanism in China is inextricably linked with the historical process of China's integrating into the international community.

Generally, China hasn't attended or signed any specific treaties specialized in the disputes settlement, and there are only provisions related to trea-

ty disputes settlement which are scattered in the bilateral or international treaties China attended. These provisions can be generally devidied into the following three kinds:

1. To resolve the treaty disputes through negotiations and consultations. Political and diplomatic bilateral treaties China signed, concerning extradition, mutual legal assistance, visa abolition, consular treaties and others related to sovereignty; as well as technical bilateral treaties, in the area of civil aviation, transportation, shipping, and taxation, generally regard negotiations and consultations as the only way to cope with the treaty disputes.

2. To resolve the treaty disputes through negotiations, consultations and arbitrations. Non-political bilateral treaties China attended concerning foreign investment protection, trade, commercial, economic, scientific and technological, cultural and relevant affairs as well as some technical international conventions china attended or signed about economy and trade, science and technology, transportation, aviation, marine, environment, health, cultural and so on generally provide the parties an arbitration mechanism after they have failed to settle disputes through negotiations and consultations. But under treaties concerning human rights, counter-terrorism, transnational organized crime, there is always a reservation that the disputes cannot be settled by arbitration.

3. To resolve treaty disputes through negotiations and consultations, arbitration, and mediation or conciliation by third party intervention.

From the perspective of China's practices, there are the following traits China's treaty dispute settlement mechanism shows:

(1) Negotiations and consultation is the priority and main way to resolve treaty disputes.

(2) Voluntary arbitration is an important supplement to resolve treaty disputes.

(3) Cautiously using of third party intervention in the dispute through mediation or reconciliation and other solutions.

(4) Avoiding the compulsory jurisdiction of international judicial institutions.

The treaty dispute settlement mechanism is a concrete manifestation and an inevitable requirement of China's independent and peaceful foreign policy. And it is an embodyment of the essence of traditional Chinese culture.

Countless facts prove that resolving treaty disputes through negotiations and consultations has high utilization, effective validity, and is a short cut as well as an ideal way to resolve the treaty disputes.

条约纠纷：国际争端解决*

Datuk Azailiza Mohd Ahad**
林建荣　凌波　孙超　译

"争端解决对于国际法的重要性，就如病理学在医学中的地位。最坏的情况莫过于各国制定规则的共识不复存在，争端各方对规则的实质意思各有分歧，对于谁违反了国际规则，在多大程度上违反国际规则以及因此造成的后果各方也争持不下这些情况是各方都不愿看到的结果。"①

一、导论

条约在国际关系中发挥着基础性的作用。条约是一个或多个的主权国家之间，或者一个或多个国际组织间签订的国际协议，它是依照国际法且以书面形式订立的。如果在这样一个条约下产生争端，缔约国就需要一个合适的途径来解决争端。为此，国际社会通过建立国际争端解决机制，来处理由于国际义务而引起的纠纷，更重要的是维护国际和平与安全。

联合国宪章呼吁主权国家通过自主选择的方式和平解决国际争端。这个理念在《联合国宪章》的宗旨中有所体现，正如其第 1 条所说：

"联合国的宗旨是：

1. 维持国际和平与安全，一直到本条末尾……遵循正义和国际法的基本原则，调整或解决国际争端以及任何足以破坏和平的国际情势。"

第 2 条　更详细地阐述了应该如何解决国际争端：

"为求实现第 1 条所述各宗旨，本组织及其成员国应遵行下列原则：

3. 所有成员国应该以不危及国际和平、安全和正义的方式，妥善地解决

---

* 本文系第五届"中国一东盟法律合作与发展高层论坛"上的发言整理。

** 作者是马来西亚总检察长办公室官员。

① Cesare Romano 教授：《国际纠纷解决》，载《牛津大学国际环境法指南》，2007 版。

他们之间的国际争端。”

第 33 条也规定了解决国际争端的合理途径：

“1. 任何争端之当事国，若争端持续状态足以危及国际和平与安全，应首先通过谈判、调查、调停、调解、仲裁、司法程序、区域性机关或区域性协议的利用，或当事国自行选择的其他和平方式，求得解决。”

争端解决机制的类型的范围广泛，涵盖从包括谈判、调查、调停或调解等“外交手段”到那些有法律约束力的方式，即通过诸如仲裁或将争端提交至国际司法机构等司法途径。

二、国际司法机构

国际司法机构可以被分为国际法庭、仲裁法庭和准司法机构。国际法庭是永久性机构，争端适用预先确定的程序性规则。

仲裁法庭则在处理每个争端时重新建立。这些程序规则通常是预先确定的，尽管在某些情况下，当事人双方通过协商一致，改变相关程序。

国际法院和仲裁法庭是通过一个国际法律协议建立，它们作出的判决具有法律约束力的。

准司法机构与国际法院和仲裁法庭不同，它一般是对争端事项进行调查进而对案件作出裁决。但是这些裁决都不具有法律约束力。联合国人权公约下的各种规范机制便是这些准司法机构的主要例子。这些不同的司法机构和准司法机构列举如下：国际法庭有海牙国际法庭、国际海洋法法庭、国际刑事法庭；仲裁法庭有常设仲裁法院、WTO 争端解决专家组和上诉机构、国际投资争端解决中心等；准司法机构有人权委员会，消除种族歧视委员会，消除对妇女歧视委员会，经济、社会、文化权利委员会等。国际司法机构的特点可以归纳如下：(a) 常设性机构；(b)由独立的法官构成；(c)裁决两个或两个以上国际法主体之间的纠纷，其中至少一方要么是国家，要么是国际组织；(d)其运行是基于先定的程序规则；(e)作出的判决具有约束力。这些国际司法机构的其他共同点还有：“首先，所有这些实体机构都作出法律裁决，这使他们区别于其他机构，例如都以‘公正的世界’为愿景但都具有典型政治性特点的联合国大会或欧洲理事会议会大会。确切地讲，这 125 个机构确定某些行为是否与特定的规范相一致。这就引出了其第二个共性，即它们都采用相同的法律体系——国际法作出裁决。第三，所有这些国际组织都直接或间接(例如，通过一个依条约建立的机构所作的决定)通过国际协议建立。由此可见，他们依

据不同于国内司法系统的法律规则建立，但同时又主要有赖于各个主权国家的支持。最后，或许更重要的是，它们共同表达了人们普遍的一个愿望，即摈弃'国家至上，强权至上'的国际旧秩序，并支持建立一个新的秩序，即人们拥有某些基本的共同价值观，在国际社会大群体中受到所有成员的保护并加以执行，包括国家、国际组织和个人（非政府组织、民族、公司、自然人等等）。"①

在传统的国际法中，自然人或非政府组织并不享有国际法上的法律地位，因为国际法上的主体一般指传统意义上的主权国家，在某种程度上，包括国际组织。② 这是可以理解的，因为只有具有国际权利和义务以及有能力通过国际主张维护其权利的实体才可以成为国际法调整的对象。③ 然而，越来越多原本由国内法管辖的领域提升至国际层面，伴随着环境、贸易、劳务和人权方面等一系列国际协议的出现，国际法的新主体应运而生了。

例如，根据双边投资条约，如果一个主权国家违反该条约，自然人投资者有权以其为被告将争端提交国际仲裁。其之所以成为可能，是因为当事的主权国家在国际协议中明确表示同意这一做法，从而保证了个人或非国家实体获得了该项权利，并使这项权利国际法庭中具有效力。

三、国际贸易争端解决机制的典型架构

大多数国际条约中规定的争端解决机制旨在实现以下两个目标中的一个：首先，争端解决机制应该为当事方提供足够的磋商和信息交换的途径来避免争端；其次，第一个目标如果没有实现，则应通过友好和高效的方式解决争端。

解决任何潜在的争端的第一步通常是要求当事方本着友好解决争端的目的进行磋商。这个过程通常是解决争端的第一阶段。如果争端仍悬而未决，则进入下一个步骤，即诉诸争端解决机制下建立的司法机构。为进一步推动这一进程，争端解决机制通常要求当事一方将与争端有关的信息告知对方，尤其是，磋商的要求必须伴随着对于讨论中措施的确认，以及显示该争端的事实和法律依据。为此，缔约国必须提供足够的信息，以确保对该措施会在多大限

---

① 《概要》(第3版)，http://www.pict-pcti.org。

② Reparation for Injuries cases, *ICJ Reports*(1949), p. 179.

③ Brownlie, *Principles of Public International Law*(6* Edition), Oxford University Press(2003), p. 57.

度上对协议的运作产生影响进行充分检查。为了鼓励双方充分利用协商程序,争端解决机制通常会要求协商程序开始并经过一定时间后,争端各方才能将此争端提交到仲裁法庭。

如果协商在规定的时间内未能解决争端,申诉方便可以进行下一步了。根据争端解决机制,他可以直接将争端提交双方一致同意的或既定的法庭,或通过向另一方提出要求,组成一个仲裁庭来裁决此争端。

若需要建立仲裁庭,争端解决机制会委任仲裁员,规定任命仲裁员的一些必要的要求和条件。任命最后一个仲裁员的日期即为仲裁法庭成立的日期(特别是在由三名仲裁员组成仲裁庭的情况下)。

法庭会遵循争端解决机制规定的程序进行。这将包括会议的进行、场所、当事方提交书状、法庭裁决过程以及法庭最终裁决的形式与内容。

一旦做出裁决,必须允许一个合理的时间来实现争端的解决。如果在实施仲裁裁决时发生争议,当事方可以进行下一步,即寻求补偿、暂停让步或根据协议应得到的利益。这需要通过进一步的裁决来确定适当的补偿标准或暂停让步或得利。

四、双边争端解决机制和世界贸易组织争端解决谅解

在国际贸易环境中,世界贸易组织多边平台——多哈回合谈判因其冗长和无成果,使得双边和地区性自由贸易协议如雨后春笋般涌现,进而创造了大量的双边和地区性争端解决机制。这催生了针对各种国际贸易对象的国际管辖权的扩散,即通过订立独立但又相互重叠的协议来规范商品、服务贸易和投资。各种国际仲裁机构的成倍涌现,反映了在各种国际法律协议下,争端当事方寻求解决争端的途径也大大地增加了。

相互重叠的管辖权增加了解决争端可选择的机构,更明显重要的是,也增加了滥诉的可能性。滥诉有违正义,因为一项争端的公平解决取决于不同仲裁机构之间的技术性差异,因此,且申诉方总会寻求就本案对他们最有利的机构。仲裁机构过多也会增加这样一种可能性,即申诉方会在每一个机构都提起诉讼进而寻求于己最有利的裁决结果。因此,为了缓解这种担心,许多国际协议契约,都有关于一旦一个裁决机构被选定则排除其他机构管辖的规定。然而,这种方法并不总是有效的,因为义务的违反可能基于一个独立的国际协议的规定,由此产生独立的诉因。

尽管如此,双边贸易协议中的争端解决机制继续寻求提供双边解决争端

的方法。通常由于双边贸易协定包含了世界贸易组织附加承诺义务的内容，因为如果不这样的话，这些承诺则没有保障。世界贸易组织附加承诺义务的范围不仅包括比世界贸易组织多边贸易承诺更为完善的要约，以及覆盖了多边框架没有规定的领域，如承诺投资、劳务、环境和竞争政策。各方还通常寻求双边争端解决机制，因为它被公认为是更为省时，更为灵活而不僵化的争端解决程序。

五、挑战

能够有效地和高效地管理避免争端是维持国际友好关系的关键。我们怎样才能改进争端避免程序呢？

双边争端解决机制的兴起是不是预示着多边框架争端解决机制的消亡呢？在贸易环境中，双边争端解决机制通常被认为是比世贸组织框架更为“有效”的争端解决方式，因为通过 WTO 框架解决争端往往会耗费大量的人力、物力和时间。双边的、区域性的和多边的争端解决机制的扩散也使得国际法的变得零散，因为这些争端解决机制不是一个协调统一的系统，而是各自相互独立的。

处理世界贸易组织附加承诺需要双边和区域争端解决机制的参与。然而，这将如何影响世界贸易组织附加承诺义务的长期增长和发展呢？

在确保商业、贸易和投资环境的平衡并具有吸引力方面，争端解决机制起着全面地保障作用。

当司法管辖权或国际法庭的裁决优先适用发生冲突时，那一种会被普遍接受呢？世界贸易组织的法律体系一直被认为没有法律约束力，但仍然很有说服力，因为专家组和上诉机构努力确保其能和世界贸易组织的法律体系保持一致。条约所引起的争端能不能提交到国家法院呢？对于像马来西亚这样坚持二元论的国家来说，违反国际义务不能当然地被认为违反了国内法。

我们如何避免各种纠纷被重复提交到不同法院呢？对任何国家来说，案例准备和纠纷管理是都一个巨大的挑战。一些常见的挑战包括数据收集不足，缺乏时间、金钱和人力等资源，以及纠纷管理本身。

六、马来西亚的贸易争端案件

1. WTO：DS1—聚乙烯、聚丙烯禁止进口措施

原告:新加坡

被告:马来西亚

案情简介:

- 1995.1.10—磋商请求
- 1995.3.16—成立专家小组
- 1995.7.19—撤诉

2. WTO: DS58—美国虾案

原告:印度、马来西亚、巴基斯坦、泰国

被告:美国

争议措施:美国禁止从非认证国家进口虾及虾类产品(即未利用海龟隔离器进行捕虾的国家)

案情简介:

- 1996.10.8—磋商请求
- 1998.5.15—专家组作出专家组报告
- 1998.10.12—上诉机构作出上诉机构裁决
- 2001.6.15—专家组下发专家组报告
- 2001.10.22—上诉机构下发上诉机构报告

3. 投资条约争端:菲律宾 GRUSLIN 诉马来西亚

事实摘要:

- 原告要求赔偿他在吉隆坡交易所(KLSE)的投资损失;
- 原告认为这些损失是由于被告违反了马来西亚—贝尔各、卢森堡经济联盟 IGA 所造成的;
- 被告提出了管辖权异议。

主要争点:

- 争端的议题是否覆盖在 IGA 第 10 条第 1 款中,如:原告所做的投资是否是被 IGA 所保护?
- IGA 第 1 条第 3 款规定的"投资"包括每一种资产……这种在马来西亚的投资是投资在一种被马来西亚相应部门批准的,并且基于法律规定和行政程序的一种事业上。

判决:

- 在吉隆坡股票交易所的上市证券所进行的投资只有在符合了第 1 条第 3 款但书(i)(如果它是一项"被批准的事业")的情况下才受到 IGA 的保护。
- 证券主管机关的批准仅仅考察一个公司的业务活动,而不是根据 IGA

的投资保护规定。

·法庭判决吉隆坡股票交易所投资不满足第1条第3款关于投资的定义

4. 投资条约争端:MHS诉马来西亚政府

事实摘要:

·1991年签署的海上救助协议中写有“普查,鉴定,分类,调查,整修,保藏,估价,销售或拍卖,并对提出了科学的方法,对戴安娜号的残骸和内物品进行打捞”。

·1995年7月12日,由于拍卖和评估的利益分配引起纠纷。

·进入ICSID之前的诉讼程序:

1995年7月,MHS向吉隆坡仲裁中心提起争端仲裁,请求独任仲裁员。

1998年7月,起诉被驳回。

1998年8月,MHS起诉到吉隆坡高等法院,请求取消KLRCA的仲裁。

1999年2月4日,吉隆坡高等法院驳回起诉,之后并没有提起上诉。

·2000年12月,MHS向英国伦敦特许仲裁协会提起诉讼(对于判决或者不当行为的国际审查)。

·2001年1月,起诉被驳回。

·2004年9月30日,MHS向国际投机争端解决中心递交仲裁请求。

·判决依据:违反了马来西亚—英国IGA(签署于1981年5月21日,于1988年10月21日生效)。

·IGA第7条——适用于ISDS,且只适用于国际投资争端解决。

·马来西亚根据国际争端解决中心仲裁规则第41条,提出管辖权异议。

马来西亚的争论:

·MHS的诉求完全基于合同违约,而不是违反条约,因为其不属于一种“投资”。

·因此诉求不能受理——

根据ICSID司法管辖权的规定因为它不是ICSID条约第25条规定的“投资”;并且根据马来西亚—英国IGA第7条规定的“投资”的范围,它也不在其内。

判决:

·法庭认为“投资”的特点为“典型的特征”或“管辖权的需求”。

·法庭总结出了由这些案件所建立起的以下几种“投资”的特征:

利润和回报的规律性;原告的贡献;合同的有效期;合同承载的风险;对于东道国经济发展得贡献

·法庭判决,海上救险合同不符合“投资”的特点。

废除程序

·MHS 要求废除基于第 52(1)(b)条所规定的对于司法管辖区的判决 à 明显超出法院职权

·关于申请废除程序的决定(2009 年 4 月 16 日下发到了涉诉各方):申请在 2∶1 的多数决下被许可(Shahabudeen 法官持反对意见)

七、意见

随着越来越多的条约的签订,各国需要更加谨慎,并做好充分实现其义务的准备,否则国家必须诉诸争端解决机制。至于条约的实施,为了能够立即和有效实施它们的条约义务,国家资源和措施必须物尽其用,无论是通过法律或行政手段。经常遭遇国际争端的国家会咨询私人国际律师,因为并不是所有的国家都可以分配专用的国家资源来处理国际争端。因此有限的资源意味着国家可能并不总是有必要的国际法律专业知识。通常对于任何国家来说,争端解决都是一件非常消耗成本的事务。因此,在平衡是否需要一个有效的争端解决机制来避免争端时需要考虑许多因素。

结　论

理想情况下,争端应该不惜一切代价加以避免。但国际关系的现实,如观点上的差异、对权利和义务的不同解释,以及未能采取必需的措施等,使得纠纷的避免有时候变得不可能。通常情况下,主权国家需要注意它在确保和平和有效地解决争端中的角色。

Treaty Disputes: The Settlement of International Disputes

Datuk Azailiza Mohd Ahad*

"Dispute settlement is to international law what pathology is to medicine. It is about the worst-case scenario, when the consensus that made it possible for rules to be created does not exist anymore, and parties argue as to what these rules actually mean and if, by whom, to what extent, and with which consequences, they have been violated. It is a place where parties hope they will never have to go."

—Prof Cesare Romano, "International Dispute Settlement", Oxford Handbook of International Environmental Law (2007).

A. Introduction

Treaties play a fundamental role in international relations. A treaty is an international agreement entered into between one or more sovereign States and one or more international organizations, which is governed under international and concluded in written form. In the event a dispute arises from such a treaty, parties would need a suitable avenue in which to settle their dispute. Thus international disputes settlement mechanisms have been put in place in order to deal with disputes arising out of international obligations, and more importantly, to maintain international peace and security.

The United Nations Charter calls upon sovereign States to settle inter-

* Datuk Azailiza Mohd Ahad: Head of International Affairs Division, Attorney General's Chambers, No 45, Persiaran Perdana, 62100 Putrajaya.

national disputes peacefully by means of their own choice. This ideal is postulated in the objectives of the UN Charter, wherein Article 1 states:

"The Purposes of the United Nations are:

1. To maintain international peace and security, and to that end: ... in conformity with the principles of justice and international law, adjustment or settlement of international disputes or situations which might lead to a breach of peace."

Article 2 further elaborates on how such disputes should be settled:

"The Organization and its Members, in pursuit of the Purposes stated in Article 1, shall act in accordance with the following Principles:

3. All Members shall settle their international disputes by peaceful means in such a manner that international peace and security, and justice, are not endangered."

Article 33 also prescribes the ideal approach to international dispute settlement:

"1. The parties to any dispute, the continuance of which is likely to endanger the maintenance of international peace and security, shall, first of all, seek a solution by negotiation, enquiry, mediation, conciliation, arbitration, judicial settlement, resort to regional agencies or arrangements, or other peaceful means of their own choice."

The types of dispute settlement mechanisms range the whole gamut from those by "diplomatic means", including negotiations, enquiry, mediation or conciliation, to those with legally binding outcomes, namely through adjudicative means such as arbitration and submitting the dispute to established international judicial bodies.

B. International Judicial Bodies

International judicial bodies could be categorized into international courts, arbitral tribunals and quasi-judicial institutions. International courts are permanent bodies, and disputes are subject to pre-determined rules of procedures.

Arbitral tribunals on the other hand are constituted a new for each

dispute brought. The rules of procedure are generally pre-determined, although under some circumstances, parties may vary the procedures subject to mutual agreement.

Both international courts and arbitral tribunals are established by an international legal instrument, and make legally binding decisions.

Quasi-judicial bodies, unlike international courts and arbitral tribunals, make enquiries into issues and rulings on cases, however, these rulings are not legally binding. Main examples of these quasi-judicial bodies are the mechanisms provided for under the various UN human rights conventions.

Examples of these various judicial and quasi-judicial bodies are as follows:

- International Courts

International Court of Justice (ICJ)
International Tribunal for the Law of the Sea (ITLOS)
International Criminal Court (ICC)

- Arbitral Tribunals

Permanent Court of Arbitration (PCA)
WTO Dispute Settlement Panel and Appellate Body
International Centre for the Settlement of Investment Disputes (ICSID)

- Quasi-judicial institutions

Human Rights Committee
Committee on the Elimination of Racial Discrimination
Committee on the Elimination of Discrimination Against Women
Committee on Economic, Social and Cultural Rights

The features of international judicial bodies could be summarized as follows:

(a)permanent institutions;

(b)composed of independent judges;

(c) adjudicate disputes between two or more entities, at least one of which is either a State or an International Organization;

(d)work on the basis of predetermined rules of procedure; and

(e)render decisions that are binding.

Other commonalities of international judicial bodies have been expressed as follows:

> "First, all of these entities make legal determinations, and this sets them apart from other bodies, such as the UN General Assembly or the Parliamentary Assembly of the Council of Europe, which share the same aspiration towards a 'just world' but are of a quintessentially political nature. To be precise, these 125 bodies determine whether certain acts are congruous with certain norms. And this leads to a second commonality, which is the fact that in order to make their determinations they all resort to the same body of law: international law. Third, all of these international bodies have been established directly or indirectly (i.e., through a decision taken by a body established by treaty) by international agreements. It follows that they are subject to a legal order that is different from that of national systems, but, at the same time, that they are subject to (and materially dependent on) State support. Finally, and perhaps more importantly, collectively they are the expression of a widely shared need to abandon a world where only States count and the mighty rule, in favor of an order where certain fundamental common values are shared, protected and enforced by all members of a wide society, composed of States, International Organizations and individuals in all their legal incarnations (NGOs, peoples, corporations, natural persons, etc.)."①

In conventional international law, individuals or non-State entities do not enjoy legal standing, as the subjects of international law were traditionally sovereign States and, to some extent, international organizations.② This is understandable as only entities which possess international rights and duties and have the capacity to pursue its rights by bringing international

① Synoptic Chart (Version 3.0), available at http://www.pict-pcti.org.

② Reparation for Injuries case, *ICJ Reports*(1949), p. 179.

claims can be subjects of international law. [①] However, as more and more areas usually reserved for domestic law transcends into the international plane, following successive conclusions of international instruments on environment, trade, labour and human rights, new subjects of international law are created.

For example, under bilateral investment treaties, private investors are given the right to bring a sovereign State to international arbitration for a breach of that treaty. This is made possible through the States' consent expressed in an international instrument, that such right is granted to the private individual or a non-State entity, and for that right to be enforceable in an international tribunal.

C. Typical Structure of Dispute Settlement Mechanism in International Trade

Dispute settlement mechanism (DSM) in most international instruments aims to achieve one of these two objectives: firstly, DSM should seek to avoid disputes by providing sufficient avenues for consultations and exchange of information, and secondly, where the first objective is not met, to settle the dispute amicably and efficiently.

The first step to any potential disputes is usually to require that Parties enter into consultations with each other with a view to settling the disputes amicably. This process is often a pre-cursor before the dispute, if it remains unsettled, could be brought to the next step, which is to refer to the matter to the adjudicating body established under that DSM. To further facilitate this process, DSM would typically require that pertinent information pertaining to the dispute is made available to the other Party, particularly, the request for consultation be accompanied by an identification of the measure at issue and an indication of the factual and legal basis of the complaint. To that end, Parties are required to also provide sufficient information to enable

---

① Brownlie, *Principles of Public International Law* (6th *Edition*), Oxford University Press (2003), p. 57.

a full examination of how the measure might affect the operation of this Agreement. In order to encourage both sides to utilize the consultation process fully, DSM would often require that a period of time has passed after the consultation process has begun before either Party could refer the matter to tribunal.

If the consultation process fails to resolve the dispute within the stipulated amount of time, then the complaining Party may proceed to the next step. Depending on the DSM, this may either be through the direct submission of the dispute to the agreed or established forum, or through request made to the other Party that a tribunal be established to adjudicate the matter.

Where a tribunal needs to be established, DSM would provide for the appointment of arbitrators, specifying the necessary requirements and conditions for the appointment of such arbitrators. The arbitral tribunal would be established on the date of the appointment of the final arbitrator (especially in a three-arbitrator tribunal).

The proceedings of the tribunal will then follow the procedures as prescribed in the DSM. This would include conduct of meeting, venues, submissions by parties, decision-making process of the tribunal as well as the form and content of the final decision of the tribunal.

Once a decision is rendered, it is necessary to allow for a reasonable period of time necessary to implement the resolution of the dispute. In the event a dispute arises from the implementation of the tribunal decision, Parties may have recourse to the next step, which is to seek compensation or a suspension of concessions or benefits granted under the agreement. This would lead to further adjudication to determine the appropriate level of compensation or a suspension of concessions or benefits.

D. Bilateral DSM v WTO DSU

In the international trade context, the prolonged and unfruitful negotiations of the Doha Round at the multilateral platform of the World Trade Organisation has resulted in the rapid quantitative increase in the number of bi-

lateral and regional free trade agreements, which in turn has created a plethora of bilateral and regional dispute settlement mechanisms.

This has given rise to the proliferation of international jurisdictions over the various international trade subjects, namely over trade in goods and services and investment through the conclusion of separate but overlapping agreements. Thus the multiplication of international judicial fora reflects the increase of distinct causes of action available under the various international legal instruments.

Overlapping jurisdictions increases the choices of forums available in which to handle the dispute, and more significantly, increases the possibility of forum shopping. Forum shopping offends the sense of justice as the fair resolution of a case depends upon the technical difference between one forum and another, and the complaining party would seek a forum which is most favourable to their case. Multiplicity of forums also gives rise to the possibility that the complaining party will initiate a case in every forum to seek a favourable outcome. Thus, to mitigate this concern, a number of international instruments include language to exclude recourse to other forums once a forum is chosen. However, this approach is not always effective, as the breach of obligations may arise from a separate international instrument giving rise to a separate cause of action.

Be that as it may, DSM in bilateral trade arrangements continues to seek to provide bilateral resolution to the dispute. Often this is unavoidable as bilateral tradearrangements incorporate WTO-plus commitments, and these commitments could not otherwise be secured. WTO-plus commitments range not only from improved offers compared to the multilateral commitments on trade at WTO, but also increased coverage over areas not regulated under the multilateral framework, such as commitments on investments, labour, environment and competition policy. Parties also commonly seek bilateral DSM as it is perceived to be quicker due to the reduced timelines, and are often less systemic and more flexible on the settlement procedures.

E. Challenges

• The ability to effectively and efficiently manage the avoidance of disputes is key in securing and maintaining amicable international relations. How can we improve dispute avoidance procedures?

• Does the surge in bilateral DSM signal the death of the multilateral framework DSM? In the context of trade, bilateral DSM is often perceived to be a more "efficient" way of dealing with disputes compared to going to WTO, which is perceived to be laborious, expensive and prolonged.

• Proliferation of bilateral, regional and multilateral DSM has also led to a fragmentation of international law, as these DSMs are not an integrated system and are each a separate DSM of their own.

• Dealing with WTO-plus commitments necessitates the existence of bilateral and regional DSM. However, how would this affect the long-term growth and development of these WTO-plus commitments?

• DSM is integral in ensuring a balanced and attractive environment for business, trade and investment.

• Where there is a conflict of jurisdiction or precedence in international court decisions, which would prevail? WTO jurisprudence have long been recognized to be non-legally binding but continue to be highly persuasive as panels and Appellate Bodies strive to ensure consistency in the WTO jurisprudence.

• Could a dispute arising out of a treaty be referred to the national courts? For a dualist system country such as Malaysia, international obligations, and therefore breaches of such international obligations are not automatically implementable under domestic legal system.

• How do we avoid multiplicity of disputes being brought to various forums?

• Case preparation and dispute management is a monumental challenge for any State. Some of the common challenges faced include insufficient data collection, lack of resources in terms of time, money and manpower, management of the dispute itself.

F. Malaysia's Trade Dispute Cases

1. WTO: DS1 - Prohibition of Imports of Polyethylene and Polypropylene

Complainant: Singapore

Respondent: Malaysia

Status:

- 10 Jan 1995—Request for consultation
- 16 Mar 1995—Request for Est. of Panel
- 19 July 1995—Complaint withdrawn.

2. WTO: DS58—US-Shrimp

Complainant: India; Malaysia; Pakistan; Thailand

Respondent: US

Measure at issue: US import prohibition of shrimp and shrimp products from non-certified countries (i. e. countries that had not used turtle-excluding device in catching shrimp)

Status:

- 8 Oct 1996-Request for consultation
- 15 May 1998-Panel Report circulated
- 12 Oct 1998-AB Report circulated
- 15 June 2001-Article 21. 5 Panel Report
- 22 Oct 2001-Article 21. 5 AB Report circulated

3. Investment Treaty Dispute: Philippe Gruslin v Malaysia

Summary of facts:

- The Claimant claimed for the alleged loss of the value of his investments which he made on the Kuala Lumpur Stock Exchange (KLSE).
- The Claimant argued that the losses were allegedly caused by the Respondent's imposition of exchange restrictions which constituted a breach of the Malaysia-Belgo Luxembourg Economic Union IGA.
- Respondent filed a jurisdictional objection.

Main issue:

• Whether the subject matter of the dispute falls within Article 10(1) of the IGA i. e. whether the Claimant had made an investment that is protected under the IGA?

Article 1(3) of the IGA →the term "investment" shall comprise every kind of assets ... provided that such assets when invested in Malaysia, are invested in a project classified as an "approved project" by the appropriate Ministry in Malaysia, in accordance with the legislation and the administrative practice, based thereon.

Award:

• An investment in the KLSE listed securities would only enjoy the protection of the IGA if proviso (i) of Article 1(3) of the IGA was satisfied i. e. if it was an "approved project".

• The approval of the securities authority was only an approval concerning the business activities of a company, not for investment protection under the IGA.

• The Tribunal found that the KLSE investment did not satisfy the definition of an investment under Article 1(3) of the IGAà objection to jurisdiction upheld.

4. Investment Treaty Dispute: MHS v Government of Malaysia

Summary of facts:

• Salvage Contract signed in 1991 "to survey, identify, classify, research, restore, preserve, appraise, market, sell/auction, and carry out a scientific and salvage of the wreck and content of Diana".

• 12 July 1995—Dispute arose → share of proceeds (auction and appraised value)

• Proceedings prior to ICSID:

July 1995—MHS referred the dispute to Kuala Lumpur Regional Centre for Arbitration (KLRCA) → sole arbitrator

July 1998—claims dismissed

August 1998—MHS applied to the High Court, Kuala Lumpur to set a-

side KLRCA award

4 February 1999—Application dismissed by the High Court & no appeal filed to the Court of Appeal

• December 2000—MHS filed a complaint to the Chartered Institute of Arbitrators, London (internal review of award & misconduct)

• January 2001—complaint dismissed entirely

• 30 September 2004—MHS submitted request for arbitration to ICSID

• Basis of claims—breach of the Malaysia-UK IGA (signed 21 May 1981 & entered into force on 21 October 1988)

• Article 7 of the IGA—forum for ISDS = ICSID only

• Malaysia raised jurisdictional objection—Rule 41, ICSID Arbitration Rules

Malaysia's arguments:

• MHS's claims are based purely on a contractual breach and not a treaty breach as they do not pertain to an "investment".

• Therefore the claim does not fall -

under the jurisdiction of ICSID as it is not an "investment" under Article 25 the ICSID Convention; and

within the scope of Article 7 in the Malaysia-UK IGA as it is not an "investment" under the IGA.

Award:

• The Tribunal approached the hallmarks of "investment" as "typical characteristics" or "jurisdictional requirements".

• The Tribunal concluded that the cases established the following characteristics of "investment":

Regularity of profit and returns

Contributions by Claimant

Duration of the contract

Risks assumed under the contract

Contribution to the economic development of the Host State

• The Tribunal found that the Salvage Contract does not fulfill the characteristics of "investment".

Annulment Procedure:

- MHS applied to annul the Award on Jurisdiction based on Article 52 (1)(b) →manifest excess of power by the Tribunal.
- The Decision on the Application for Annulment (dispatched to Parties on 16 April 2009): Application allowed by a majority of 2－1 (Judge Shahabudeen dissented).

G. Observations

As more treaties are signed, States need to be more cautious and be prepared to fully implement its obligations, as otherwise States may be subjected to DSM. With regards to the implementation of treaties, States' resources and measures will have to be in place, whether through legal or administrative means, in order to be able to immediately and effectively implement their treaty obligations.

States subject to international dispute oftentimes consult private international lawyers, as not all States can allocate dedicated national resources to handle international disputes. Thus limited resources mean States may not always have the necessary international legal expertise.

Disputes are generally a very costly affair for any State. Thus, numerous considerations need to be taken into account in balancing the need for an effective dispute settlement mechanism, and avoiding disputes.

H. Conclusion

Disputes ideally should be avoided at all costs. But the realities of international relations dictate that differences in views, and interpretation of rights and obligations and failure to take the required measures means that disputes cannot always be avoided. States in general need to be mindful of its role in ensuring a peaceful and effective settlement of disputes is achieved.

Prepared by:
Datuk Azailiza Mohd Ahad
Norhayati Raihan Wahab
International Affairs Division
Attorney General's Chambers.

中国、东盟国家法律制度问题各论

LEGAL SYSTEM ISSUES OF CHINA AND ASEAN COUNTRIES

中国的“有余文化”和金融法

吴志攀[*]　林建荣 译

内容摘要　本文解释了中国高储蓄率的原因，并从中国传统文化和金融法律系统的角度探讨了中国稳步发展的原因。本文认为中国的“有余文化”深深植根于自己的传统之中，深刻影响着政府的决策，并已成为社会习惯，融入中国的法律体系中。

中国的储蓄率在世界上位于前列，人们习惯于把他们大部分的收入存进银行，而不是通过借贷来维持他们入不敷出的消费。这一做法和大部分西方国家的人民大相径庭。

大部分经济学家认为：在中国过去 30 年经济快速发展的进程中，高储蓄率发挥着积极作用。同时，这一现象也影响着全球经济。例如，一些人认为：正是由于中国的储蓄才更加滋长了美国的过度消费心理。据他们所称，这些(中国人储蓄的)钱为美国提供了廉价的债务，导致其财政失调、债务危机以及全球金融市场的动荡。

笔者并不支持这个观点，因为它是不公平的。然而，今天，本文并非要反驳该观点，而是要解释中国高储蓄率的原因，并从中国传统文化和金融法律系统角度来谈谈中国稳步发展的原因。

中国和东盟国家之间在文化方面有很多相似的地方，我们也在积极促进法律方面的交流和金融市场上的合作。

中国人民崇尚“有余文化”，他们认为自己应该调整开支和收入的比重，并保留一定的存款。在汉语中，“有余”这一词中的发音“Yu”，和汉字“鱼”的读音一样。基于此，中国人民将鱼看作“有余”的象征。旧时的春节有这样一个

* 吴志攀，北京大学常务副校长(正局级)、党委常委，教授、博士生导师，兼任中国法学会副会长。

传统——每家每户都在门上贴年画。其中最受欢迎的主题之一,就是在图片上画着一个孩子抱着一个鲤鱼,这也意味着"年年有余"。

"有余文化"也体现在我们的日常生活中。当一中国主人招待他的客人时,他会在桌子上放好几盘菜。四盘凉菜和四盘热菜通常是基本标准。而客人们通常不会把菜吃光,他们会故意留下一些,让人觉得他们已经吃饱喝足,也让主人面上有光。

关于这个习俗,有个笑话。一个中国人请一个美国人共进晚餐,那位美国人奋力地吃完他的食物,而中国人却认为可能是食物不够,便不停地给美国人添加食物,美国人只好继续不停地下咽,这期间对他来说简直是"活受罪"。这体现了不同的餐桌礼仪,但更重要的是体现了两种不同的文化背景。

笔者经常回忆起30年前发生的那件事情。那时笔者还很小,中国也正处于计划经济时代,政府将其政策描述为"整体考虑,调整收支和保持适当的有余"。收音机上也经常听到这样的语录,"中国政府既没有内债,也没有外债"。人们对此很自豪,因为他们认为没有债务的政府是一个强有力的政府。1949年以前,由于战争,西方国家成为中国的债权人。近代历史就是一部巨额债务的历史,它终结于中华人民共和国的成立。

改革开放后,西方经济理论在中国成为主流。西方经济学的主要观点认为赤字财政能够加速经济增长。中国政府所采取的谨慎政策被认为是保守的。历史的经验教训让中国政府在很长一段时间担心通货膨胀。现代历史也曾经有严重的通货膨胀,因此中国政府在实施控制通货膨胀措施时保持谨慎的态度。这也被认为过于保守。

现在,中国政府已经有大量的债务,尤其是借钱来促进快速发展的地方政府。一些经济学家甚至声称这些债务会导致新的金融危机。然而,经过客观和认真的分析之后,我们可以看到:与美国和欧洲国家相比,中国政府要谨慎得多,特别是中央政府,它竭尽全力控制债务的数额和消除通货膨胀。

因此,我们可以得出结论:中国的"有余文化"深深植根于自己的传统之中,并深刻影响着政府的决策。

统计数据显示,2011年1月,中国商业银行的储蓄金额是15万亿元,大约2.3万亿美元。这个数字远高于美国,尽管美国有一个规模更大的经济。2011年8月的统计数据表明,大约60%的美国居民储蓄少于1000美元。也就是说,大多数美国人借钱,而大多数中国人存钱。

一些学者认为:一方面,中国在社会福利方面的支持力度不够,包括教育、医疗保健、养老金和就业,这也解释了家庭储蓄率高的原因。另一方面,由于

美国人享受更好的福利,所以没有必要存钱。

一定程度上来说,这个解释还是蛮合理的,但并不是最终答案。笔者的问题是:美国政府资金从何而来?我们可以确信,大量的资金(约 1.16 万亿美元)是从中国借来的。如果中国人停止储蓄,美国政府如何获得资金来提供社会福利?显然,如果美国没有国内储蓄,那么,它就不得不依靠中国人民的储蓄。

中国的“有余文化”已成为社会习惯。它也融入中国的法律体系之中。

例如,根据《中华人民共和国中国人民银行法》第 29 条的规定,中国人民银行不得对政府财政透支,不得直接认购、包销国债和其他政府债券。

根据《中华人民共和国商业银行法》第 27 条规定:有下列情形之一的,不得担任商业银行的董事、高级管理人员……(四)个人所负数额较大的债务到期未清偿的。第 41 条则规定:任何单位和个人不得强令商业银行发放贷款或者提供担保。商业银行有权拒绝任何单位和个人强令要求其发放贷款或者提供担保。

《中华人民共和国票据法》第 74 条规定:本票的出票人必须具有支付本票金额的可靠资金来源,并保证支付。第 87 条规定:支票的出票人所签发的支票金额不得超过其付款时在付款人处实有的存款金额。出票人签发的支票金额超过其付款时在付款人处实有的存款金额的,为空头支票。禁止签发空头支票。

类似的例子还有很多。最重要的一点是:就连中国法律通常也禁止政府实施赤字政策。《中华人民共和国中国人民银行法》第 3 条规定:货币政策目标是保持货币币值的稳定,并以此促进经济增长。相比之下,其他国家的法律几乎没有类似规定。

中国的法律也禁止银行削减利率为零。《中华人民共和国商业银行法》第 29 条规定:商业银行办理个人储蓄存款业务,应当遵循存款自愿、取款自由、存款有息、为存款人保密的原则。相较之下,其他国家的法律很少提及银行是否应该付利息给储蓄人。这些国家赋予银行或相关协会组织来确定利率政策。

这些法律都旨在鼓励储蓄和抑制通货膨胀。然而,在日常经济运作中,有时通货膨胀上升是不可避免的。所以中国法律如何处理它?今年 6 月以来,中国的居民消费价格指数一直高于银行的储蓄率。中国政府积极实施政策,包括提高基准利率和存款准备金率来减少货币供应,希望尽一切努力控制通货膨胀。其他有关部门也通过提高工资和福利,增加养老金和释放商品储备

等来干预市场。

西方经济学家和政治家们经常批评中国法律和“有余文化”中的这些规则。他们认为中国政府操纵汇率。他们进一步推测:由于人民币贬值,中国获得了巨大的贸易顺差,而美国反过来就遭受贸易赤字。他们主张美国政府应印刷更多的钱来拯救其制造业,以及应该实施量化宽松政策来维持其就业和社会福利。

这类批评完全忽视了事实。我们认为:任何法律体系应该尊重本国的传统文化,保护本国人民的利益。中国不出口其“有余文化”,但我们希望西方发达国家可以学会尊重我们的文化。这种文化,尽管它不能消除人类内心的邪恶,却可以激发他们的美德。中国人一直奉行“己所不欲,勿施于人”的原则。中国专注于自身的发展,不会损害其他国家的利益。我们试图限制我们的膨胀的欲望和提倡适当、节俭的生活方式。中国政府努力增加就业和保护本国企业的利益。这有错吗?

长期以来,美国政府一直通过征收铸币税,发行债券和输出通货膨胀来保持其巨额费用。这种行为损害了包括中国在内的东亚国家。在2008年金融危机后,美国议会曾两次实施了量化宽松政策,印刷大量的金钱,而其他国家却因此利益受损。即使在标准普尔下调美国债率后,中国政府仍在更多的购买。

中国政府现在拥有3.2万亿美元的外汇储备,其中1.16万亿是用于购买美国债务。还有一个非常重要的组成部分,是用于购买房利美和房地美的债务,以及用于中国的美元储备。自2005年7月起,美元对人民币贬值了26%,美国储蓄利率仅为1%,债券收益率只有5%。因此,中国已经成为美国通货膨胀最大的受害者。损害程度已越来越严重,也有可能引发两国金融法律系统之间的冲突。

自从第二次世界大战起,美元成为世界货币。这是美国债务评级首次被下调。此解释至关重要。它意味着由美国法律系统维持的货币政策正在成为一个糟糕的政策,并可能损害别国利益。

实际上,美国现行政策只能维持一个短期的经济增长。从长远来看,它不仅将损害其他国家的利益,自己也会蒙受损失。美国不可能永远享受这样的低利率和无限制地印刷美元。在这种无限制的政策下,美国金融法律系统已经开始衰败,次贷危机就是一个典型的后果。

中国和美国经济之间的关系是非常密切的。要么双赢,要么双输。笔者不认为中国政府的宽容态度是软弱行为,此态度恰是一种对美国政府做出良

好回应的期待。

最后,笔者想用两个小故事来说明本文的观点。

大约 30 年前,也就是中国的改革开放初期,一个上海商人挣了一些钱,一个浙江温州的商人向他借了些。除夕之夜,温州的那位商人飞到上海来支付利息。当然,当时中国商人没有大规模的资本,利息当然也只有几百元。那么,在航班价格更高的情况下,商人为什么还要专程来支付利息呢?其原因就是中国的"有余文化"。"春节也被认为是一年的终了。中国人认为他们应该在年底前偿还所有的债务,尽管有时数额相对较小。这种"有余文化"也是中国人的信用的一个例证,同时也是我们中国人民牺牲很多来维持的。温州商人现在之所以获得了如此巨大的成功,归根结底就是他们对信用以及中国传统文化的重视。

第二个故事和美国有关。

在 2011 年上半年,美国苹果公司的账面余额已经达到 790 亿美元,高于美国政府的财政余额。苹果公司的信用评级也高于美国政府。苹果公司的成功并不依赖借贷和投资,而是依靠技术创新和思想创新。笔者相信真正的美国精神在于像苹果之类的公司,而不是华尔街。这是美国未来的真正发展方向。

China's "Surplus Culture" and Financial Law

Wu Zhipan*

China's saving rate is one of the highest in the world. People deposit the majority of their income into banks instead of taking out loans for consumption beyond their means. This contrasts sharply with a majority of western countries.

Most economists agree that China's high saving rate has been playing an active role during the rapid growth of the past 30 years. Meanwhile, this phenomenon is also affecting the world economy. For example, some people believe it is China's saving that indulges the United States to consume excessively. They're saying the money is providing cheap debt for the US, causing its fiscal disorder, debt crisis and turbulence of world financial market.

I'm not a supporter of this opinion because it is unfair. However, instead of debating about it, today I'm going to explain some reasons for the high saving rates in China and China's stable development from the perspectives of traditional Chinese culture and financial law systems.

There are a lot of cultural similarities between China and ASEAN countries. We are also promoting communication in law and cooperation in financial markets.

Chinese people hold a "surplus culture". People believe they should adjust expenses to their income and keep a certain amount of balance. In the Chinese language, the character "surplus" is pronounced "Yu", same as the character "fish". For that reason, Chinese people consider fish as a symbol of surplus. We have a tradition on our ancient spring festival, that every

* Executive Vice President and professor of Peking University, China.

family posts New Year Pictures on their door. One of the most popular themes on the picture is a child holding a carp, which means gaining surplus for every year.

"Surplus culture" can be observed in our daily life. When a Chinese host treats his guests, he will serve many dishes on the table. Four cold dishes and four hot dishes would be the basic standard. The guests, on the other hand, do not eat up the food. They will intentionally leave some to show they're full, so that the host will gain face.

There is a joke about this custom: A Chinese treats an American to dinner. The American eats very hard to finish his food, while the Chinese host thinks maybe the food is not enough. He keeps adding food. The American has to keep eating and hasa very hard time.

This is a difference of table manners, but more importantly of two different cultural backgrounds.

I often recall things that happened 30 years ago, when I was very young and China was in the era of planned economy. Back then, the Chinese government described its principle as "making overall consideration, adjusting expenses to income and keeping appropriate surplus". There was always such sayings on the radio that the "Chinese government has neither domestic nor foreign debt". People were proud of it because they considered a government with no debt a powerful government. Before the year 1949, western countries were China's creditors as a result of the war. Huge debt was a staple of history, which was brought to an end by People's Republic of China.

After the Reform and Opening, western economic theory gained prominence in China. Major views of western economics believed that deficit financing was able to accelerate economic growth and China's cautious policy was considered conservative. By learning from its own experience, Chinese government feared inflation for a long time. In modern history, there was once severe inflation, and therefore the Chinese government maintains a cautious attitude when implementing measures to control inflation. This is considered to be conservative as well.

Nowadays the Chinese government has relatively large amounts of debt, especially local governments who borrow money to promote rapid development. Some economists even claim that these debts will lead to a new financial crisis. However, after objective and careful analysis, we can see the Chinese government is more cautious compared with the US and European countries, especially the central government, which makes every effort to control the amount of debt and eliminate inflation.

Therefore, we can conclude that China's "surplus culture" is deeply planted in its tradition and is still strongly affecting government decisions.

Statistics show that in January, 2011, Chinese commercial banks' saving amount is 15 trillion Yuan, about 2.3 trillion dollars. The number was much bigger than that of the US, while the US has a much larger economy. Statistics of August, 2011 show that around 60% of American residents save less than 1000 dollars. That is to say, most of Americans are borrowing money while most of Chinese are saving.

Some scholars believe China has insufficient support of social welfare including education, medical care, pension and employment, which explains the high household saving rate. On the other hand, American people do not have to save, since they enjoy better welfare.

The explanation is somewhat reasonable, but it can't be the final answer. My question is: where do US government funds come from? We can be sure that a great amount of it, about 1.16 trillion dollars, is borrowed from China. How can the US government get the money to provide social welfare if Chinese people stop saving? The statement is clear: if there is no domestic saving, it has to rely on savings from Chinese people.

China's "surplus culture" has become a custom in society. It is also taken into China's law system.

For example, according to article 29 of Law of the People's Republic of China on the People's Bank of China, "The People's Bank of China may not make an overdraft for the government, and may not directly subscribe or underwrite state bonds or other government bonds".

According to article 27 of Law of the People's Republic of China on Commercial Banks, "In any of the following circumstances, a person shall not be appointed as a director or senior management personnel of a commercial bank ... 4. Failing to pay large amounts of personal debts due". According-

ing to article 41, "No entity or individual may coerce a commercial bank into granting loans or providing guarantee. A commercial bank shall have the right to refuse any entity or individual to force it to do so".

According to article 74 of Law of the People's Republic of China on Negotiable Instruments, "The drawer of a promissory note shall have a reliable source of funds for paying the amount of the promissory note and ensure payment". According to article 87, "The amount of the check issued by the drawer shall not exceed the actual amount deposited by the payer at the time of payment. If the amount of the check issued by the drawer has exceeded the actual amount deposited by the payer at the time of payment, the check is a dishonorable check, which is strictly forbidden".

There are many more such examples. The most crucial point is that even Chinese law often prohibits government from implementing a deficit policy. According to article 3 of The Law of the People's Republic of China on the People's Bank of China, "The aim of monetary policies shall be to maintain the stability of the value of the currency and thereby promote economic growth". Other countries' laws, on the other hand, hardly include such regulation.

Chinese law also prohibits banks from cutting the interest rate to zero. According to article 29 of Law of the People's Republic of China on Commercial Banks, "Commercial banks shall follow the principles of voluntary deposit and free withdrawal, paying interest to depositors and keeping secret for depositors in handling individual savings deposits".

In contrast, other countries laws hardly mention whether banks should pay interest to depositors. They let banks or banking associations determine interest policies.

These laws all aim to encouraging savings and inhibit inflation. However, sometimes in the day to day economy, the rise of inflation is inevitable. So how do Chinese laws deal with it? Since June this year, China's CPI has been higher than banks' saving rate. The Chinese government is making every effort to control the inflation, implementing policies that include raising the benchmark interest rates and required reserve ratio to reduce money supply. Other economy-related departments are also intervening in the market

by raising wages and welfare, increasing pension and releasing merchandise reserves.

Western economists and politicians often criticize these principles of China's laws and the "surplus culture". They believe the Chinese government is manipulating exchange rates. They further speculate that due to the undervaluation of Chinese Yuan, China is gaining huge trade surpluses while the US in turn is suffering trade deficit. They declare the US government has to print more money to save its manufacturing industry and has to implement quantitative easing to maintain its employment and social welfare.

This sort of criticism totally ignores the facts. We believe any law system should respect traditional cultures of its own country and protect the interest of its own people. China does not export its "surplus culture", but we hope western developed countries can learn to respect our culture. This culture, though it cannot eliminate evil within human beings, can stimulate virtue in it. Chinese people believe one should not do to others what he does not want others to do to him. China focuses on its own development and does not harm the interest of other countries. We try to limit our inflating desire and advocate a moderate and thrifty lifestyle. The Chinese government tries to increase employment and protect the interests of Chinese enterprises. Is there anything to blame in it?

For a long period, the US government has been maintaining its huge expenses by imposing seigniorage, issuing bonds and exporting inflation. This behavior is harming the interest of East Asian countries including China. After the financial crisis in 2008, the US conference has implemented QE twice, printing a huge amount of money, while other countries were suffering. Even after Standard & Poor's downgraded US debt, the Chinese government is still buying more of it.

The Chinese government now has foreign exchange reserves of 3.2 trillion dollars, among which 1.16 trillion is used for buying US debt. There is also a significant part of it that is used for debt of Fannie Mae and Freddie Mac, and for dollar reserves within China. Since July, 2005, the US dollar to Chinese Yuan has depreciated by 26%, and US saving interest rate is only 1%, debt yield only 5%. Therefore, China has become the biggest victim of

US inflation. The harm has already developed to a severe extent and might also cause conflict between the financial law systems of the two countries.

Ever since World War II whenthe US dollar became a world currency, this is the first time US debt is downgraded. The interpretation is critical. It means the monetary policy maintained by the US law system is becoming a bad policy that may damage others.

Actually, the present policy of the US can only maintain a short-term growth. In the long run, it will harm not only other countries' interests, but also its own. It is impossible for the US to enjoy such low interest rates forever and print dollars unlimitedly. Under this unrestrained policy, US financial law system has begun to fail. The subprime mortgage crisis is a typical result.

The relationship between the Chinese and the US economy is very close. There can only be either win-win or lose-lose result. I consider the Chinese government's tolerant attitude not as weakness, but as an expectation of US's kind response.

At last, I want to support my point with two little stories.

At the beginning of China's Reform and Opening, about 30 years ago, a businessman from Shanghai earned some money, and a merchant from Wenzhou, Zhejiang province borrowed some from him. On New Year's Eve, the merchant from Wenzhou flew all the way to Shanghai to pay the interest. Of course, back then Chinese businessmen did not have large scale of capital. The interest must be merely several hundred Yuan. Then why must the merchant pay the interest when the price of flight was much higher? The reason is China's "surplus culture". Spring festival is also considered as the end of a year. Chinese people believe they ought to pay back all the debt before the end of each year, even though sometimes the amount is relatively small. This "surplus culture" is also an evidence of Chinese people's credit, which we will sacrifice a lot to maintain. The emphasis of credit and Chinese tradition is the exact reason why merchants from Wenzhou have gained such great success nowadays.

The second story is about America.

In the first half of the year 2011, the book balance of the American company Apple had reached 79 billion dollars, higher than the balance of the US government. The credit rating of Apple is also higher than that of the US government. Apple's success does not rely on borrowing and investing. It relies on technological innovation and new ideas. I believe the real American spirit lies in companies like Apple instead of Wall Street. This is the real direction of US's future development.

基于对东盟宪章理解论国际条约的实践*

Zatil Aqilah Metassan* 常铮 孙超 译

简介 当我们想到2008年12月15日生效的东盟宪章，我们马上面临的问题即本份重要的法律文书将如何改变东盟作为一个政府间国际组织的性质。大多数法律学者把注意力放在东盟宪章第3条，即赋予东盟以"法律人格"，随后，我们面临的另一个法律困惑便是此"法律人格"对于东盟的意义。只有国家在国际法中享有"法律人格"或"国际法律人格"，可以以其名义享有权利，并遵守国际体系下所赋予的义务，如向国际法庭提出权利主张，享有作为国际法主体的主权豁免，缔结国际条约。而现在，国际组织特别是联合国，被承认具有"国际法律人格"，但是不同于国家，国际组织并不享有完全的"国际法律人格"。

然而，国际组织一项最常见到属性则是具有订立国际条约的能力。1986年订立的《国家与国际组织间以及国际组织间的维也纳条约法公约》进一步确认了这一项权利。

虽然东盟宪章授予东盟以"法律人格"，但是有些人会怀疑根据东盟宪章所赋予的"法律人格"并非一个具有确实意义的人格，因此我们应当深入到国际组织本身的运行与实践中寻找答案。本文的目的并非评估法律人格是否存在。因为东盟宪章已经声称东盟"协定决议由国家、次区域、国际组织、机构作出"，因此本文将继续推定东盟确实具有"国际法律人格"并有能力签订国际条约。

本文的目的，亦为本文主题，旨在放眼未来，探寻东盟将如何实施国际条约。自从东盟宪章生效至今，东盟还没有代表其成员国订立国际条约。2009

---

* 本文是作者在东盟法律协会举办的第十一届国际会议期间形成的。2012年2月15—17日，努沙杜瓦，巴厘岛，印尼。

* 作者系印度尼西亚总检察署国际事务处官员。

年2月27日签署的东盟—澳大利亚—新西兰自由贸易协定(AANZFTA)是由东盟成员国作出的决议,而并非是由东盟作为代表作出的。因此,关于东盟将如何实施其与第三国或国际组织作出的国际条约仍然是一个理论问题。

本文将首先解释由东盟达成的国际条约之所以应被视为其由东盟订立,并且据此所产生的权利义务被直接归属于作为一个独立实体的东盟的原因。为揭示此原因,本文将参考东盟宪章第41(7)条和东盟关于订立国际条约程序规则的决议。接下来将通过进一步分析东盟机关的组织运行,以评估其是否可以实施其决议。最后,本文将考虑决议与实施国际条约对于东盟对外关系的重要性。

一、什么是东盟达成的国际条约

《国家与国际组织间以及国际组织间的维也纳条约法公约》将国际条约定义为"称'条约'者,谓以下主体间所缔结而以国际法为准之国际书面协定(i)一个或多个国家和一个或多个国际组织之间;或(ii)国际组织之间……"

在东盟的语境下,可以划分为三种国际条约:

1. 由东盟成员国订立的国际条约;
2. 由东盟与其成员国订立的国际条约;
3. 由东盟与第三方当事国或国际组织订立的国际条约。

对于与东盟有关的国际条约没有什么可说的,更不必说执行情况了。东盟宪章第41(7)条指出:"与国家,次区域,区域和国际组织、机构的协议",但也有其他参照资料,比如"东盟决议与协定峰会"、"东盟决议"、"东盟协议与决定"。东盟关于订立国际条约程序规则的决议,寻求进一步澄清东盟订立的国际条约——"任何书面协议,无论其特定名称,东盟均作为独立的实体在国际法规则的框架下享有权利与承担义务"。这将成为我们对于第三种国际条约认识的指导。由于第41(7)条指称的"国家"为通常意义上的国家,所以东盟成员国也可以与东盟达成国际条约,即第二种国际条约也被包含在内。

然而,如果我们通读第41条,该条似乎表明为建立任何有意义的对外关系,东盟均需要越过其10个成员国圈。因此,本文仅考虑第三种国际条约的实施,即由东盟与第三方当事国或国际组织订立的国际条约。

二、东盟是否为区别于其成员国的独立实体

若一个国际组织具有独立于其成员国的法律人格，则在国际法上应为自己的行为负责。但是，东盟作为一个独立的实体是否可以对其实施的国际条约或对东盟与其成员国均有与约束力的条约负责，仍不清楚。对于欧盟而言，与第三方订立的国际条约对其机构和其成员国均有与约束力。

在那些为作为独立实体的东盟创造权利义务的国际条约和对那些为单独的东盟成员国创造权利义务的国际条约之间，ROPCIAA 作出了一个区别。尽管 ROPCIAA 做出了区别，我们仍然不确定东盟与第三方当事国或国际组织订立的国际条约仅仅约束东盟，还是对东盟和其成员国均有约束力。由于问题过于复杂，东盟宪章在国际条约抑或其他条约如何被实施上保持了沉默。无论如何，确定的是东盟达成的国际条约应为具有独立"法律人格"并作为独立实体有能力签订国际条约的东盟创立权利与义务。

根据查尔斯观点，无法遵守国际条约的原因之一是缔约方在开展事务方面的能力限制。我们应该审视东盟的内部结构与运行，特别是其在东盟宪章规定下的组织机构。据此评估当东盟作为一个独立的实体去实施行为时，其是否具有真正的能力，特别是在实施国际条约方面。

东盟的 7 个重要机构：

1. 东盟首脑会议；
2. 东盟协调理事会；
3. 东盟共同体委员会；
4. 东盟部长级会议；
5. 东盟常驻代表委员会；
6. 东盟国家秘书处；
7. 东盟秘书长和东盟秘书处。

其他机构如东盟政府间人权委员会和东盟基金会。由于这些机构的角色与职能过于具体，并且不涉及东盟的整体运作，所以并不在本文的研究范围内。

(一)东盟首脑会议

东盟首脑会议由东盟成员国的国家元首或政府首脑组成，是东盟的最高决策机构。在各成员国无法达成共识之时，东盟首脑会议将作出决定。也是

在出现未解决争议，不配合调查情况时被移交纠纷，提出建议或作出决定的东盟争端解决机制的核心。并且，也被公认为是作为决定某项行为是否符合宪章第20(4)条所界定的严重违反宪章规定行为的机构。

(二)东盟协调理事会

东盟协调理事会由东盟成员国的外长组成，是直接向东盟首脑会议报告的东盟主要协调机构。它负责对向东盟首脑会议作出的，东盟共同体委员会报告和东盟秘书长年度报告的协调，也负责确保东盟共同体委员会政策的一贯性，监督东盟秘书处在东盟秘书长报告指导下的工作。同样，它也是东盟首脑会议决议与其相关实施机构的联系渠道。不过东盟宪章并没有明确界定“东盟首脑会议决议”这一概念，也没有指出国际条约是否属于此范围。

东盟协调理事会作为东盟首脑会议的直接协助机关，在东盟宪章规定下的争端解决机制中也发挥着重要作用，此争端解决机制主要是针对东盟成员国对于东盟机构决定的解释和适用理解上的争议(应当指出的是，DSMP尚未生效)。虽然待解决的争端和违反规定的行为最终被提交给东盟首脑会议，但是，在其被提交之前东盟协调理事会也会起到一定的解决争端的作用。

(三)东盟共同体委员会

东盟共同体委员会由东盟政治安全共同体理事会、东盟经济共同体理事会和东盟社会文化共同体理事会组成。这些理事会分别负责东盟关于这三个领域的事务，即在政治安全领域、经济领域和社会文化领域。各个委员会都由东盟成员国指派的专员所代表。各委员会辖下的东盟部长级会议包括相关领域的各项机构。委员会的职责是协调这些东盟部长级会议，并向东盟首脑会议提交报告与建议。

东盟共同体委员会也负责确保东盟首脑会议相关决议的实施。同样，东盟宪章中也没有具体界定“东盟首脑会议决议”的范围，回避了东盟订立的国际条约是否包括在内的问题。

(四)东盟部长级会议

正如前面所提到的，东盟部长级会议在东盟共同体委员会的管辖范围内。它的根本职责是统管对各领域的各种倡议的实施。每个会议都有自己的职责，并且赋有向共同体委员会提交报告与建议的职责。不可避免的，各个会议也负责东盟首脑会议决议和条约的执行。但此处的“决议和条约”是否包括东

盟订立的国际条约仍不得而知。

在ROPCIAA下的部长级会议与东盟常驻代表委员会(CPR)负责对东盟订立国际条约提出建议,也针对国际条约的谈判,与CPR一起制定东盟的共同立场。从此我们可以看出,部长级会议对于国际条约的订立以及之后的实施都产生影响。不幸的是,ROPCIAA只提供了缔结的国际协议的规则,而对于其进一步的实施,则没有更多的说明。

(五)东盟常驻代表委员会(CPR)

在东盟总部雅加达,每个东盟成员国委任一名常驻代表。CPR一项最重要的责任就是支持东盟共同体会议的工作,协调东盟国家秘书处与东盟部长级会议的工作,联络东盟秘书长与东盟秘书处。之外,它也促进东盟与外部伙伴的合作,CPR的角色更着重于协调各个部长级会议,并对重点工作进行监督。

(六)东盟国家秘书处

东盟国家秘书处由各个东盟成员国建立,作为东盟事务的国家联络点,也有助于在国家层面上协调东盟决议的实施。但是这是否意味着国际条约在国家层面上的实施仍有待观察。虽然不了解它将如何建立、在哪建立,但它作为一个国家联络点和东盟国家层面上的智囊团都有重要意义。截至目前,东盟国家秘书处尚未被确定。有些人认为,建立一个国内的(domestic)东盟国家秘书处需要立法。这个机构是否将是一个独立的实体,与其服务宗旨仍不确切。东盟宪章并未明确规定,国际条约关于东盟的特权与豁免也没有提及国家秘书处。它代表东盟,但东盟国家秘书处是否可被视为东盟是有疑问的,特别是从它是由其成员国在其国内自行建立的角度上来讲。

(七)东盟秘书长和东盟秘书处

在东盟宪章生效之前,东盟秘书处由东盟外长签订的条约成立。当时,由印度尼西亚共和国政府主办东盟秘书处,现生效的东盟宪章将秘书长与东盟秘书处作为东盟的一个机构——由成员国组成的政府间组织。另一个变化是,东盟秘书长与东盟秘书处被授予特权与豁免。虽然,此条约尚未生效,成员国仍有义务避免实施违背此条约的行为。

然而,东盟秘书长的能力在东盟宪章生效后并没有什么变化。虽然东盟宪章第11(2)(d)条规定,秘书长是“与外部主体一起参与会议并表达东盟的立场”,它仍需要“依据批准的政策指导方针与授权进行”。此外,ROPCIAA并未赋予秘书长订立国际条约的能力。东盟的共同立场由东盟部长级会议、东盟常驻代表委员会、东盟外长会议决定。决议并签署国际条约的权力在依据ROPCIAA规定下的东盟常驻代表委员会或东盟外长会议。秘书长的职责仅仅是基于东盟常驻代表委员会或东盟外长会议的决定签发全权谈判证书、签署正式确认书上。

三、订立国际条约:东盟与东盟成员国

在东盟宪章生效前,东盟已与其他国际组织作出了协议与备忘录,并由东盟秘书长代表东盟秘书处签署。但是这些协议与备忘录都只是一般的合作,没有像其他协议一样对权利与义务进行详解,比如自由贸易协定。

2009年2月,仅仅在东盟宪章生效后几个月,东盟—澳大利亚—新西兰自由贸易区协议(AANZFTA)由东盟成员国签署,而不是由东盟代表。也许因为AANZFTA的谈判过于接近东盟宪章生效的时间,此时对于AANZFTA的任何改动都是不切实际的。

根据东盟宪章第41(7)条,它使东盟“得以与国家或次区域、区域、国际组织和机构缔结条约”。在推动东盟宪章起草工作时,专家小组曾建议秘书长被授权“代表东盟成员国签订非敏感条约”。这对于东盟订立国际条约有什么样的意义?西蒙·切斯特曼在讨论东盟是否大于或小于其部分的总和时写道,许多外国观察家会说“除非它提供的更多,其成员国与东盟的直接联系将不会减少其与不同国家的双边外交需求,它的全部作用就是增加了另一层外交关系”。考虑到这一点,我们应当问自己东盟作为一个单独的实体缔结国际协定将有什么前景?在东盟宪章对国际条约的实施保持沉默的情况下,评估变得异常困难。

让我们考虑这样一个场景:东盟与外部实体一起订立国际条约。根据ROPCIAA,国际条约的谈判由东盟代表完成,其谈判立场依据东盟常驻代表委员会或东盟外长会议的指示而作出。国际条约的订立在东盟常驻代表委员会或东盟外长会议(AMM)的决议下作出。谁将实施国际条约?鉴于条约的谈判基于东盟常驻代表委员会或东盟外长会议的决议,所以这些机构将由利益攸关方负责条约的执行。

官员们在谈判立场的发展中常有原因去采用远视的态度,虽然在条约的订立中他们应具有操作性的责任。一旦条约生效,他们在谈判桌上的言行均

可能困扰他们。

东盟常驻代表委员会在东盟宪章规定下的角色更在于协调而非是实施，这与东盟部长级会议不同，从东盟宪章第10(1)(b)条“在各自的职权范围内实施东盟首脑会议的决议和条约”可以看出。

那么东盟部长级会议将如何实施国际条约？东盟部长级会议并不像欧盟委员会和欧洲议会一样有制定法律的权力，也没有强制其成员国执行国际条约的权力。它基于东盟首脑会议决议和条约工作。换句话说，他们无权代表东盟，东盟首脑会议仍为主要决策机构。除东盟首脑会议外，东盟外长会议也被认为是另一个可能参与外部关系事宜决策的机构。东盟首脑会议和东盟外长会议的决议也应基于协商并达成的共识之上。鉴于东盟部长级会议缺乏实施的能力，宪章在此项上保持沉默，并且决策的做出基于最高机构的共识，似乎对于实施任何一个潜在的国际条约来说都需要经历一个长期并艰难的过程。这将使任何实施行为都难以被实践。

除了东盟宪章规定的不切实际的实施框架，宪章对于东盟与其成员国订立的国际条约的效力也保持了沉默。正如前面提到的，欧洲联盟里斯本条约明确指出，其与第三国或国际组织订立的国际条约同时约束其机构与成员国。尽管里斯本条约并未具体说明如何实施国际条约，这通常在其判例法中阐明，国际条约仍被认为是二级惯例与协定。因此，东盟成员国可能需要制定实施性的国内法以期执行国际条约。所以，没有一种集中的主权以赋予东盟机构能力代表东盟独立实施行为。如果真的如此，那么缺少宪法性规定、司法决议、学理阐明的国际条约之实施将更为复杂。

四、东盟未来的外部关系与国际条约

考虑到东盟实施国际条约的困难，我们想知道是否需要赋予东盟机构更多的能力，使其享受国际条约下的权利义务。例如欧盟，有效地进行二分，在一些领域汇集主权权力，而在另一些领域保有它。然而，任何将东盟转变为超国家机构的观念都已被东盟领导人明确否定。

大概目前关于改变的答案是否定的。但是，即使是由东盟成员国共同而非东盟代表他们签订的自由贸易协定，外部主体仍对与东盟建立多方关系展示了兴趣。欧洲经济和社会委员会对于欧盟—东盟关系的评论是，在东盟与澳大利亚、新西兰、中国和印度签订自由贸易协定之后，其将在国际上扮演一个更加重要的角色。它进一步提到，作为欧盟仅次于美国与中国的第三大贸

易伙伴,取消关税与非关税壁垒对欧盟具有重要意义。东盟被认为是平衡中美力量的战略合作伙伴。2009 年 7 月 22 日,美国加入《东南亚友好合作条约》。据东盟秘书处的新闻发布,东盟秘书长素林·比素万博士说,这代表着美国新政府对东盟具体政策的一项转变。东盟对于美国的利益是显而易见的——美国总统奥巴马出席最近的第三次东盟—美国领导人会议;7 月 16—28 日,美国国务卿希拉里·克林顿出席巴厘岛的第 18 届东盟地区论坛。

现在东盟订立的国际条约与其后续执行可能不那么令人担忧。如果这样能更有效地实施的话,东盟可能继续以其成员国共同的方式订立国际条约。大概建立在一般合作基础上的协议与备忘不能创立使东盟作为独立实体而享有承担并且可以实际实施的具体权利义务。

对于东盟,还有其他更加需要关注的问题,比如东盟条约的执行。条约所规定东盟的特权与豁免以及争端解决机制仍未建立。另外还包括东盟货物贸易协定(ATIGA)所企求的使东盟在 2015 年成为一个单一市场和生产基地,这个目标在东盟宪章中也有体现。此外,还有东盟全面投资协议,其目的是通过使成员国建立开放的投资机制,加强对投资者的保障,以此创造有利的投资环境并促进东盟作为一个综合投资区域的发展。在这些领域均需要采取优先行动,以期在 2015 年实现东盟共同体。

然而,由东盟的成员国而不是东盟代表其订立国际条约可能引发东盟的分裂的危险。其外部的合作伙伴可能不会将东盟看作一个可靠的功能性的组织。因此,虽然在执行国际条约上还有许多问题,此问题应当首先被考虑。东盟宪章 21(1)条在执行与程序规定上规定,各东盟共同体委员会应规定自身的议事规则。这将是关于执行规定发展的出发点。

结　　语

截至目前,东盟还没有准备好像东盟宪章第 41(7)条和 ROPCIAA 所期许的一般订立国际条约。早些时候它已经表明东盟还没有能力履行国际条约所规定的义务,这仍然需要成员国进行相关国内立法。东盟大部分的注意力可能将放在提升其内部的整合度,优先实现东盟内部机构和议事规则的发展。然而由各会员国订立的国际条约的泛滥可能会对东盟作为一个独立于其成员国的国际组织的可信度产生疑问。虽然东盟已经拒绝了成为超国家共同体的建议,但是,对于在不危及其会员国利益的前提下,东盟自主订立并以其自身权利有效执行国际条约的能力仍需进一步的研究。

Implementation of International Agreements in the Basis of the ASEAN Charter*

Written by Zatil Aqilah Metassan**

Introduction

When we think of the ASEAN Charter, which entered into force on 15 December 2008, we are immediately faced with the question of how this primary constituent instrument has changed ASEAN as an intergovernmental organization. Most legal scholars would then direct their attention to Article 3 of the ASEAN Charter, which conferred "legal personality" to ASEAN. We are then faced with another legal quandary on what this "legal personality" means for ASEAN. Before the *Reparations* case, only States enjoyed "legal personality" in international law or "international legal personality", and could avail itself of the rights and to be subject to all of the duties known to the international system, such as the ability to bring claims before an international tribunal, to enjoy immunities attaching to international legal persons and to conclude international agreements. Now, international organisations, notably the United Nations, have been recognized to have "international legal personality". Unlike States, international organisations do not

* This paper was written in conjunction with the 11th General Assembly of the ASEAN Law Association (ALA GA) held at the Bali International Convention Centre, Nusa Dua, Bali, Indonesia on 15th-17th February 2012.

** All views stated herein are those of the author alone.

Officer from Internatinal Affairs Division, Attorney Gerenal's Chambers.

enjoy the full breadth of "international legal personality". ①

However, one of the most common attributes that international organisations enjoy is the ability to enter into international agreements. The 1986 Vienna Convention on the Law of Treaties between States and International Organisation or between International Organisations further recognizes this right. ②

Although the ASEAN Charter had granted ASEAN with "legal personality", some would argue that conferring ASEAN with "legal personality" under the ASEAN Charter does not necessarily mean that it possesses personality in a meaningful sense, and instead we should look deeper into the practice and operation of the international organization itself. ③ This paper is not aimed at assessing the existence of legal personality. The ASEAN Charter has already asserted that ASEAN "may conclude agreements with countries or sub-regional and international organisations and institutions ... " as such this paper will continue with the presumption that ASEAN does posses "international legal personality" and the capacity to enter into international

---

① Reparation for Injuries Suffered in the Service of the United Nations, Advisory Opinion, *ICJ Rep.* (1949) p. 174, [*Reparations case*], p. 179: "the Court has come to the conclusion that the Organization is an international person. That is not the same thing as saying that it is a State, which it certainly is not, or that its legal personality and rights and duties are the same as those of a State. Still less is it the same thing as saying that it is "a super-State", whatever that expression may mean ... Whereas a State possesses the totality of international rights and duties of an entity such as the Organization must depend upon its purposes and functions as specified or implied in its constitutent documents and developed in practice. "

② Vienna Convention on the Law of Treaties Between States and International Organizations or Between International Organizationa, [*VCLTIO*], 21 March 1986, (not yet in force), preamble paragraph 11: "*Noting* that international organizations possess the capacity to conclude treaties, which is necessary for the exercise of their functions and the fulfillment of their purposes. "

③ Simon Chesterman, Does ASEAN Exist? The Association of Southeast Asian Nations as an International Legal Person, *ASEAN*: *Life after the Charter*, Edited by S. Tiwari, p. 20.

agreements. ①

The purpose of this paper rather, as the topic has so prescribed, is to look further ahead into how ASEAN would implement international agreements. Since the entry into force of the ASEAN Charter, there had been no international agreements entered into by ASEAN on behalf of its member states. The ASEAN-Australia-New Zealand FTA (AANZFTA) signed on 27 February 2009, was concluded by the individual member states rather than ASEAN on their behalf. Hence, the question on how ASEAN will implement international agreements that it has concluded with a third party State or international organisation is rather a theoretical one.

This paper will begin by explaining why an international agreement concluded by ASEAN should be regarded as those agreements entered into by ASEAN and that creates rights and obligations for ASEAN as a distinct entity from its Member States. In demonstrating this, the paper will refer to Article 41(7) of the ASEAN Charter and the Rules of Procedure for Conclusion of International Agreements by ASEAN. ② It will then proceed to analyse the operation and functionality of ASEAN's organs to assess whether they could execute implementation. Towards the end, this paper will then consider the importance of concluding and implementing international agreements in ASEAN's external relations.

---

① ASEAN Charter, Article 41(7): "ASEAN may conclude agreements with countries or sub-regional, regional and international organisations and institutions. The procedures for concluding such agreements shall be prescribed by the ASEAN Coordinating Council in consultation with the ASEAN Community Councils."

② The Rules of Procedure for Conclusion of International Agreements by ASEAN (ROPCIAA) was drafted by the ASEAN Senior Officials' Meeting Working Group on the High Level Legal Experts Group's Remaining Legal Instruments. It was then adopted by the ASEAN Coordinating Council in Cambodia. The Rules were drafted in accordance with Article 41(7) of the ASEAN Charter: "ASEAN may conclude agreements with countries or sub-regional, regional and international organisations and institutions. The procedures for concluding such agreements shall be prescribed by the ASEAN Coordinating Council in consultation with the ASEAN Community Councils."

International agreements concluded by ASEAN? What is it?

The 1986 Vienna Convention on the Law of Treaties between States and International Organisation or between International Organisations defines international agreements as an agreement "governed by international law and concluded in written form: (i) between one or more States and one or more international organizations; or (ii) between international organizations ... "①

In the context of ASEAN, three types of international agreements come into mind:

1. International agreements concluded between ASEAN Member States;

2. International agreements concluded between ASEAN and a Member State; and

3. International agreements concluded between ASEAN and a third party State or international organisation.

There is nothing much said in the ASEAN Charter regarding international agreements, even less on its implementation. Article 41(7) of the ASEAN Charter refers to "agreements with countries or sub-regional, regional and international organisations and institutions", but there are also other references such as "agreements and decisions of the ASEAN Summit"②, "ASEAN decisions"③ and "ASEAN agreements and decisions"④. The Rules of Procedure for Conclusion of International Agreements by ASEAN sought to further clarify international agreements of ASEAN as "any written agreement, regardless of its particular designation, governed by internation-

---

① VCLTIO Article 2-Use of Terms: "1(a) "treaty" means an international agreement governed by international law and concluded in written form: (i) between one or more States and one or more international organizations; or (ii) between international organizations ... "

② ASEAN Charter, Article 10(1): "ASEAN Sectoral Ministerial Bodies shall: ... (b) implement the agreements and decisions of the ASEAN Summit under their respective purview ... "

③ ASEAN Charter, Article 13: "Each ASEAN Member State shall establish an ASEAN National Secretariat which shall: ... (c) coordinate the implementation of ASEAN decisions at the national level ... "

④ ASEAN Charter, Article 11(2): "The Secretary-General shall: ... "

al law which creates rights and obligations for ASEAN as a distinct entity from its Member States". This would point us in the direction of international agreement types 3. Since Article 41(7) refers to "countries" in its general sense, each ASEAN Member State could also be said to conclude international agreements with ASEAN and so international agreements could also include type 2.

However, if we were to read Article 41 in its entirety, it would seem that in order to have external relations in any meaningful sense, ASEAN would need to establish relations beyond its circle of 10 member states. Thus, this paper will only consider the implementation of international agreements type 3—international agreements concluded between ASEAN and a third party State or international organisation.

Who is ASEAN? Is it a distinct entity from its member states?

Where an international organisation has international legal personality separate from its member states, it is responsible in international law for its own acts, but does ASEAN act as a distinct entity from its member states in order to be responsible for say, the implementation of international agreements by ASEAN, or could the agreement bind both ASEAN and its Member States?① For the European Union, international agreements that it concludes with third countries or international organisations would bind its institutions and member states. ② Having said that, there are those who would caution on making any comparison between ASEAN and the EU. ③

---

① *Anthony Aust*, *Modern Treaty Law and Practice*, 2nd Edition, Cambridge University Press.

② Treaty of Lisbon (Amending the Treaty on European Union and the Treaty establishing the European Community), Article 188L: "2. Agreements concluded by the Union are binding upon institutions of the Union and on its Member States."

③ Simon Chesterman, Does ASEAN Exist? The Association of Southeast Asian Nations as an International Legal Person, *ASEAN: Life after the Charter*, supra note 4 at p. 32.

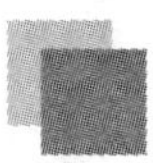

A distinction is made in the ROPCIAA between international agreements that create rights and obligations on for ASEAN as a distinct entity from its Member States, and those that create rights and obligations upon individual ASEAN Member States. ① Despite the distinction made in ROPCIAA, it is still uncertain whether international agreements between ASEAN and third party States or international organisations would bind ASEAN only, or both ASEAN and individual ASEAN member states. ② To further complicate matters, the ASEAN Charter is silent on how international agreements, or any agreements, are to be implemented. Regardless, what remains certain is that the international agreement entered into by ASEAN should create rights and obligations on ASEAN as it is an international organisation with "legal personality" with the capacity to enter into international agreements as a separate entity from its member states. ③

According to Chayes and Chayes, one of the causes for non-compliance of an international agreement is limitations on the capacity of parties to carry out their undertakings. ④ We shall now look at the internal structure and operation of ASEAN, specifically its organs, as prescribed under the ASEAN Charter. We would need to assess whether there is any real competence for ASEAN as a distinct entity from its member states to act on its own, especially on the implementation of international agreements.

---

① See ROPCIAA, Rule 1:"1. These Rules specify the procedure for the conclusion of international agreements by ASEAN as an intergovernmental organisation in the conduct of external relations as provided in Article 41(7) of the ASEAN Charter. 2. These Rules shall not apply to the conclusion of international agreements concluded by all ASEAN Member States collectively and which create obligations upon individual ASEAN Member States."

② Michael Ewing-Chow, Translating the Design into a Bloc: The Domestic Implementation of the ASEAN Charter, *Life after the Charter: ASEAN*, p. 76.

③ Supra note10.

④ Abram Chayes and Antonia Handler Chayes, On Compliance, *International Institutions: An International Organization Reader* (edited by Lisa L. Martin and Beth A. Simmons), p. 260.

There are 7 main organs of ASEAN:①

(1)ASEAN Summit;

(2)ASEAN Coordinating Council;

(3)ASEAN Community Councils;

(4)ASEAN Sectoral Ministerial Bodies;

(5)Committee of Permanent Representatives to ASEAN;

(6)ASEAN National Secretariat; and

(7)ASEAN Secretary-General and ASEAN Secretariat.

Other organs also include the ASEAN Human Rights Body and the ASEAN Foundation. However, this paper will not commit to studying these organs as their roles and functions are too subject specific and do not relate to the overall functioning of ASEAN.

ASEAN Summit

The ASEAN Summit is comprised of Heads of State or Government of the ASEAN member states and it represents the highest policy and decision-making body within ASEAN.② The ASEAN Summit's decision is needed where consensus cannot be achieved.③ It is also the highest body within ASEAN for referral of disputes where there is an unresolved dispute and non-compliance with the findings, recommendations or decisions, recommendations or decisions resulting from an ASEAN dispute settlement mechanism.④ However, it is yet to be known how this would reconcile with Article 20(4) where cases of serious breach of the Charter or non-compliance

---

① ASEAN Charter, Chapter IV-Organs.

② ASEAN Charter, Article 7-ASEAN Summit.

③ ASEAN Charter, Article 20(2): "Where consensus cannot be achieved, the ASEAN Summit may decide how a specific decision can be made."

④ ASEAN Charter, Article 26—Unresolved Disputes: "When a dispute remains unresolved, after the application of the preceding provisions of this Chapter, this dispute shall be referred to the ASEAN Summit, for its decision" and Article 27(2): "Any Member State affected by non-compliance with the findings, recommendations or decisions resulting from an ASEAN dispute settlement mechanism, may refer the matter to the ASEAN Summit for a decision."

should be referred to the ASEAN Summit for decision.

ASEAN Coordinating Council

The ASEAN Coordinating Council is comprised of the ASEAN Foreign Ministers, and it is the main coordinating body within ASEAN, which reports directly to the ASEAN Summit. It is responsible for coordinating the reports of the ASEAN Community Councils and the annual report of the Secretary-General on the work of ASEAN to the ASEAN Summit. ① It is also responsible for ensuring policy coherence amongst the ASEAN Community Councils, and also oversees the function and operations of the ASEAN Secretariat by considering the report of the Secretary-General. ② It also channels the agreements and decisions of the ASEAN Summit to the relevant organs for implementation. ③ The ASEAN Charter is not clear on what it means by "agreements and decisions of the ASEAN Summit" and whether it could also include international agreements.

The ACC, as a body directly assisting the ASEAN Summit, also has a significant role to play under the Protocol to the ASEAN Charter on Dispute Settlement Mechanisms (DSMP) in the settlement of disputes between ASEAN Member States concerning the interpretation or application of ASEAN Instruments (it should be noted that the DSMP has yet to enter into force). ④ This includes moving the dispute settlement process forward, where the member states in dispute opts for its assistance. Although unre-

---

① ASEAN Charter, Article 8: "The ASEAN Coordinating Council shall: (d) coordinate the reports of the ASEAN Community Councils to the ASEAN Summit; (e) consider the annual report of the Secretary-General on the of ASEAN ... "

② Ibid, Article 8: "(f) consider the report of the Secretary-General on the functions and operations of the ASEAN Secretariat and other relevant bodies ... "

③ Ibid, Article 8: "(b) coordinate the implementation of agreements and decisions of the ASEAN Summit ... "

④ See Protocol to the ASEAN Charter on Dispute Settlement Mechanisms, Article 9—Reference to the ASEAN Coordinating Council ad Annex 4—Rules of Arbitration, Rule 4(a) and (b): The ACC may be requested to appoint the third arbitrator where there is no agreement between the Parties to the dispute.

solved disputes and non-compliance are to be referred to the ASEAN Summit, the ACC also has a role to play to assist in such cases with the intention of settling the dispute, before it is submitted to the ASEAN Summit. ①

ASEAN Community Council

The ASEAN Community Council consists of the ASEAN Political-Security Community Council, ASEAN Economic Community Council, and ASEAN Socio-Cultural Community Council. Each of the Council is responsible for the implementation of the three community pillars of ASEAN, namely the ASEAN Political-Security Community, ASEAN Economic Community and ASEAN Socio-Cultural Community. ② The Community Councils are each represented by the nationals of ASEAN Member States who are designated by them. ③ Each of this Community Council has under its purview the ASEAN Sectoral Ministerial Bodies covering various sectors under the relevant community pillar. ④ It is the responsibility of the Community Councils to coordinate the work of these ASEAN Sectoral Ministerial Bodies, and

---

① DSMP, supra note 19, Article 26. Also see ASEAN Charter, Article 8(2): "The ASEAN Coordinating Council shall: (a) prepare the meetings of the ASEAN Summit ... (h) undertake other tasks provided for in this Charter or such other functions as may be assigned by the ASEAN Summit ... " Although the decision on unresolved dispute and non-compliance ultimately rests on the ASEAN Summit, the ACC is given a role to assist settling the dispute, before it is submitted to the ASEAN Summit.

② These community pillars together form the ASEAN Community. Following the Cebu Declaration on the Acceleration of the Establishment of an ASEAN Community by 2015, signed on 13 January 2007, ASEAN's goal for establishing of the ASEAN Community was further accelerated from 2010 to the year 2015.

③ ASEAN Charter, Article 9: "3. Each Member State shall designate its national representation for each ASEAN Community Council meeting."

④ ASEAN Charter, supra note 26, see sub-paragraph 2: "Each Community Council shall have under its purview the relevant ASEAN Sectoral Ministerial Bodies."

submit reports and recommendations to the ASEAN Summit. ①

The ASEAN Community Council also needs to ensure the implementation of the relevant decisions of the ASEAN Summit. Again, there is nothing said in the ASEAN Charter on what "decisions of the ASEAN Summit" would include, and it begs the questions on whether such decisions could also mean international agreements entered into by ASEAN.

ASEAN Sectoral Ministerial Bodies

As mentioned earlier, the ASEAN Sectoral Minsiterial Bodies (ASMB) comes under the purview of the relevant ASEAN Community Councils. This organ is essentially responsible for the groundwork of various initiatives under each community pillar. Each ASMB has its own mandate and submits reports and recommendations to its respective Community Councils. ② Inevitably, each ASMB would be responsible for implementing agreements and decisions of the ASEAN Summit. ③ Whether or not such "agreements and decisions of the ASEAN Summit" could include international agreements entered into by ASEAN is also unknown.

Under the ROPCIAA the ASMB, in coordination with the CPR are responsible for making a proposal for ASEAN to enter into an international agreement. It is also responsible for formulating ASEAN Common positions

---

① ASEAN Charter, supra note 26, see sub-paragraph : "(b) Coordinate the work of the different sectors under its purview, and on issues which cut across the other Community Councils; and (c) submit reports and recommendations to the ASEAN Summit on matters under its purview."

② ASEAN Charter, Article 10: "1. ASEAN Sectoral Ministerial Bodies shall ... (d) submit reports and recommendations to their respective Community Councils."

③ ASEAN Charter, supra note 29 see subparagraph (1)(b): "1. ASEAN Sectoral Ministerial Bodies shall ... (b) implement the agreements and decisions of the ASEAN Summit under their respective purview ..."

with the CPR for the purposes of negotiating the international agreement. [①] From that we could derive that the ASMB would have a stake in the conclusion of the international agreement and its further implementation. Unfortunately, ROPCIAA only provides rules for the conclusion of international agreement, there is not much said on the further implementation of such agreements even in the ASEAN Charter.

Committee of Permanent Representatives to ASEAN

Each ASEAN Member State is to appoint a Permanent Representative to ASEAN with the rank of Ambassador based in Jakarta. [②] The Committee of Permanent Representatives to ASEAN (CPR) has one of the most responsibilities within ASEAN. It supports the work of the ASEAN Community Councils and the ASMB, coordinates with ASEAN National Secretariats and other ASMB, and liaise with the Secretary-General of ASEAN and the ASEAN Secretariat. [③] In addition to these functions, it is to facilitate ASEAN cooperation with external partners. [④] The CPR's role is more on coordinating with various ASEAN organs, and focused on monitoring actions taken at the groundwork level.

ASEAN National Secretariat

The ASEAN National Secretariat is to be established by each ASEAN

---

① ROPCIAA, Rule 3: "The proposal to commence a negotiation of an international agreement shall be coordinated with the Committee of Permanent Representatives to ASEAN by the relevant ASEAN Sectoral Ministerial Bodies at the senior officials level. The ASEAN Foreign Ministers Meeting, on its own or through the Committee of Permanent Representatives to ASEAN, shall decide on the proposal and shall appoint the appropriate representative(s) to commence the negotiation on behalf of ASEAN." And Rule 4: "2. Such ASEAN common position shall be formulated by the relvant ASEAN Sectoral Minsiterial Bodies ... 3. The representative(s) as referred to in Rule 3 shall adhere to an ASEAN common position which serves as a basis for negotiation."

② ASEAN Charter, Article 12(1).

③ ASEAN Charter, Article 12(2).

④ Ibid 32.

Member State, and it would serve as a national focal point for all ASEAN matters. ① This National Secretariat would also serve to coordinate the implementation of ASEAN decisions at the national level. ② Whether this could mean the implementation of international agreements at the national level is yet to be seen. Although there is nothing much said on how it will be established and where, the fact that it is to act as a focal national point and repository of all ASEAN information at the national level as well as responsible for disseminating ASEAN information, indicates that it would serve at the domestic level within the territory of each member state. ③ As of now, these ASEAN National Secretariats have not been identified yet. Some would argue that establishing a domestic ASEAN National Secretariat requires implementing legislation. ④ Whether or not this national secretariat will be an independent body from the member state with the purpose of serving ASEAN remains unclear. The ASEAN Charter is silent on this. The Agreement on the Privileges and Immunities of ASEAN make no reference to the ASEAN National Secretariat. ⑤ It refers to ASEAN, but whether or not ASEAN National Secretariat could be considered as ASEAN is questionable, especially since it is to be established by Member States in its domestic sphere.

---

① ASEAN Charter, Article 13: "Each ASEAN Member State shall establish an ASEAN National Secretariat which shall ..."

② ASEAN Charter, supra note 35, Sub-paragraphs: "(c) coordinate the implementation of ASEAN decisions at the national level ..."

③ ASEAN Charter, supra note 35, Sub-paragraphs: "(b) be the repository of information on all ASEAN matters at the national level; (c) coordinate the implementation of ASEAN decisions at the national level ..." (e) promote ASEAN identity and awareness at the national level ... "

④ Supra note 13, at p. 77: Michael Ewing-Chow argued that the establishment of an ASEAN National Secretariat would require an outlay of fiscal expenses, and hence it may require implementing legislation for its establishment.

⑤ Agreement on the Privileges and Immunities of ASEAN was signed on 25 October 2009. It has not come into force yet.

Secretary-General of ASEAN and ASEAN Secretariat

Before the entry into force of the ASEAN Charter, the ASEAN Secretariat existed in 1976 with the signing of the Agreement of the Establishment of the ASEAN Secretariat by the ASEAN Foreign Ministers. At the time, the Government of the Republic of Indonesia hosted the ASEAN Secretariat. Now with the entry into force of the ASEAN Charter, the Secretary-General and ASEAN Secretariat exists as an organ of ASEAN, an intergovernmental organization with distinct identity from its Member States. The other significant change for the Secretary-General of ASEAN and the ASEAN Secretariat is that they are now granted privileges and immunities. Although this Agreement has yet to enter into force, the member states are obliged to refrain from acts which would defeat the object and purpose of the treaty. ①

However, not much has changed in the competence of the Secretary-General after the entry into force of the ASEAN Charter. Although Article 11(2)(d) of the ASEAN Charter provides that the Secretary-General is to "present the views of ASEAN and participate in meeting with external parties", it has to be "in accordance with approved policy guidelines and mandate given to the Secretary-General ... " Furthermore, the ROPCIAA does not give the Secretary-General a big role to play in the process of concluding international agreements. The ASEAN Common position is formulated by the ASMB, the CPR and the ASEAN Foreign Ministers to a certain extent. Decision on signing and concluding the international agreement also lay with the CPR or the ASEAN Foreign Ministers, depending on the circumstances as prescribed under the ROPCIAA. The Secretary-General's role is merely to issue full powers for negotiation, signing and instrument of formal confirmation, upon receiving approval from the CPR or the ASEAN Foreign Ministers to do so.

---

① VCLTIO, Article 18.

Conclusion of International Agreements: ASEAN vs ASEAN Individual Member States

Prior to the entry into force of the ASEAN Charter, ASEAN had concluded Memorandas and Agreements with other international organisations, and signed by the Secretary-General of ASEAN on behalf of the ASEAN Secretariat. ① However, these Memorandas or Agreements were focused on general cooperation only, lacking any rights or obligations in detail unlike

① The following memorandas and agreements are available at http://www.asean.org/20198.htm: See Agreement of Cooperation between the Association of Southeast Asian Nations (ASEAN) and the United Nations Educational, Scientific and Cultural Organization (UNESCO), signed by the Secretary-General of ASEAN on 12 September 1998. ASEAN was named as the party to the Agreement even before it was conferred legal personality under the ASEAN Charter.

See Memorandum between the Secretariat of the Association of Southeast Asian Nations (ASEAN Secretariat) and the Secretariat of the United Nations Economic and Social Commission for Asia and the Pacific (ESCAP Secretariat), signed by the Secretary-General of ASEAN on 2 January 2002.

See Memorandum of Understanding between the Secretariat of the Association of Southeast Asian Nations (ASEAN Secretariat) and the Secretariat of the Shanghai Cooperation Organization (SCO Secretariat), signed by the Secretary-General of ASEAN on 21 April 2005.

See Memorandum of Understanding for Administrative Arrangements between the Association of Southeast Asian Nations Secretariat and Asian Development Bank, signed by the Secretary-General of ASEAN on 24 August 2006. The MOU provides that it is not meant to be legally binding.

See Cooperation Agreement between the Association of Southeast Asian Nations (ASEAN) Secretariat and the International Labour Office, signed by Secretary-General of ASEAN on 20 March 2007.

See Memorandum of Understanding between the Association of Southeast Asian Nations (ASEAN) and the United Nations (UN) on ASEAN-UN Cooperation, signed by the Secretary-General of ASEAN on 27 September 2007.

Even after the entry into force of the ASEAN Charter, the Secretary-General continued to conclude international agreements between the ASEAN Secretariat and other international organisations. See Memorandum of Understanding between the Secretariat of the Association of Southeast Asian Nations and the Secretariat General of the Cooperation Council for the Arab States of the Gulf, signed by the Secretary-General on 30 June 2009.

other agreements such as the FTAs.

On February 2009, just a few months after the entry into force of the ASEAN Charter, the ASEAN-Australia-New Zealand Free Trade Area Agreement (AANZFTA) was signed by the individual member states collectively, rather than ASEAN on its behalf. ① Perhaps the AANZFTA negotiations were too close into completion at the time the ASEAN Charter entered into force, that any changes to the arrangement on the conclusion of the AANZFTA was probably impractical or impossible. ②

Looking at Article 41(7) of the ASEAN Charter, it provides that ASEAN "*may* conclude agreements with countries or sub-regional, regional and international organisations and institutions". ③ In facilitating the drafting of the ASEAN Charter, the Eminent Persons Group recommended that the Secretary-General be "delegated the authority to sign *non-sensitive agreements* on behalf of ASEAN Member States". ④ What does this mean for ASEAN when concluding international agreements? Simon Chesterman, in discussing whether ASEAN is more than the sum of its parts or less, wrote that many outside observers would say that "*unless and until it (ASEAN) offers something more, then liaising directly with ASEAN does not reduce the need for bilateral diplomacy with the various states. All it does is to add another layer of diplomacy*". ⑤ With this in mind, we ask ourselves what prospects is there for ASEAN to conclude international agreements as a

---

① The AANZFTA was signed at the side-lines of the 14th ASEAN Summit on 27 February 2009 in Cha-am Hua Hin, Thailand. It is the single most comprehensive economic agreement entered into by ASEAN to date. Most economic agreements with dialogue partners are concluded in separate agreements such as those concluded to establish the ASEAN-China Free Trade Area.

② Negotiations on the AANZFTA began as far back as 2004, when it was launched by the ASEAN-Australia and New Zealand Commemorative Summit.

③ Supra note 6.

④ The Eminent Persons Group on the ASEAN Charter, *Report of the Eminent Persons Group on the ASEAN Charter* (Jakarta, December 2006), para. 37. Available at http://www.aseansec.org/19247.pdf.

⑤ Supra note 4, p. 32.

separate entity? This is especially difficult to assess where the ASEAN Charter is silent on the implementation of international agreements.

Let us consider a scenario where ASEAN will enter into an international agreement with an external party. According to ROPCIAA, the international agreement would be negotiated by the ASEAN representative(s), who would receive instructions from the ASMB and CPR on the position for negotiations. The international agreement would then be concluded upon the decision of the CPR or the AMM. Who would then implement the international agreement? Since the agreement was negotiated on the basis of common positions formulated by the ASMB and CPR, it is assumed that these organs would be the interested parties and hence, would be responsible for the implementation of that agreement. As Chayes and Chayes would argue:

"Officials engaged in developing the negotiating position often have an additional reason to take a long-range view, since they may have operational responsibility under any agreement that is reached. What they say and how they conduct themselves at the negotiating table may return to haunt them once the treaty has gone into effect. "①

The CPR's role, as provided in the ASEAN Charter, is more focused on coordination, rather than implementation. This is unlike the ASMB, which according to Article 10(1)(b) of the ASEAN Charter shall "*implement the agreements and decisions of the ASEAN Summit under their respective purview*". How then will the ASMB implement the international agreement? The ASMB do not have the power to enact laws unlike the EU Commission and Parliament, nor does it have the power to impose enforcement of an international agreement on member states. It works on the basis of agreements and decisions of the ASEAN Summit. In other words, they do not have the power to decide on behalf of ASEAN, and the ASEAN Summit continues to be the main organ for decision-making. Apart from the ASEAN Summit, the ASEAN Foreign Ministers Meeting (AMM) is also recognized as another forum that could partake in the decision-making on matters re-

① Supra note 16, pp. 253～254.

garding external relations. ① Decisions made by the ASEAN Summit and the ASEAN Foreign Ministers would also need to be based on consultation and consensus. ② With the ASMB lacking the power to act, as the Charter is silent on the matter, and decision-making based on consensus left to the highest body, it seems that any action for implementation of a potential international agreement would need to go through a long and arduous process. This could make any action for implementation either impractical or impossible.

Apart from the impracticality of implementation under the framework provided in the ASEAN Charter, it should also be noted that the Charter is also silent on the effect of international agreements on ASEAN or its member states. As mentioned earlier, the European Union the Treaty Lisbon clearly states that international agreements that it concludes with third countries or international organisations would bind its institutions and member states. ③ Although the Treaty of Lisbon does not specify how international agreements would be implemented, as this is normally elaborated in their case laws, the international agreements are still considered as secondary conventions and agreements. ④ Hence, there may be a need for implementing domestic legislation to be enacted by each ASEAN Member State for such international agreements. Since, there is no pooled sovereignty within ASEAN that would give ASEAN organs the competence to act on behalf of

---

① ASEAN Charter, Article 41: "5. The strategic policy directions of ASEAN's external relations shall be set by the ASEAN Summit upon the recommendation of the ASEAN Foreign Ministers Meeting. 6. The ASEAN Foreign Minsiters Meeting shall ensure consistency and coherence in the conduct of ASEAN's external relations."

② ASEAN Charter, Article 20: "1. As a basic principle, decision-making in ASEAN shall be based on consultation and consensus. 2. Where consensus cannot be achieved, the ASEAN Summit may decide how a specific decision can bemade ... "

③ Supra note 14.

④ See Case C-69/89 *Nakajima All Precision Co. Ltd v. Council*, [1991] E. C. R. I-2069, [Nakajima Doctrine]. See also Case C-70/87 *Fediol v. Commission* [1989] E. C. R. 1781 [Fediol Doctrine]. Both cases are regarding direct effect of GATT as a pre-condition for using these Agreements as a ground for judicial review in a direct action brought before the European Court of Justice or the Court of Fist Instance.

ASEAN, implementation would then be left with the member states. If this is so, then implementation of international agreements becomes more complicated, as there is a lack of constitutional clarity, judicial decisions and elucidating academic writing about the implementation of treaties within ASEAN. ①

International Agreements and the Future of ASEAN's external relations

After considering the difficulties of implementing international agreements by ASEAN, we ask again whether there is a need for change and whether more competence should be given to ASEAN organs, so it could assume rights and obligations under an international agreement. The European Union, for example, has effectively dichotomized itself as it has pooled its sovereignty in some areas whist keeping sovereignty in other areas. ② However, any notion of transforming ASEAN into a supra-national body had already been firmly rejected by the ASEAN leaders. ③

Perhaps the answer for change would be a no, for now. Even as ASEAN concludes Free Trade Agreements as individual member states collectively rather than ASEAN on its behalf, its external partners have still shown interest in engaging with ASEAN. An opinion made by the European Economic and Social Committee on "EU-ASEAN Relations" had commented that ASEAN has greater international role following the Free Trade Agreements that it has concluded with Australia and New Zealand, China and In-

---

① Supra note 13, p. 73.

② European Integration: Sharing of Experiences, Jorgen Orstrom Moller.

③ Tan Lay Hong, Will ASEAN's Economic Integration Progress Beyond a Free Trade Area, 53 *ICLQ* (2004) 935 at 949 and 967.

dia.① It further commented that the removal of significant tariff and non-tariff barriers would "entail clear benefits for the EU", whilst stating that ASEAN is currently EU's third trading partner after the USA and China. ASEAN is also seen as a strategic partner in the balance of power between the U. S and China. On 22 July 2009 the U. S acceded to the Treaty of Amity and Cooperation in Southeast Asia. According to an ASEAN Secretariat press release Dr. Surin Pitsuwan, Secretary-General of ASEAN said, "This represents in concrete terms, a shift of strategy on the part of the new US administration towards ASEAN".② U. S interest in ASEAN was apparent with the presence of President Barack Obama in the recent 3rd ASEAN-US Leaders' Meeting, and the attendance of Secretary of State Clinton to the 18th ASEAN Regional Forum and Post Ministerial Meeting held in Bali, July 16 to 28.

The conclusion and subsequent implementation of international agreements by ASEAN may not be of concern now. ASEAN may well continue with the practice of entering into international agreements as individual member states collectively, if these were to lead to faster and more effective implementation. Perhaps agreements or memorandas based on general cooperation that do not create elaborate rights or obligations could be entered into by ASEAN as a distinct entity, where implementation would not be as complicated.

There are other more pressing matters that require the urgent attention of ASEAN, such as the implementation of ASEAN Agreements. The Agreement on Privileges and Immunities of ASEAN and the Protocol on Dispute Settlement Mechanism has yet to come into force. Others include the

---

① The opinion of the European Economic and Social Committee on "EU-ASEAN Relations" was adopted at it 463rd plenary session held on 26 to 27 May 2010. The FTA referred to here are the ASEAN-Australia-New Zealand Free Trade Area (AANZFTA), China-ASEAN Free Trade Area (CAFTA) and ASEAN-India Trade in Goods Agreement (TIG).

② Press release available at http://www. asean. org/PR-42AMM-US-Signed-TAC. pdf.

realization of the ASEAN Trade in Goods Agreement (ATIGA) that is aimed at turning ASEAN into a single market and production base by 2015. This goal has also been enshrined in the ASEAN Charter. ① Also, there is the ASEAN Comprehensive Investment Agreement which aims to achieve free and open investment by 2015 through liberalization of the investment regimes of member states, enhancing protection to investors, creating favorable conditions for investment and to promote the ASEAN region as an integrated investment area. ②These are the areas that require priority action as it aims at achieving ASEAN's goal of realizing an ASEAN Community by 2015.

However, there is a fear that entering into international agreements by individual member states instead of ASEAN on its behalf may cause the fragmentation of ASEAN. Its external partners could see ASEAN less as a credible and functional grouping. Thus, even with the considerable problems for ASEAN in implementing international agreements, there may be a need to consider this matter soon. Article 21(1) of the ASEAN Charter on implementation and procedure provides that "*Each ASEAN Community Council shall prescribe its own rules of procedure*". This could be starting point for developing rules on implementation.

Conclusion

As of now, ASEAN is not ready to enter into international agreements as envisaged by Article 41(7) of the ASEAN Charter and ROPCIAA. Earlier it was demonstrated that ASEAN alone does not have the capacity to carry

---

① Article 1-Purposes: "The purposes of ASEAN are ... 5. To create a single market and production base which is stable, prosperous, highly competitive and economically integrated with effective facilitation for trade and investment in which there is free flow of goods, services and investment; facilitated movement of business persons, professionals, talents and labour; and freer flow of capital ... "

② Yap Lai Peng, The ASEAN Comprehensive Investment Agreement 2009: Its objectives, Plan and Progress, *ASEAN: Life after the Charter*, Edited by S. Tiwari, p. 102.

out obligations that requires affirmative action set forth in an international agreement, and hence enforcement of relevant domestic implementing legislation by member states is still needed. Most of ASEAN's focus and attention would probably be best spent on enhancing integration within ASEAN, and thus prioritizing the realization of various ASEAN instruments and developing relevant rules of procedure. However, the proliferation of international agreements entered into by individual member states may bring into question the credibility of ASEAN to act as an independent international organization that is separate from its member states. Although ASEAN has rejected the idea of supranationality, there is a need to further study on the level of competence that is acceptable for ASEAN to have in order for it to conclude international agreements and effectively implement them in its own right, without jeopardizing the interests of member states.

中国律师服务业对外开放刍议[*]

王公义[**]

内容摘要 任何一个国家法律服务领域的开放都是循序渐进的,是与其国情和国内律师业的发展状况相适应的。伴随着中国经济的快速发展和对外开放的不断深入,中国法律服务业特别是律师服务业的对外开放也取得了重要进展。

一般来说,在同一个法系之内,法律制度或法系依据的都是相同的法律传统,法律彼此之间,如判例法或者成文法,也相互影响。因此来自不同国家,但属于相同法系的律师之间,在法律思维方面较为相近,除了语言的障碍之外,就法律问题的沟通并没有太大的困难。另外,一国法律的最大特性在于,需要结合当地的文化、风俗、制度与语言,因此国内法往往不是外国人所能深入了解与运用的。包括律师业在内的法律服务业的开放,也因此会受到很大的限制。所以,各国开放本国法律服务市场特别是律师行业都不是一蹴而就的,大多都经历了一个循序渐进,逐步放开的过程。

世贸组织秘书处关于法律服务的背景说明中指出,随着国际贸易的兴起和新领域的出现,尤其是商事法律的产生,法律服务行业在近几十年中得到了长足发展。日益扩大和深化的国际贸易联系以及发展中国家经济高速发展的势头,都对法律服务提出了全球化的需求,并刺激着各服务实体在中国等快速发展的新兴市场设立分支机构。

全球法律服务行业在过去十多年里经历了收入的显着增长期和发展巩固期,萌生了越来越多的跨国律师事务所和律师团体。从全球法律服务业发展

---

* 此文是作者在第五届"中国—东盟法律合作与发展高层论坛"上的发言材料。

** 王公义,研究员,法学博士、经济学博士,中国社科院研究生院毕业,《中国司法》总编辑,司法部研究室主任、司法研究所所长。

水平看，美国的法律服务业发展最为成熟，基本占据了全球法律服务的一半份额；欧洲地区的法律服务业发展也比较成熟，占据的市场份额仅次于美国；亚太地区法律服务业发展水平与美国和欧盟相比尚有较大差距，占据的市场份额也较小，但近年来随着亚太经济的快速发展，国际知名的法律服务公司（律师事务所）纷纷在亚太地区扩展业务，促使亚太地区的法律服务业得到迅速发展，成为全球法律服务业发展最快的地区，而中国在法律服务领域已成为亚太最具吸引力的地区之一。

纵观全球，国际律师事务所主要有两种扩张模式：其一为“跟随客户”（follow your client）模式，即律师事务所与其主要客户公司在国外市场的扩张实现同步。这些以客户为中心的扩张主要发生在20世纪80年代和90年代的发达国家市场，律所主要为其客户公司提供全面、排他的法律建议。近年来此模式已扩展至许多拥有大型跨国企业的发展中国家。上述律师事务所通常处理公司内部法律事务，不从事纯粹的国内法律服务。

其二为“法律服务本土化”（local legal service）模式。20世纪90年代起，部分国际律师事务所通过吸收本国律师提供本国法律服务或兼并本国律师事务所的方式实现其人员多元性、多样化及本土法律服务。不管采用何种扩张模式，拥有成熟组织构架和高效律师管理制度的国际律师事务所，都能凭借其国际化优势和专业服务经验，在今天竞争愈加激烈的法律服务市场中不断发展壮大。

改革开放以来，中国律师服务业的对外开放取得了重要进展，为国家对外开放做出了重要贡献，为律师业扩大国际交流合作提供了良好基础。尽管中国的律师制度恢复重建仅有20多年的时间，但律师服务业的对外开放却有近20年的时间。1992年外国律师事务所在中国设立办事处的试点工作正式启动后，试点范围逐步扩大，试点城市由最初的5个增加为现在的19个。

伴随着中国经济的快速发展和对外开放的不断深入，中国法律服务业特别是律师服务业的对外开放也取得了重要进展。入世以后，我们严格履行WTO承诺，推动法律服务领域的对外开放。外国律师事务所驻华代表处发展迅速，以每年30～40家的速度递增，截至目前，已有来自20多个国家和地区的律师事务所在我国设立了300多家代表处，其中，新加坡律师事务所在中国境内已经设立了7家代表机构，近几年的年均收入超过了2000万元人民币。这些代表机构的业务范围不断拓展，涉及投资、资本、融资、诉讼仲裁、国际贸易、知识产权、股票债券、保险、生物技术和信息工程等众多领域。

中国始终坚持加入世贸组织时在法律服务部门作出的承诺：一是允许外

国律师从事允许该律师从事律师执业业务的国家/地区的法律，以及就国际公约和惯例提供咨询服务，并对跨境交付和境外消费两种服务提供模式不作限制。二是外国律师事务所可以代表处的形式提供法律服务，代表处可从事营利性活动，业务范围如下：(1)就该律师事务所律师允许从事律师执业业务的国家/地区的法律及就国际条约和惯例向客户提供咨询；(2)应客户或中国律师事务所的委托，处理该外国律师事务所律师允许从事律师执业业务的国家/地区的法律事务；(3)代表外国客户，委托中国律师事务所处理中国法律事务；(4)订立合同与中国律师事务所保持长期的委托关系办理法律事务；(5)提供有关中国法律环境影响的信息。三是代表处可以按照与中国律师事务所达成的协议约定，直接向受委托的中国律师事务所的律师发出指示。四是外国律师事务所驻华代表处的代表应为执业律师，为WTO成员的律师协会或律师公会的会员，且在中国境外执业不少于2年。首席代表应为WTO成员的律师事务所的合伙人或相同职位人员(如有限责任公司律师事务所的成员)，且在中国境外执业不少于3年。五是外国律师事务所驻华代表处的代表在华居留时间每年不得少于6个月。代表处不得雇佣中国国家注册律师。

由此可见，根据我国入世承诺和《外国律师事务所驻华代表机构管理条例》，外国律师事务所驻华代表处在中国境内开展业务的范围越来越广泛，可就本国法、第三国法和国际法提供咨询服务，也可通过订立合同的形式与中国律师事务所建立长期的委托关系，开展业务合作，较好地满足了外国律师事务所适应经济全球一体化趋势，提供跨法域法律服务的实际需求。目前，东盟律师事务所驻华代表处在中国的业务范围涉及投资、资本、融资、诉讼仲裁、国际贸易、知识产权、股票债券、保险、生物技术和信息工程等众多领域，为中国—东盟各国经贸领域的交流合作和共同繁荣作出了积极贡献。

多年来，中国内地律师不断开拓涉外业务，逐步介入外商投资、国际贸易、国际金融等涉外商事活动，境外企业来华、内地投资贸易抑或境内企业到国外、境外投资贸易，竞相聘请中国内地律师作为代理人或提供相关的法律帮助。许多中国内地律师以其熟悉国内法律环境、熟练掌握国际惯例的优势和娴熟的语言交际和业务能力，赢得了国内外客户的信任和尊重。外国和香港律师事务所驻华和驻内地代表机构，通过为境内外客户提供优质高效的法律服务，也为吸引境外投资、促进对外贸易以及帮助中国内地企业走向国际市场做出了积极贡献。外国和香港律师事务所与中国内地律师事务所的合作不断加强，不少外国和香港律师事务所已经与中国内地律师事务所建立了长期的业务合作伙伴关系，在众多大型国际项目中密切配合、分工合作。外国和香港

律师事务所先进的内部管理制度、高效优质的运行机制、细致的专业分工、协调的业务协作、完善的律师业务培训制度等，为深化中国内地律师制度改革提供有益的借鉴。

今后，中国律师服务业的发展将围绕为构建社会主义和谐社会服务的总体目标，积极推进律师制度改革，完善律师制度：继续改革和完善律师的组织结构和组织形式，特别是完善律师事务所的组织形式，加强律师事务所建设，充分发挥律师事务所自我管理、自我约束的作用，进一步改革和完善“两结合”的律师管理体制，强化司法行政机关对律师、律师事务所和律师协会的指导监督职责，充分发挥律师协会在律师行业自律管理中的作用，加强对律师执业的行政监督、行业监督和社会监督，努力维护当事人的合法权益，等等。

与此同时，随着中国经济的不断发展以及与国际经济更加紧密地融合，中国也将进一步推动中外（包括内地与港、澳）律师事务所和律师的交流与合作，特别是加强与东盟法律服务行业的合作。在巩固已有成果的基础上积极创新，不断充实交流合作内容，拓展交流合作渠道，提高交流合作质量，为促进中国与其他国家和地区特别是东盟的经贸往来和民商事交往做出贡献。

同时我们认为，任何一个国家法律服务领域的开放都是循序渐进的，是与其国情和国内律师业的发展状况相适应的。为此，我们会进行深入的调查、研究和论证，在对外开放中国律师业的过程中遵循循序渐进原则，立足本国国情，努力在开放要求与国内律师业发展状况之间寻求一种最佳的平衡，逐步地、有序地提高法律服务领域的开放水平，从而满足外界对于中国律师业对外开放的希望，推动中外法律服务业建立良好的合作关系，相互促进、共谋发展。

Thought on the Opening of Legal Service in China

Wang Gongyi

The rising of international trade and the emergence of the new field have promoted the global legal service industry. The global legal service industry of Asian-Pacific region grows quick, accompany with the fast developing economy, China is the most attractive country in this area. Since the reform and open-door policies, legal services in China has made important progress.

Since entering into the WTO, China strictly adheres to its promises and endeavors to promote the opening up in the legal service area. Nowadays, representative offices of foreign law firms enjoy a rapid development, and continuously expand their business scopes. For example, the business scope of Asean law firm representative offices involves various areas such as investment, capital, financing and litigation arbitration. All these interactions made positive contributions to common prosperity and further cooperation in China-Asean economic and trade fields.

For years, mainland lawyers are devoted to develop international business, and gradually engage in the foreign trade affairs. Moreover, they have constantly strengthened the bilateral and multilateral cooperation with law firms between the U. S. and Hong kong, drawing on the advanced international business management, promoting the reforms of legal service in China Mainland.

In the future, the legal services of China will:

(1) Actively promote the reform of the lawyer system and improve it;

(2) Further facilitate communication and coordination with foreign law firms, especially the law firms from ASEAN;

(3) Based on the present conditions, devote to balancing the domestic development status and the opening up requirement, and promoting the development and prosperity of international legal service.

统一东盟各国投资法的制度基础
——以印度尼西亚为视角

Melli Darsa* 陈超洁 译 WTO 实验班 校

内容摘要 统一东盟成员国之间的投资法被认为是实现东盟经济共同体前景的先决条件，只有东盟各国在一个更加开放的贸易和投资制度下，才能促进更有利的贸易和投资环境。如果东盟可以统一各国之间的投资法的话，它将保护每个成员国的国家利益，同时将东盟发展成为一个经济发展更为公平、社会贫富差异更少的区域，并增进区域之间的商品、服务、技术劳动力和投资的自由流动。

尽管致力于在 2015 年创建一个东盟经济共同体，一些东盟成员国仍相互竞争，统一各国投资法的进程也面临着挑战。本文从印度尼西亚的角度，讨论了统一各国投资法所存在的问题，旨在讨论和分析印度尼西亚与东盟其他成员国在统一投资法的过程中将会面临到的挑战，本文还为未来能够更有效地统一提供了建议。在阐述主要议题之前，作者先讨论隐藏在统一各国投资法背后所存在的理论和现实问题，以使本文所阐述的议题被放在一个适当的背景下。

一、法律统一化的简介

法律统一化的概念通常是基于标准化将加快法律融合的进程，能为跨国投资者降低交易成本和提高一些法律制度尚不发达的国家的法律制度质量。标准化通过确定共同原则和标准，以及使用“示范法”等各种形式实现。

法律统一化和法律移植已成为法律与发展运动的关键性工具，并被国际机构（如世界银行和国际货币基金组织）作为“最佳的实践方法和机制”常年大

* 作者系印度尼西亚 Meui Darsc & Co.（MDC）律师事务所创业人及管理合伙人。

量地使用。在呼吁"国际新秩序"和经历亚洲金融危机的背景下,世界银行和国际货币基金组织对法律统一化的努力是印度尼西亚当下普通法司法管辖区的某些原则与主要的民事法律传统和平共存的原因之一。同时,过去只涉及外国专家对印度尼西亚法律现实情况缺乏理解的法律统一化进程,最近变成了将印尼法律(特别是经济法)统一入其他运作良好的司法管辖区的法律本土化进程,因为有几位印度尼西亚关键的高级专家作为此进程中的领导人。虽然有时它仍缺乏足够的透明度,印尼法律的现代化进程已经取得了可圈可点的进步。

"法律统一化"的倡导者声称:统一的法律规范会减少交易成本,以此加快国际间的贸易频率。他们进一步指出,法律统一化不仅引导法律融合和法律统一,还会减少法律的不确定性,同时增强法律的可预测性,并提高法律制度的质量。"法律统一化"也被认为有益于解决"法律冲突的问题和国际私法与外国实体法难以运用的问题……增强法律的可预见性和安全性"。

与提倡"统一法律"相反的是提倡"监管竞争"。"监管竞争"的倡导者认为在监管竞争过程中,法律和政策制定者将试图找到最佳、最有效的规则以构建一个高质量的法律体系,而不是仅仅在最低的共同标准中作选择的移植。监管竞争不会冲击到现有的法律文化和国家的历史,也不会存在为适应社会和政治而支出的潜在的高昂费用。

此外,在一个充满持不同意见的法律专家和实践者的国家,法律协调化产品也可能导致法律的不确定性。这些专家可能会对应该如何执行由"法律统一化"进程而引入的移植法律有不同的意见,到了一定的时候这些不确定性就会引起法院裁决的争议。一般来说,将法律条文与法律实践相分离是很罕见的,每个法律条文都应该参照其他法律,也许这些所参照的法律并不一定通过"法律统一化"或者"法律监管竞争"成为了现代化法律。

另外,有效的法律统一化需要某些先决条件。

首先,一个国家在有效地进行法律统一化之前,应该已经拥有一个相当发达和运作良好的法律基础设施,这是因为法律统一化的过程本身不会一蹴而就,若进行不佳可能变成了只是停留在翻译外来法律的层面。律师和当局官员作为一国法律基础设施的重要部分必须对移植法律有充足的理解,从中寻求更大利益的保护。此外,如果法律实施过程中不能得到预想中法律基础设施的支持,那么寻求改革可能只不过是表面文章而已。

第二,将各个国家的社会经济发展理想地当作是在相似的水平线上。倘若各国的基本需求完全不同,那么各国抛开法律统一化的呼声、抵触法律统一

化的想法是再自然不过的事了。这个观点将会在之后关于东盟统一化的文段中阐明。

第三,法律统一化的法律原则或法律规范应该得到哲学、实践、技术这三个层面的承认。从哲学层面来看,必须要解释投资法统一化在何种程度上可以真正符合 1945 年宪法所阐明的国家利益,或者说在何种程度上能够使国家利益最大化。从实践层面来看,国家应该设立怎样的机制和运用怎样的谋略来完善法律统一化,因为它涉及确保某些行政程序能与其他拥有更好的官僚体系的国家一样有效率。从技术层面来看,应将现有的国内法律和法律统一化所涉及的其他国家的国内法律相对比,明确目前妨碍法律统一化进程、与法律统一化建设的价值观不符的法律条文。

需要承认的是,统一化过程确实很困难,因为它必须满足一些成员国或利益相关者,而协调的概念可能是由代表国家的政党提出的,一个国家的法律统一化能获得多大的成功取决于其他许多事情。在弗洛里金的著作《立法质量:一个法律和发展项目》中,弗洛里金认为理想的立法是无法实现的,因为法律的利用者各不相同,每一个人对法律的期望也各不相同。良好的政策必须成功地调和这些不同的观点。根据弗洛里金的观点,法律利用者包括立法者、国会议员、政治家,和有立法倡议的行政机构。通常他们会在立法机构里就相关问题自发地进行公开辩论。通过立法的法律将成为政治家更深层次的政治利益或政治议题。弗洛里金所分类的第二组法律利用者由官僚和政策制定者组成,他们通常进一步解释和制定规章或下属法规。他们创建配套政策和技术规范,通过一定的法律法规来确保预期想要实现的利益,或者出于某种原因,以其他方式制造政府想要的例外情况。弗洛里金所分类的第三组法律利用者由商界、一般大众或者一些不得不应付、遵从、承认法律效力的人。笔者想在此添加一组法律利用者,它包括执法者,法官,还有律师。法律法规会不会顺利地起草,以及捍卫谁的利益,都会对如何在实践中执行移植/统一化的法律产物有所影响。这种执行决定了任何一个统一化法律产物的效力。

二、东盟视角下的外商投资

东盟各国的总投资框架可以在《东盟全面投资协议》(简称《ACIA 协议》)中找到。2009 年 2 月 26 日之后,这个框架被正式纳入协议中,旨在加强各成员国的经济合作。《ACIA 协议》的目标是建立一个自由开放的投资体制,这个目标将通过以下三点来实现:(1)促进并保护所有成员国投资者的自由;(2)改进有利于投资的法律法规,提高这些法律法规的透明度和可预见性,通过建

立这些有利的投资条件吸引更多外商投资;(3)将东盟作为一个整体的投资环境来联合推广。为了鼓励外商到东盟各国投资,《ACIA 协议》通过具有广泛基础的四大支柱来建立一个自由、便利、透明、具有竞争力的东盟投资环境。这四大支柱分别是保护投资 、加强合作、提高认识、开放市场。在实施过程中,尤其是以下指导性原则常被适用:

1.使投资自由化、便利化,保护投资、促进投资;

2.以使东盟成为一个自由开放的投资环境的视角,逐步开放本国投资市场;

3.给予以东盟为主要投资对象的投资者优惠;

4.成员国之间享受优惠待遇;

5.不追溯根据以前的协议所做出的承诺;

6 .对成员国进行特殊和差别待遇,以及其他灵活处理,这些取决于各成员国在某些领域的发展水平和敏感性;

7.在适当情况下各会员国享受互惠待遇。

《ACIA 协议》期望通过保护投资、提升投资者对东盟的信心,以及通过扩张、工业互补和专业化手段发展东盟内部更深层次的投资,以使东盟的贸易繁荣起来。《ACIA 协议》还期望那些以东盟为主要投资对象的投资者在东盟各国投资时能够受益于非歧视待遇。这意味着国外投资者将会享受类似国内投资者的待遇,并且还与其他同样以东盟为主要投资对象的投资者享受同样的待遇。《ACIA 协议》将全面保护和保密外来投资者关于基金和资本的转拨、利润和红利的分配的行为。

三、印度尼西亚关于外来投资的总框架

(一)外来投资规范

外商对制造业和非金融业务的直接投资受到 2007 年第 25 号投资法和其实施条例的约束,除了某些负面清单上的业务不予以开放以外,其他大多数业务都允许外商直接投资,但有一定限制。

此外,尽管外来投资规范并不十分明确,但一家企业一旦成为上市公司,外资所有权不会受到严格限制。某些法律结构,例如控股公司,将获准发行股票,然后分发给社会,其中大多是外国人。因此印度尼西亚已出台适当的自由化政策。2007 年第 25 号投资法取代了早期的“ 1967 年第 1 号关于外国投资

法和 1968 年第 8 号国内资本投资法”，可以说它坚持了《ACIA 协议》的指导性原则。例如，在第 12 条中可以找到投资自由化的指导性原则：所有业务均对投资开放，除非有附带封闭或开放的条件。这些附带条件一般会在 2007 年第 76 号的政府规章中查阅到，这份规章阐明了资本投资已关闭的业务和附条件开放的业务的标准，并按照 2010 年第 36 号总统令《禁止类和限制类投资产业目录》(即所谓的“负面清单”)执行。但是为了确定某业务是否对外国投资者开放，投资统筹委员会或技术部的澄清和确认就显得尤为必要。

为了扩大经营或吸引新的投资者，第 18 条在一定条件下认可了“刺激或鼓励投资者原则”。这种刺激/奖励可通过法律允许范围内的减少各类税收或关税的形式实现，这些问题一般由财政部长管理。此外，为便于取得外国劳动力许可牌照和许可证的行为在第 23 条中予以认可，它类似于《ACIA 协议》第 22 条中所记载的。

投资法第 25 条至第 26 条还引入了被称为 PTSP 的一站式服务体系，其目的是帮助投资者更易于找到在印尼投资的服务、财政设施和信息的途径。它进一步根据 2009 年第 27 号总统令条例规范了资本投资的一站式服务。投资协调委员会(简称 BKPM)目前也宣布，PTSP 通过国家唯一投资窗口(简称 NSWI，其试点在巴淡岛)得到极大促进。这是一个电子投资平台，投资者可以进行在线投资申请许可和非许可服务。

PTSP 的目的在于促进投资者获得有关投资的服务、金融设施和信息。例如，在申请许可证的过程中，BKPM 将与相关政府和部门机关合作来发布业务许可证，这使发放给投资企业许可证的过程更权威也更有效。

投资法的另一个重要特征是中央政府保证，除了法律明确规定以外，不会将外来资本收归国有或者取消投资者享有外来投资的权利。如果中央政府将外来资本收归国有或者取消投资者享有外来投资的权利，国家将根据投资者所投资的市场价值给予一定的赔偿。随着这个保证应运而生的是第 8 条规定：外国投资者有权将其拥有的外币、利润、银行利息、分红以及其他收入转移或者遣送回国。

第 32 条规定：任何有关投资的争端应先商议调解，若调解不成，再由双方指定的国际仲裁或法院解决。

投资协调委员会主席颁布了许多重要条例，特别是投资协调委员会主席颁布的 2009 年第 12 号关于投资申请的指导方针和程序条例、2009 年第 13 号关于资本投资绩效的指导方针和程序条例(该条例由 2010 年第 7 号条例修订)和 2009 年第 14 号关于信息服务系统和电子投资应用条例。

(二)外商投资流程

1. 在非上市/私营公司

外商对非商业银行/金融服务的非公开上市公司的投资由投资协调委员会负责审批，投资协调委员会主要审批是以下两类投资企业：国内投资企业、外国投资企业。国内投资企业归印度尼西亚自然人或法人所有，而外国投资企业归外国自然人或法人所有。

若要在印度尼西亚直接投资非金融业务，外国投资方必须设立一家外资企业。在企业设立之前，外国投资方必须提交投资登记的申请，登记后6个月内，外国投资者必须与其他股东设立印度尼西亚的有限公司并取得司法和人权部长的批准。从申请设立外资企业到外资企业有效运作，这个过程要花费将近4个月的时间。投资登记的有效期存续到取得初步执照或者准备开始经营或投入生产之前，当外资企业准备开始经营或投入生产，则应当申请营业执照。

基于对建立新的外资企业的时间跨度和商业方面的考虑，外国投资方会选择先兼并一家非经营性的有限公司，再将其转换为外资企业。这个过程可以节省时间和成本，因为法人实体已经是有限公司的形式，而唯一要做的就是获得投资协调委员会的相关许可。根据投资协调委员会条例，从收到填好的申请到颁布投资批准证书全过程最多只需7个工作日。但实际操作中，这一过程会花费大约两个星期之久。

2. 在公开上市公司

除了法律明文规定需要管制的行业(如商业银行、金融、外资矿业)之外，对公开上市公司的投资一般没有管制程序的设置。因为所有交易记录都会被股票交易透明地记载，并可以酌情披露或报告。

需要牢记于心的一条最重要的规定是：当投资者想要获得一间上市公司50%以上股份的所有权，根据印尼的资本市场和金融机构监督局颁布的条例，这种行为将视为“收购行为”。此外，如果新的控股人持有超过80%的公开上市公司股票，不论是初步收购还是强制要约收购，都应在两年内将自己超过80%的股票向公众转让销售，所有的新控制人最多只能持有80%的股份。因为该规例假定少数股东有权和前控股者以同样的价格买进股票，但新的控股者不应使公司的公众持股量太少以至于该公司的资金流动不足。虽然该条例只规定了两年的年限，但它在东盟其他国家证券监管条例中仍然是一种特例。

一旦投资者成为了控股者，他就可以提名公司董事会和监事会的人选，并

确保他所提名的人能成为董事会和监事会的成员。通常，董事和监事都是由一些股东提名的，但是他们仍需对公司尽忠实义务。作为一家好的公司管理原则，它要求每位股东都被同等对待（尽管资本市场和金融机构监督局不喜欢这种做法），哪怕是上市公司的股东也有可能在合同里让他们参与管理公司事项（例如就某项决策组织投赞成或反对票），以便他们可以对这些事项产生更积极的影响。

上市公司需要监事会里至少有 30 ％是独立成员，一名董事必须是“独立董事”，还有审计委员会（如监事会下属的审计薪酬委员会）进一步确保高管人员以负责任的态度管理公司。尽管存在某一方拥有多数股权，独立董事会成员和独立委员会应确保上市公司的运作方式保护大众股民利益。“保护大众股民利益”的概念在其他附属条例及要求披露的重大交易中被发现。进行这类交易前，应提出公平的意见。

四、印尼的外国联合管理机构投资问题的法律和规则

尽管全面的投资法律的存在符合东南亚联盟全面投资协议，但是其可能会受区域和国家层面的某些因素影响。

（一）区域挑战

在区域层面，有许多的事实表明东南亚联盟的全面投资协议不能客观反映应有的民主化和自由化。例如，并非所有的成员国在其本国内有全面的、适时的外商投资法。大多数东南亚国家仍然依赖少数落后的投资条款或者其他限制性政策，来保护某些业务，使其免于向外国人全面开放。

事实上，每个人不可能完全忽视东盟合法化、和谐化缓慢进程的事实。东盟各国可能不被认为是真正意义上推进文明化建设的国家，而仅仅只是试图保护他们自己地区建立的企业不受威胁的西方国家。区域性法律一致化的其他影响因素是由于不同的金融市场发展、基础设施和劳动力的技能导致成员国间不平等的市场捕获能力。在某些方面，东南亚联盟国家间还是存在明显的差距。

例如，新加坡被认为是一个有着现代化的、世界级的基础设施的国家。许多人认为，这些使得新加坡成功地转变成为一个强大的、拥有有效的组织机构和法律确定的金融中心。在某种程度上，对于大多数公司来讲，新加坡已经成为一个较好的投资地点和解决地点。在司法实践中，人们也注意到，新加坡法

律已经越来越多地被选择用来调整总部位于印尼的公司的事务。事实上,许多东盟国家也有类似的自然优势和潜力,但是可能导致他们之间的监管竞争,成员国之间缺乏共同的机构会进一步使得投资者在选择投资地上更多依赖于他们的偏好。在汇率和财政政策方面没有足够的对话也给我们这样一个疑问:东南亚联盟何时才能达到经济一体化。

新加坡、马来西亚和泰国这三个国家有着现代化的基础设施建设,这些使得这三个国家成为有吸引力的投资中心,尽管我们知道实际的市场(尤其是在消费产品的情况下)可能存在于印度尼西亚。这种差异在劳动力方面也预示着,某些国家的劳动者只能从事低技能的工作,而其他国家的公民却是拥有全球化的生物技术或生产技术的员工。

最后一个阻碍东南亚联盟一体化的因素我们不得不面对,即地区主义的协议能在多大程度上适用于发展的全球化。那就是,地区性的交流确实能影响他们以外的其他国家,因此有更多国家呼吁全球化。某些东南亚联盟国家的政府已经把合作化放在全球化水平而不是地区水平。总之,全面实现东南亚联盟议程是不可能,但是在这个全球化的世界,须尽最大可能在某些观点上达成共识。

(二)国家所面临的挑战

就印尼这个国家而言,若其欲充分发挥潜力,以期达到东盟投资统一局面,还需处理很多领域的问题与事务。其中,很多都是历史遗留问题,或者是亚洲金融危机后改革和印尼向完全民主国家转型过程中的结果。不管这个国家的历史如何,除非印尼有能力解决这些问题,否则该国还需要一段时间才能完全对投资统一开放。

1. 地方的分权缺乏明确界限

早在1999年,印尼正式通过了关于政府的法令第22条,而在此之前,区域政府早已下放相关权限至已经行使权力的地方政府。自此,当地政府被授权在一定限度内征税以及批准投资。然而,至于哪些中央或地方的部门享有此项权力,依然不明确。

许可证的发放通常成本高,耗时长且不确定。中央和地方政府之间权限分配的模糊性,导致了基础设施建设和发展的重复以及许可证发放要求之间的冲突。

就外国投资而言,当讨论到地方政府与省政府所做决定或政策之间延续性缺失时,地方分权所引起的问题依然赫然存在。

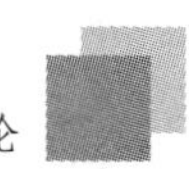

尽管印尼投资协调委员会起着主要作用，地方的协调委员会依然负责诸如地点，防干扰许可证的签发。即使是支持外国投资的一站式服务或者国家单一窗口的贸易模式，也无法完全扫除这些问题。对地区政府而言，相关事务依然亟待解决，或者通常技术部还需要继续投入时间。

2. 法律(不)确定性

关于一些经常应用于经济交往当中的，诸如关于某些安全利益以及权利转让的关键法律概念(例如强制性或可执行性)，经常会出现法律上的不确定性。按照印尼所秉承的大陆法传统，法官仅充当只要懂法律，便能作出良好判决的人。事实上，政策的起草，政策之间的关联通常是不明确的，从而导致了法律一定程度上的不确定性。

就外国投资而言，针对其开放的产业缺乏明晰性。通常情况下，对于裁定某一企业部门是否真正关闭，不准进口商品单并不可靠，因为印尼技术部门与投资协调委员会的官员对此可能持不同的观点。尽管如此，外国投资依然坚持不准进口商品单涵盖了对外国投资开放的产业。值得注意的是，近来，印尼的几个诸如银行业，电信业和媒体业等重要领域也出现了关于外国投资的法律上的不确定性。

(1)银行业

早在1999年，一个银行99%的股份都可能由外国人持有，开放度很高，趋近自由化。因此，亚洲金融危机前的主要私人银行现今均被各家外国银行，战略性投资者和私人股票持有者所控制。而如今，由于成本太高，印尼当事人无法重新获得这些银行。同时，一些印尼银行试图开办离岸分行，却面临着极大困难。这些分行声称，在其他国家并未实行互惠制度。这导致了印尼央行发表声明，宣称其并不包含银行收购申请，因其旨在分析与银行相关的外国投资政策。在此之前，市场早有传言，认为央行将会在2011年的某个时候，推进有关外国对印尼银行所有权政策的重大改革举措。尽管不久之后，印尼央行行长否认将会对外国在印尼银行所有权设限，但他确实承认央行正从良好的社团法人管理角度去审视这些问题。最近，大部分外国投资者均认为，印尼即将制定法律用以使外国对其所有权政策更加严厉，甚至可能导致该些政策的逆向适用。

换言之，受财务业管理局管制的其他行业(例如，保险业，证券业和跨国金融等)也将受到同样的限制，该现象引起了各界的极大关注。对于极有可能“不受欢迎”的政策，草草发出宣告，只会引起政策的模糊与不确定性。对于创建有利的外国投资环境，政策之间的良好作用有着至关重要的意义。

(2)电信业

根据不准进口商品单,电信业通常受到关于外国所有权49%到95%不等的限制。故而,电信业将外国投资拒之门外。然而,一些公开上市的公司利用其结构,已经成功地避过这一限制。

关于电子交易和门户网站服务是否应当被认定为不准进口商品规定当中的多媒体服务,依然存在广泛争议。然而,外国投资者至多只能掌握49%的股份。鉴于电子交易和门户网站服并未在不准进口商品单之列,故不准进口商品单未明确规定是否此二者也拒绝外国投资。根据2001年《电子通信与工业技术法令》以及《电信服务运营法规》第21条,电子交易和门户网站服务包含于多媒体服务当中。在2008年9月第三次修订的MOCIT法令第21条中,电子交易和门户网站服务被认为不再属于多媒体服务。近期,就电子交易和门户网站服务是否也应受“49%”规定的限制,MOCIT与印尼投资协调法协调委员会存在分歧。

(3)私营电视广播业

依据印尼2005年颁布的关于私营电视广播公司(PBC)法规第24条第1段,私营电视广播公司仅能由印尼公民或法人团体设立,且由印尼公民完全持有股份。外国公民或法人团体可以直接或间接地持有该公司已发行和缴纳资本的20%,该公司应该拥有两个或两个以上自然人或法人作为其股东,已发行和缴纳资本剩余的80%必须由百分之百的印尼公民或法人持有。任何一个使得外国在私营电视广播公司持股超过20%标准的交易,都应当进行调整,使其符合规定(即不得超过20%)。

另外,根据政府报告第27条第2段规定,这样的公司在证券交易所可以仅将其已发行和缴纳的资本的20%在证券交易所进行公开发行。而第27条第3段则更进一步明确规定,若私营广播公司在证券交易所发行其股本的20%,外国公民或法人仅能认购发行的股票,才可以成为私营广播公司的股东。

在实践中,经常出现这样的情况,即市场操控者会设立一个公开发行的私营广播公司,使其免受外国自然人或法人对其股份持有的相关规定与限制。印尼信息交流部的部长已同Bapepam-LK讨论过,讨论的内容是针对公共控股公司在私人广播公司中20%外国持股权限制有关部门将采取的措施,但是,相关结果并未公开。

(4)种植园经济

在种植园经济中,只要该种植园在25公顷或以上,可以作为农产品加工

业独立运行，不管它有没有加工场，外国人可以持有其95%的股份，而面积小于25公顷或者更小规模的加工场则留给中小型和微型企业。在印尼经营种植园经济的外国自然人或法人必须同印尼本国人通过在印尼确立法定地点，建立合资公司。这一项要求是为了防止已享受政府设施的种植园将其财产转移到外国实体名下，而无意提高当地社区居民的收入。

尽管如此，在实践中，依然存在由外国实体完全控股的种植园经济，这是因为印尼人至少需持有种植园经济5%股份的法规2007年才生效。因此，先于2007年不准进口商品单的发布的，外国实体对种植园经济的完全控股依然有效。但是，若该些公司中的外国人在2007年不准进口商品单出台以前或之后，持股低于其规定的95%的最低限度，则在该些公司内的投资者则最多只能持有该公司95%的股份，无法再增加持股份额。

法律明确的法规也可能引发法律的不确定性。最近就有这样的实例，于2011年6月28日生效的《汇率法》规定，一些在印尼的司法管辖区内进行的贸易，须使用卢比作为支付工具。《汇率法》第21条规定，在印尼领域内发生的支付贸易，金融结算以及其他的金融交易（存在于其他人中间的存款等），须使用卢比进行交易。然而，这条规定存在许多适用例外，包括一些与市预算、收入、对外国授权、外国存款汇率以及与国际金融相关的交易，可以不要求使用卢比。《汇率法》第23条规定，在印尼境内，卢比作为一种用来履行付款、结算义务的支付工具，不得被拒绝接受，除非所支付的卢比真假难辨。但是，在双方已经就付款预结算书面达成一致的交易中，上述条款不适用。《汇率法》被认为依然存在模糊性，尽管其第21条规定，支付手段非卢比不适用，但是第23条又宽范围地规定适用例外。

为了解决公众关心的这个问题，印尼财政部财监委员会于2011年年底发行了一本关于《汇率法》（也就是《财政部解释》）执行的小册子。《财政部解释》规定，汇率法仅适用于支票和信用证以外的现金交易（纸币和硬币）和电子付款。该解释还规定，只要双方签订合同，接受卢比作为上述《汇率法》第23条所规定交易中支付工具的义务可以不履行。这点其实与《汇率法》本身明确的用词有别。

由于财政部的这个解释并非立法，它可以提供在实务中的便利，但同时，它也将在法庭适用中面临着挑战。也正因为如此，该解释为那些本应在《汇率法》规定下明晰的问题开了一个不好的先例。

3. 劳动力问题

印尼的劳动法倾向于保护劳动者，相比泰国，越南，孟加拉和中国，它的劳

动法并不那么受到赞誉。这主要是由于印尼劳动法对下岗、精简成本以及短暂性雇佣(劳动力外包)限制进行了详尽的规定。印尼劳动者的劳动技能并不符合更高科技的生产或作业要求。为了吸引外资,印尼必须改善法制环境和提高劳动者教育水平与就业技能。如此,同其他国家劳动者相比,印尼劳动者便能更具竞争优势。

4. 基础设施

印尼至今没有现代化机场,且经常性出现电力断供、交通拥堵、饮用水供应不足等状况,印尼政府已经在全国范围内拨出大量资金用于能源和基础设施的项目建设。然而,这些项目是否能够顺利完成或者是否能够顺利扩展,却取决于很多因素,包括寻找支持项目的资金和专家等。此外,工程的怠慢源于法律的不确定性以及应对2003年市金融法大调整的限制措施,因而印尼政府不得不制定另一看似创新,实则平平的金融项目,该项目对投资者和金主而言,并无吸引力。生效不久的《土地采购法》为用于公共用途事业的顺利执行提供了更有效的保障。

鉴于长久以来,印尼的基础设施建设一直落后于其周边邻国,尽管存在远大的市场前景,外国投资者可能并不愿意在印尼设立工厂。

5. 腐败

腐败一直以来都是印尼的顽疾。地方分权以及从总统制到议会制的制度转变,衍生了比以往更加猖獗的腐败。此外,投资者一般都会质疑印尼法院的公平公正性以及不相信印尼司法系统对其条约所赋予财产权的执行力度。因此,当有纠纷产生时,许多商业合同都选择仲裁(包括国外仲裁)。

五、如何加快东盟投资法律统一化进程

鉴于上述讨论,我们可以清楚了解到,统一化的目标并不是单一的,而是受许多因素和条件的影响。然而,一般来说,要达到统一化的目标,可以采取以下步骤:

1. 创造一个公平竞争舞台,以便东盟各成员国法院,金融机构在小规模基础设施上与最发达的国家公平竞争

创造公平竞争舞台将会耗时很长,但是却必须经历,特别是对印尼这个由17000个岛屿组成的国家而言。

2. 确保每一东盟成员国就法律协调事务给予政治支持和一致的观点

对那些政治上并未形成共识的国家而言,将统一原则转化为法律是极具

挑战性的。若每个国家都能在政治上给予支持，那么在投资法律法规统一过程中，便可以形成一套适用模板。

3. 赋予并提高相关政府以及部门的行政力，使其有效行政

我们可以把投资程序统一、简化、加快，至于达到何种程度取决于每个国家政府部门处理这种程序的难易程度。同时还取决于，对外国投资具有前瞻性的政府在法律的各个领域，或者仅仅是在某些商业领域，是否被充分授权。更重要的是，处理投资的部门必须具有现代化眼光，负责任以及具有理智与逻辑。某种程度上，一些政府部门对技术部门并不了解，故而有可能在投资委员会与技术部门之间存在政策上的分歧，导致统一化进程的不确定以及缓慢性。

4. 加强一站式服务以及东盟单一窗口制度的建立

一站式投资中心对吸引和支持潜在的投资是至关重要的。一站式服务是与分权有关的一个概念，而此处的"分权"则是指由中央政府向任一投资决定所授予的权限。

5. 加强投资领域(受暂时例外清单/敏感清单规制)的指导性合作

通过统一暂时例外清单/敏感清单，使得东盟各成员国都拥有类似名单，可以更进一步地强调东盟之间外国投资的自由化。

6. 加深东盟各成员国之间激励政策的统一

研究表明，一些东盟成员国在建立成本高昂的激励机制，以吸引和保持外国投资方，展开了白热化的竞争。

7. 避免东盟各成员国之间双重征税协议

8. 在东盟成员国之间建立相互监督机制，以确保各成员国享有平等地位

9. 建立一个普遍的东盟机制，用于了解各成员国就其根据东盟协议和《东盟经济共同体蓝图》(AEC Blueprint)制定目标实施过程中的进展或者阻碍

10. 扩大投资统一化进程中的私营企业参与度

若没有私营企业的充分参与和建议，统一化进程不可能有效推行。私营企业的反馈也许有时并不恰当，然而，知悉参与者参与解决外国投资者面对的各种问题，可以给政府官员在推进统一进程中提供更多不同的视角。

11. 加强政策之间的沟通，保证法律规定的内容与实际执行的措施之间没有模糊或不确定甚至偏离

统一预示着自由化，各国政府须更加珍视这个市场，以国家利益的名义逆向适用一些限制性政策只会导致困扰。即使各国政府停止适用限制性政策，也并不意味着投资没有因为法律的不确定性有所下降。

12. 对于许可证发放和司法行使过程中的腐败行为绝不姑息

许可证发放中的腐败增加了交易的成本和不确定性,特别是当不同的政府部门不仅仅根据法律规定的内容来颁发许可证,还因腐败而颁发许可证的时候。故而,对于腐败,必须加以遏制。对于这种行为,绝对不能姑息,尤其是许可证发放和司法行使过程中的腐败,尤其不能宽待。

13. 就印尼而言,由于在其他任何司法管辖区内的不存在性,修订强制性邀约收购规定,在获取多于80%的销售额后,让出20%的销售额

如果是为了拥有足够数量的上市公司,而且这些公司运作良好,资金流动性强的话,承担强制性要约收购的义务也应因此做出调整,不是要求从公众处强制收购,而是要求投资者两年内再次出售。

虽然达到投资统一化没有捷径,笔者依然坚信,如果上述步骤得以实行,东盟各国之间将会更顺利地达到统一局面。上述步骤能实行到何种程度,取决于各成员国的政治意愿以及其采纳这些法律和政策的政治上的支持程度。

Critical Issues on Investment Law Harmonization in ASEAN: The Indonesian Perspective*

Melli Darsa**

INTRODUCTION

Harmonization of the investment laws among the ASEAN countries is assumed to be a prerequisite for implementing the vision of ASEAN Economic Community, where it is believed that a more liberalized trade and investment regime in ASEAN would encourage a more favorable trade and investment climate in the region. It is also believed that if the investment laws can be harmonized, it will also protect each member country's national interest, and at the same time, ASEAN would be able to develop into a region of more equitable economic development, a region with less poverty and socio-economic disparities, as well as a region with increased free movement of goods, services, skilled labor and investment. ①

Notwithstanding the commitment to create an ASEAN Economic Community by 2015, several ASEAN member countries continue to compete a-

---

* This paper is presented at General Assembly XI ASEAN Law Association, Bali on 17 February 2012.

** Melli Darsa practices as an advocate in Indonesia, specializing in M&A, securities and finance matters and is the founder and managing partner of the Indonesian firm "Melli Darsa & Co." or MDC.

① Thanadsillapakul, Lawan, Framework Agreement on the ASEAN Investment Area (AIA), accessed on 17 December 2011 at http://www.thailawforum.com/articles/lawanaia.html.

gainst each otherand the harmonization process has faced challenges. This paper discusses the issue of investment law harmonization from an Indonesian perspective and seeks to discuss and analyze the challenges which may be faced by Indonesia in undertaking legal harmonization in investment laws with the ASEAN countries. It also provides recommendations for more effective harmonization in the future. Prior to addresing the main topics, the writer discusses the theories and realities behind legal harmonization processes to put those topics in what she believes to be an appropriate context.

LEGAL HARMONIZATION IN GENERAL

The notion of legal harmonization is generally based on the premise that "*standardization would accelerate the process of legal convergence ... reducing transaction costs for transnational investors and increasing the quality of legal institutions in countries whose institutions are less developed*". ① Standardization is done through various ways, including identifying common principles and denominators, as well as using "model law" forms.

Legal harmonization and transplantation have become the key tools for the Law and Development movement, and have been largely used for many years by international institutions such as the World Bank and IMF on the "best practices and institutions" approach. The legal harmonization efforts of the World Bank and IMF during the New Order era and following the Asian Financial Crisis has been responsible for creating a situation in Indonesia where certain principles of Common Law jurisdiction now live peacefully with a primarily Civil Law tradition. Meanwhile, many of the legal harmonization processes in the past often involved only foreign experts with lack of understanding of Indonesian legal realities or stumbling blocks. More recently, the process of harmonizing particularly economic laws in Indonesia into laws of other well-functioning legal jurisdictions have become a more indigenous process involving key senior Indonesian experts as their leaders. E-

---

① Pistor, The Standardization of Law and Its Effect on Developing Economics, *G-24 Discussion Paper*, K. ,(2000)4, p. 1.

ven though at times, it still lacks sufficient transparency, the process to modernize Indonesian law has seen commendable progress.

Generally, advocates of legal harmonization claim that harmonized legal rules will cut transaction costs and therefore foster international trade and commerce. ① They further say that legal harmonization leads to not only legal convergence and unification of laws, but also less legal uncertainty, while enhancing legal predictability, and increasing the quality of legal institutions. It is also believed that legal harmonization is useful in resolving "*conflict of laws problems and the often difficult application of private international law and foreign substantive law ... generating greater legal predictability and security*". ②

The opposite of legal harmonization among nations is "regulatory competition". Advocates of the regulatory competition process take the view that in a regulatory competition process, law and policy makers will try to identify the best and most efficient rule resulting in a high quality legal system, instead of making a mere transplantation involving the choosing among the lowest common denominators③. Legal traditions will remain distinct and not affected by the other. Regulatory competition does not threat the existing legal culture and history of a country. Nor does it involve potentially high social and political adaptation costs. ④

Furthermore, in a country with a non-unified group of legal experts and practitioners, legal harmonization products may also result in legal uncertainty. These expertsmay have such different views on how transplanted legal products brought in through the legal harmonization process should be enforced. These may create controversial court decisions in due course. Generally, this is because it is rare that a provision of law can be seen in isola-

---

① Ibid, p. 4.

② Carbonara, E. &Parisi, F. ,The Paradox of Legal Harmonization, *University of Minnesota School of Law and University of Bologna Department of Economics Working Paper* (2007),p. 369.

③ Ibid, p. 4.

④ Faria, Future Directions of Legal Harmonization and Law Reform: Stormy Seas or Prosperous Voyage,J. A. E. ,(2009), p. 370.

tion, and in practice, it should be seen in the context of other laws which may not have been modernized through the process of harmonization or regulatory competition.

Moreover, there are certain prerequisites for effective legal harmonization.

First, a country should already have a fairly developed and well-functioning legal infrastructure before it can effectively undertake legal harmonization. This is because the process of legal harmonization itself does not immediately create the intended results just upon the introduction of a new transplanted law or regulation. Legal practitioners and bureaucrats who are parts of the legal infrastructure of a nation must also have sufficient understanding as to the larger interests sought to be protected through a transplanted law, as harmonization may possibly result in laws which is "lost in translation". Further, if the legal infrastructure is not able to support its implementation as intended, then the sought reform may become largely cosmetic. ①

Second, countries should ideally have similar level of socio-economic development. In a situation where the basic needs between countries are distinctly different, it is only natural that despite the call for harmonization, countries naturally tend to conflict the idea of harmonization. This point will be further illustrated in the context of ASEAN harmonization later in the paper.

Third, the principles or norms of laws that would become the objects of harmonization should be acceptable from philosophical, practical as well as technical standpoints. From a philosophical standpoint, the question which must be addressed is; to what extent the harmonization of investment laws truly accommodates the national interests as stated in the 1945 Constitution, or to what extent it is believed by the country at large. The practical question would be; to what extent a country should establish the institutions and resources to develop adequate legal harmonization, as it involves ensuring certain administrative processes to be as efficient as those in other countries which may have better bureaucracies. From a technical standpoint, one

① op. cit. , p. 2.

should compare the existing national laws with those of the countries which are the objects of harmonization, and then identify the items in the national laws which still hinder the harmonization process and the construction of values that should be realized through such harmonization.

It is perhaps worth remembering that harmonization may indeed be difficult because it must please a number of constituents or stakeholders. While the notion of harmonization may have been proposed by parties representing a nation state, to what extent harmonization can succeed in that nation will depend on many other things. In his writing "*Quality of Legislation: A Law and Development Project*", Florijin states that ideal legislation cannot be achieved because there are different users of law, each of whom may have different expectations. Good policies must be successful at reconciling those various points of view. According to Florijin, users include the lawmakers; meaning the parliamentarians, politicians, or the executive branch of a (political) party which may have the law making initiative. They generally set the initial public debates in legislative bodies pertaining to those issues. Law which passes the legislation should become the politician's further political interests or agenda. The second set of users identified by Florijin comprise of the bureaucrats and policy makers who generally interpret and create further bylaws or subordinate regulations of the legal harmonization products. They create supporting policies and technical regulations to ensure that the interests regulated by a certain law or regulation can be implemented as intended or, otherwise create carve outs which the government may, for some reason, want to create. The third set of users comprise of business communities, the public at large or those who will have to deal with, comply with, and face the effects of the legislation. Finally, I would add a final set of users which includes the law enforcers, court officers, also legal practitioners. Depending on how well-drafted a law or regulation may or may not be, as well as whose interests it is defending, it will have an impact on how such transplanted/harmonized legal product is enforced in practice. Such enforcement will, in the final analysis, determine the effectiveness of any legal harmonization product.

FOREIGN INVESTMENT UNDER ASEAN PERSPECTIVES

The general investment framework for the ASEAN countries can currently be found in the ASEAN Comprehensive Investment Agreement (ACIA). The framework was officially included in the agreement since 26th of February 2009, to intensify economic cooperation between and among the ASEAN member states. ACIA's objective is to create a free and open investment regime in ASEAN which would be realized through (i) progressive yet protective liberalization for investors of all Member States, (ii) improvement of transparency and predictability of conducive investment laws, which would become more appealing through the establishment of certain favorable conditions for investment, and (iii) joint promotion of the region as an integrated investment area. ① ACIA also aims to create a liberal, facilitative, transparent and competitive investment environment in ASEAN through its four pillars of broad-based programs for encouraging investment in the ASEAN region: (i) investment protection, (ii) facilitation and cooperation, (iii) promotion and awareness, and (iv) liberalization. In its implementation, certain guiding principles apply, particularly:

a. Investment liberalization, protection, promotion, and facilitation; ②

b. Progressive liberalization of investment with a view towards achieving a free and open investment environment in the region;

c. Benefit to investors and their investments based in ASEAN;

d. Preferential treatment among member states;

e. No back-tracking of commitments made under earlier agreements;

f. Special and differential treatments, and other flexibilities to Member States depending on their levels of development and sensitivities in certain

---

① Art. 1 (Objectives) of the ACIA.

② Liberalization is targeted to the following sectors: manufacturing, agriculture, fishery, forestry, mining and quarrying, services incidental to manufacturing, agriculture, fishery, forestry, mining and quarrying, and any other sectors, as may be agreed by all Member States (Article 3.3 of the ACIA).

sectors;

g. Reciprocal treatment in the enjoyment of concessions among Member States, where appropriate.

ACIA expects that by protecting investment and improving investors' confidence to invest in ASEAN, as well as encouraging further development of intra-ASEAN investments through expansion, industrial complementation and specialization, business would thrive. It is also expected that ASEAN-based investors would be able to enjoy the benefits of non-discriminatory treatment when they invest in other ASEAN countries. This would mean that investors would be granted similar treatments as domestic (host country) investors, and also similar treatment vis-à-vis other ASEAN-based investors. They would be granted full protection and security with regard to transfer of funds, capital, profits and dividends to be conducted by investors. ①

GENERAL FRAMEWORK FOR FOREIGN INVESTMENT IN INDONESIA

Foreign Investment② Regulations

Direct foreign investment in manufacturing and non-financial services are governed by Law No. 25 of 2007 ("Law No. 25/2007") and its implementing regulations. Except for certain sectors, specifically determined by

---

① Art. 13 of the ACIA.

② Foreign investments in Indonesia are classified into banking, financial services, securities investments, and non-financial sector investments. Generally, foreign investment in manufacturing and non-financial service activities are under the coordination of the Investment Coordinating Board (BKPM). Industries, which are subject to more stringent regulations, such as banking, securities, insurance, multi-finance, and other non-banking financial services, are regulated currently under Bapepam-LK (the Capital Market and Financial Institution Supervisory Agency), while banks are regulated under the Central Bank (BI). By January 2013, a new body called the Financial Services Authority (OJK) will be operating to take over certain functions of the Central Bank and of Bapepam-LK.

the Negative List[①] most business sectors are open for direct, foreign investment with certain limitations.

Moreover, though it has never been specifically clear, once a company becomes publicly listed, foreign ownership restrictions will not be strictly applied. Certain legal structures, such as holding companies, will be allowed to issue shares which are then distributed to the public, who are all or mostly foreigners, notwithstanding the subsidiary companies that should be operated otherwise, as their operations exclude areas of investments. Generally therefore Indonesia has liberalized policies in place.

Law No. 25/2007 which replaces earlier laws on investments as contained in Law No. 1 of 1967 on Foreign Capital Investment and Law No. 8 of 1968 on Domestic Capital Investment, can be said to already adhere to the guiding principles of the ACIA agreement. For example, the guiding principle of liberalization can be found in Article 12 of the law stating that all business sectors are open for investment unless they are stated as closed or open with conditions. This is generally found in Government Regulation No. 76 of 2007 regarding The Criteria and Establishment of Closed Business Line and Open Business with Conditions in respect of Capital Investment, as further implemented under Presidential Regulation No. 36 of 2010 regarding List of Business Fields Closed to Investment and Business Fields Open With Conditions to Investment (Negative List). However, in order to obtain certainty as to whether a business line is open to foreign investors, clarification and confirmation with BKPM or the technical ministry may be needed.

The principle of protection is reflected through Article 10 which requires investment companies to prioritize the employment of Indonesian citizens as the manpower, though they are still allowed to employ foreigners for certain expertise or positions. The principle of facilitating or giving incentives to investors that requires expansions or new investors is granted with certain conditions under Article 18. This facility/incentive can be granted in the form of reduction on various types of taxes or customs. These matters

---

① Presidential Regulation No. 77 of 2007 as last amended by Presidential Regulation No. 36 of 2010.

are generally regulated in a number of Minister of Finance decrees. Further, the facilitation for obtaining foreign manpower licenses and permits is also granted under Article 23, which is similar with the one contained in Article 22 of the ACIA agreement.

Article 25 to 26 of the Investment Law also introduces the one-stop service system known as PTSP, which is aimed at helping investors to open easier access to services, fiscal facilities and information regarding investment in Indonesia. This is then further regulated under the Presidential Regulation No. 27 of 2009 regarding One Stop Services in Capital Investment. The Investment Coordinating Board (BKPM) has also announced that the PTSP is facilitated through a National Single Window for Investment (NSWI, with the pilot project in Batam). This is an electronic platform for investments that enables investors to apply for license and non-license services online.

The purpose of the PTSP is to facilitate investors in obtaining services, fiscal facility and information related to investment. For instance, in the licensing process, BKPM will cooperate and coordinate with the relevant government or department institutions for the issuance of business license. This process is intended to make the issuance process of business licenses for the investment companies more effective and efficient.

Another important feature of the Investment Law is the Central Government's guarantee that it will not nationalise a foreign investment or revoke rights to control a foreign investment, except where it is declared by law. If the Central Government nationalises or revokes the foreign investment, it must pay compensation in an amount determined in accordance with the market price of the investment. This guarantee is accompanied by assurances under Article 8 that a foreign investor will have the right to transfer and repatriate the investment in foreign currency, profit, bank interest, dividend and other incomes, provided the legal obligations of the concerned investor have been settled.

Article 32 regulates that the dispute settlement related to any investment shall be firstly settled through the deliberation to reach consensus, otherwise, such dispute may be settled through international arbitration or

court as determined by the concerned parties.

A number of regulations were also issued by the Head of BKPM, notably Head of BKPM issued a number of key regulations, particularly Head of BKPM Regulation No. 12 of 2009 on Guidance and Procedure for Investment Applications, Head of BKPM Regulation No. 13 of 2009 on Guidelines and Procedures for Surveillance of Capital Investment Performance as amended by Regulation No. 7 of 2010, and Head of BKPM Regulation No. 14 of 2009 on Informations Service System and Electronic Investment Applciations.

Processes for Foreign Investment

In Non-Listed/Private Companies

For foreign investment in non-banking/financial services of non-publicly listed companies, the process will involve BKPM. Two types of investment companies under the auspices of BKPM include (i) Domestic Investment Companies (*Perusahaan Penanaman Modal Dalam Negeri* or "PMDN Companies"), and (ii) Foreign Investment Companies (*Perusahaan Penanaman Modal Asing* or "PMA Companies"). A PMDN Company is wholly owned by Indonesian citizens or Indonesian legal entity and a PMA Company is wholly or partially owned by foreign citizens or foreign legal entity.

To directly invest in the non-financial sectors in Indonesia, a foreign party must establish a PMA Company. ① Prior to this the foreign investor would file an application for Investment Registration. At the latest 6 months since such registration, the foreign investor must jointly establish with another shareholder an Indonesian limited liability company (*Perseroan Terbatas* or "PT Company") and obtain the approval from the Minister of Law and Human Rights ("MOLHR") for the company's deed of establishment. The process to set up a PMA Company starting from the establishment licensing

① If the foreign party only intends to promotional activities or be able to represent itself in entering into any agreements with customers in Indonesia, then the foreign party may establish a foreign representative office.

until it operates effectively takes approximately four months. The Investment Registration is valid until such time that the company obtain a In-Principle License (for PMA Company which requires facilities) or the company is ready to commence commercial operations or production at which time it should apply for the Business License. ①

Due to the length of time for the establishment of a new PMA Company and considering the commercial aspect, a foreign party may opt to acquire a non-operating PT Company and convert it to a PMA Company. This process saves time and costs because the legal entity is already in the form of PT Company. Therefore, the only remaining step is to obtain the relevant permits from BKPM. Pursuant to BKPM regulations, the issuance of such permits should l take seven working days at the latest, after the application requirements has been completed and submitted to BKPM. However, in practice, the business license issuance process may take approximately two weeks.

In Publicly Listed Company

If the investment is made for a publicly listed company, there are generally no regulated process (except for clearly regulated industries such as banking, financial, and Foreign Investment/ PMA mining), as all transactions will be construed to be done transparently through the stock exchange, and subject to disclosure or reporting as applicable.

The most important provision to be borne in mind is; when an investor seeks to obtain more than 50% of the ownership shares of a publicly listed company, such action will be construed as a takeover under the regulations of the Indonesian Capital Markets and Financial Institutions Supervisory Agency (Bapapem-LK), triggering the obligations to conduct a mandatory tender offer for all the public shares. Furthermore, to the extent of either the intial takeover or the mandatory tender offer resulting in more than 80% of the publicly listed shares being owned by the new controller(s), then they should, in a period of two years, divest their shares to the public so that

① Head of BKPM Regulation No. 12 of 2009.

they will only hold the maximum 80% shares of the company. This is because the regulation assumes that the minority shareholders have the right to be bought out at the same price as the former controller does, but that the new controller should not end up making the company's public float become so insignificant as to render the company's illiquidity. While the regulation does provide mechanisms for extending the two-year sell-down period, it still constitutes an anomaly in the midst of other ASEAN countries' securities regulation.

Once a public investor becomes the controller, he can obviously nominate and ensure the appointment of the nominees in the company Board of Directors and Board of Commissioners. ① Generally, directors or commissioners are nominated by certain shareholders but their duty of loyalty still remain with the company. As principles of good corporate governance require shareholders to be treated equally, it is possible, even for shareholders of public companies (though Bapepam-LK agency never likes such practices) to regulate matters in the contracts, such as organizing voting in favor or against certain decisions, so that they may together have better influence on the items which require shareholders' approval.

Publicly listed companies require at least, 30% independent members of the Board of Commissioners. Furthermore, one director must be an "independent director". There are also audit committees, such as the Audit and Remuneration Committees under the Board of Commissioners to further ensure the company is managed in a responsible manner. Independent board members and committees should ensure that, notwithstanding that a certain party may have the shareholding majority, the running of the public company would be done in a manner to protect the public shareholders' interests. The notion of protection of public shareholders interest is further found in other regulations pertaining to affiliated and material transactions which require disclosure. Fair opinions should be stated before such transactions take place.

---

① The Indonesian Company Law recognizes a two-tier Board system whereby the daily management and operations of the Company is entrusted to the directors, and the supervision of the Company is entrusted to the Board of Commissioners.

ISSUES PERTAINING TO INDONESIAN FOREIGN INVESTMENT LAWS AND PRACTICE

Despite the existence of a comprehensive law on investment which is in line with the ACIA agreement, its effectiveness may be affected by certain factors, on both a regional and national level.

Regional Challenges

At the regional level, there are a number of evidences indicating that the investment laws of ASEAN are not yet in a stage of harmonization or liberalization as they should be. For example, not all member states have comprehensive, up-dated foreign investment laws in place. Most ASEAN countries still rely on some sort of negative list of investments or other restrictive policies to generally protect certain business sectors from being totally opened up to foreigners.

Indeed, one cannot totally ignore the reality of the slow process of true legal harmonization in ASEAN. This was discussed at length by Darryl Jarvis who generally stated that empirically, ASEAN countries tend to prioritize the preservation of nationalism versus regionalism, particularly in investment policies, which then results in segmented/ sectional sheltering and investment protectionism. The ASEAN countries may not be perceived as really pushing liberalization, but instead perhaps only trying to protect their own regional-based enterprises against threats of the western ones. Other challenges of regional law harmonization have been identified as among others, the inequality of market capture capabilities of the member states due to differences in financial market development, infrastructure and labor skills. There are clear disparities among the ASEAN countries in this respect.

For example, Singapore is acknowledged as a country with modern, world class infrastructure which has also successfully transformed itself into a strong financial center with, many people believe, efficient institutions and legal certainty. This has, in part, made Singapore an obvious choice for investments, listing of companies, as well as a place for alternative dispute

resolution (arbitration). In legal practice, people also have noted that the Singapore laws have been increasingly chosen to regulate Indonesia-based transactions. The fact that a number of the ASEAN countries have similar natural strengths and potentials may later result in regulatory competition among them. The lack of common institutions among the member states further encourages investors to create natural preferences on where to invest. The perception that there are no sufficient dialogues in exchange rate and fiscal policies also puts into question to what extent ASEAN can truly achieve economic integration. ①

Those issues are important items of coordination to protect each of the member states against global shocks or contaminating each other. The modern infrastructures of Singapore, Malaysia and now Thailand, make these three countries attractive venues for regional hubs, notwithstanding the actual market (especially in the case of consumer products) may exist, let us say, in Indonesia. The discrepancy in labor skills also means that labor force in certain countries may only be used for lower-skilled jobs, while other jurisdictions may have their citizens actively become global employees in biotechnology or manufacturing.

Finally, the last challenge ASEAN harmonization has to face is to what extent the principles of regionalism are as relevant in a world of increasing globalization. Regional communities are proven to affect countries outside their territories, thus there has been more calls on globalization. Certain governments of ASEAN countries have put their priorities on ensuring coordination at more global, rather than regional levels. In brief, the priority to implement the ASEAN agenda may not be, in the opinions of some as high as it should, in this increasingly globalized world.

National Challenges

At the national level, there are areas of concern which must first be ad-

---

① See Jarvis, Foreign Direct Investment and Investment Liberalization in Asia: Assessing ASEAN's Initiatives 1. *Lee Kuan Yew School of Public Policy National University of Singapore*, *D. S. L.*, (2010), *pp.* 31~32.

dressed if Indonesia is expected to achieve its true potential and be able to fully embark on ASEAN investment harmonization. Many of these problems are legacies of the past, or a result of many reforms that occurred following the Asian Financial Crisis, and the transformation of Indonesia into a true democracy. Whatever is its history, until Indonesia can solve these problems, it may be some time before the country can fully open itself up to true harmonization.

Decentralization Lack of Clear Divisions

In 1999, the Government adopted Law No. 22 of 1999 concerning Regional Governments which delegated certain authorizations to the regional governments that had previously been exercised[①]. Thereafter, the local governments have been authorized to impose taxes and levies within certain limits as well as approve certain investments. The authorized divisions of the central and regional governments, however, remain unclear.

Licensing procedures are costly, time consuming and often uncertain. The ambiguous distribution of authorizations between the central and regional governments has also created overlapping infrastructure development, as well as conflicting licensing requirements.

In the context of foreign investment, the problems created by decentralizationare also apparent when discussing the lack of consistency between policies or decisions taken at a regional level versus those at the provinces.

While BKPM plays the primary role, the regional BKPMD is responsible for the issuance of some licenses such as location or anti-nuisance permits. The creation of one-stop service or national single window to support foreign investment does not completely eliminate these problems. Certain matters will still need to be dealt with at the regional level, or may often times continue to involve other technical ministries. There may also be insufficient manpower and capacity to support the activities in the regions.

---

① The Law of The Republic of Indonesia No. 22 of 1999 concerning Regional Governments.

Legal (Un)Certainty

There are often legal uncertainties pertaining to certain key legal concepts which are commonly used in economic transactions, e. g. pertaining to certain security interests and concepts (such as the enforceability of assignment of rights for security purposes or indemnity). The Civil Law tradition which Indonesia adheres to is one which assumes judges can be mere administrators who upon reading the law will be able to give good decisions. The reality is that there are often unclear drafting, or communication of policies. These result in uncertainties of laws.

In the context of foreign investment, there is often lack of clarity on business open to foreign investment. The Negative List may often not be a reliable basis for determining whether a business sector is truly closed, as technical ministries and agencies may have different views than BKPM officers on the matter. Certain principles of foreign investment will be upheld notwithstanding that the Negative List may imply the business is open for foreign investment. ①

In particular, certain legal uncertainty in foreign investment currently exists in Indonesia in certain key sectors such as the banking sector, telecommunications and media.

1. Banking

In 1999, banks were opened up to liberalization and 99% shares of a bank may be owned by foreigners. As a result, the leading private banks of the pre Asian Financial Crisis era have now been controlled by various foreign banks and strategic investors or private equities. Such banks are now too expensive to be reacquired by Indonesian parties. Meanwhile, certain Indonesian banks have faced difficulties trying to open offshore branches claiming there have been no reciprocity of facilitation in the other countries. This, in addition to nationalistic sentiments, have led to the Central Bank

① For example, a PMA company may never sell directly to end users thus any scheme which effectively enables this would not be permitted even if the Negative List may imply the business is open for majority control by foreign investor.

announcing that it would not entertain applications for bank acquisitions as it was analyzing the foreign investment policies pertaining to banks. Prior to this, there were already rumours in the market that the Central Bank would be pushing for drastic changes to the foreign ownership rules pertaining to banks by sometime in 2011. Although the Governor of the Central Bank later denied that there would be a limitation of majority foreign ownership in banks, he did admit that the Central Bank was reviewing the issue from a good corporate governance perspective. Generally foreign investors currently believe that Indonesian laws will be made to change to make the foreign ownership rules for banks more restrictive and may even possibly apply these rules retroactively.

This has caused great concern that other industries to be regulated under the OJK (eg. insurance, securities and multifinance) would also be subject to the same restriction.

Premature announcements of potentially "unpopular" policies (at least among foreign investors) only create confusion and uncertainty. Clear communication of policies is of utmost importance for creating a conducive foreign investment environment.

2. Telecommunications

Under the Negative List, the telecommunication sector is generally subject to foreign ownership limitations varying from 49% up to 95%. The telecommunication tower industry is specifically closed for foreign investment. However, the publicly listed company structure has been successfully utilized to overcome this restriction.

There are also some levels of uncertainty as to whether or not online transaction and portal services should be considered as multimedia services based on Negative List Regulation, whereby the foreign ownerships are restricted to the maximum of 49%. On the one hand, the Negative List does not regulate explicitly whether or not the online transaction and portal services are closed for foreign investment since they are not specifically listed in the Negative List Regulation. Under the 2001 Decree of the Minister of Communication and Technology, No. KM. 21 on Telecommunication Services Operation, online transaction and portal services are included as other multimedia services. In the third amendment of MOCIT Decree No. 21/2000 issued in September 2008, the online transaction and portal services were no longer regarded as multimedia services. Currently, there is a conflict of opinion between the MOCIT and Investment Coordinating Board BKPM pertaining to whether or not this matter should be a subject to the 49% restrictions.

3. Private Television Broadcasting

Pursuant to Article 24 paragraph (1) of Government Regulation No. 50 Year 2005 on Private Broadcasting Companies(PBC) Services, a private television broadcasting company may only be established by an Indonesian citizen or Indonesian legal entity, in which all of its shares are owned by the Indonesian. Foreign citizens or foreign legal entities may directly or indirectly hold only 20% of the total issued and paid up capital of the company. The company should have at least, two foreign citizens or foreign legal entities as its shareholders. The remaining 80% of the total issued and paid up capital must be owned by an Indonesian citizen and/or an Indonesian legal entity which is 100% owned by an Indonesian. Every transaction that causes the foreign ownership shares of a PBC to exceed the 20% threshold, must be adjusted to be in compliance with the foreign ownership threshold (i. e. 20%).

Furthermore, Article 27 paragraph 1 of GR 50/2005, provides that such a company may only list 20% of its total issued and paid-up capital at the stock exchange. Article 27 paragraph 3 further stipulates that in the event where the 20% of the PBC shares are listed at the stock exchange, foreign citizens and legal entities may only own PBC shares through purchasing the listed shares.

In practice, it is common for the market players to make a PBC owned by a publicly listed company, which is not restricted under the foreign shareholding regulation. The Minister of Communication and Information has conducted discussions with Bapepam-LK on the approach that will be taken by the ministry in connection to the 20% foreign shareholding restriction in a PBC by Public Hold Co. but the results have not been made public as yet.

4. Plantation Business

In plantation businesses, foreigners may own up to 95%[①] of the shares of a plantation business with an area of at least, 25 hectare or more, with or without a processing unit, or it can be operated solely as a product processing plantation business. Plantations with area less than 25 hectares, or low-scaled processing units are reserved for micro, small, and medium enterprises and cooperatives. The foreign legal entity or citizen conducting plantation business in Indonesia must establish a joint cooperation with Indonesian business actors by establishing a legal entity domiciled in Indonesia. This requirement is to prevent plantation companies that have received facilities from the government, from transferring their profit to a foreign entity with no intention or plan to improve the community income.

Notwithstanding the above, in practice, there are plantation companies which can be owned up to 100% by a foreign entity. This is because the minimum 5% Indonesia ownership obligation only started to take effect in 2007. Accordingly, plantation companies with 100% the shares have been owned by foreign investors prior to the issuance of the Negative List in 2007 can continue to do so. However, if the foreign ownerships in such companies prior to or after the enactment of the Negative List 2007 are below the maximum foreign ownership threshold as stipulated in the 2007 Negative List (95%), investors in such plantation companies will not be able to increase their aggregate shareholding above the maximum foreign ownership threshold.

Other uncertainty may be created by the law's express provisions themselves. The most recent occurrence was by virtue of Law No. 7 of 2011 (the "Currency Law") which came into effect on 28 June 2011.

The Currency Law requires the use of and prohibits the rejection of the Rupiah in certain transactions occurring within the jurisdiction of Indonesia. Article 21 of the Currency Law requires the use of the Rupiah in payment transactions, monetary settlements of obligations and other financial transactions (among others, the deposit of money) within Indonesia. However, there are a number of exceptions to this rule, including certain transactions

① Provided that Recommendation from Minister of Agriculture cq Director General of Plantation is obtained

related to the state budget, income and grants from and to foreign countries, international trade transactions, foreign currency savings deposited in a bank and international financing transactions. Article 23 of the Currency Law prohibits the rejection of the Rupiah offered as a means of payment, to settle obligations or in other financial transactions within Indonesia unless there is uncertainty regarding the authenticity of the Rupiah bills offered. The prohibition does not apply to transactions in which the payment or settlement of obligations in a foreign currency has been agreed in writing. The Currency Law was considered to create uncertainty because whilst Article 21 forbids settlement in a currency other than the Rupiah, while Article 23 provides a very broad exception to the prohibition of the rejection of Rupiah.

To address public concerns, in December of 2011, the Directorate General of Treasury at the Ministry of Finance issued a booklet of guidelines concerning the implementation of the Currency Law (the "MOF Interpretation"). The MOF Interpretation explains that the Currency Law only applies for cash transaction (coins and bank notes) while excluding payments involving demands deposits (checks and letters of credit) and electronic payments. The MOF Interpretation also explains that the obligation to accept the Rupiah as a payment for transactions, as settlement for an obligation or for any other financial transaction as mentioned in Article 23 of the Currency Law, can be avoided by contractual arrangement existing or entered into either before or after the enactment of the Currency Law. This is actually different from the express wording of the Currency Law itself.

While the MOF Interpretation may have been able to provide some practical clarity, because the MOF Interpretation does not constitute legislation, it may be subject to challenge. This also makes for a bad precedent being that those issues should have been made clear under the Currency Law itself, as the MOF Interpretation when tested in the court may be subject to challenges.

Labor Related Issues

The Indonesian Labor Law is considered to be very protective on employees and is considered to be less favorable compared to those of other

countries such as Thailand, Vietnam, Bangladesh and PRC. This is because the labor law regulates detailed lay-off procedures, significant retrenchment costs, and limits temporary hiring (outsourcing). The skills of workers in Indonesia are also considered not appropriate for higher technical productions or processes.

To make investments in Indonesia more attractive, there must be improvement in the legal framework as well as training and education of the people so that workers of Indonesia can be more competitive with those of other countries in the region.

Infrastructure

Modern airports and ports continue to be non-existent in Indonesia, and Indonesia still suffers from power outages, transport failures and inadequate clean water supplies. The Government has provided significant funding for the development of energy and infrastructure projects throughout Indonesia. However, the ability for these projects to be successfully completed and successful completion of the expansion programs will depend on numerous factors, including the ability to find the financing and expertise supports for such projects. In addition, some of the lethargies are due to legal uncertainty and restrictions occurring in reaction to the state finance law overhaul in 2003 onwards, resulting in the Government being forced to create what may be deemed as innovative, but "non-plain vanilla" project finance alternatives which may not be as attractive to sponsors and financiers. The practical problem of clearing lands for public use has been cited as one of the long standing blocks. Under the new Land Procurement Law which recently came into effect, the smooth execution of development activities on areas required for public purposes[①] can be better ensured. The Land Procurement Law introduces clear and expedited steps for the procurement of land for public interest.[②]

For so long as the infrastructure of Indonesia is lagging behind its neighbors, then notwithstanding the existence of a strong market, foreign investors may not be persuaded to locate their factories or operations in Indonesia.

---

① The Land Procurement Law specifically stipulates that the following development projects are classified as being done in the public interest: (1) national defense and security; (2) public road, toll road, tunnel, railway, train station, and train operating facilities; (3) water embankment, reservoir, irrigation, drinking water channel, water disposal channel and sanitation and other water resource management building; (4) seaport, airport, and terminal; (5) oil, gas, and geothermal infrastructure; (6) power plant, power transmission, switch yard, power network and distribution; (7) government telecommunication and information network; (8) waste disposal and processing place; (9) hospitals owned by the Central Government or Regional Government; (10) public safety facilities; (11) cemetery owned by the Central Government or Regional Government; (12) social facilities, public facilities and open public green space; (13) wild life and culture preservation areas; (14) office area for the Central Government, Regional Government or sub-districts/villages; (15) structuring of urban slum area and/or land consolidation, and rented residential for low-income communities; (16) education facilities or schools under the Central Government or Regional Government; (17) sport facilities owned by the Central Government or Regional Government; and (18) public market and public car park.

② Initially, government entities which wish to procure land for public interest must engage the Entitled Party in a public consultation on the proposed development plan until a consensus is reached. In the event no consensus can be reached, the Governor will set up a team to examine the reasons for the Entitled Party's objections, and, based on such reasons, will make a decision as to whether the targeted land is approved to be procured for public interest. To the extent the Entitled Party still has objections, it may file a legal claim to the State Administrative Court, whose decision is subject to final appeal at the Supreme Court. If the land has been approved to be procured for public interest by virtue of a legally binding court decision, the National Land Agency shall appoint an independent appraisal team to determine the compensation value to be paid to the Entitled Party. The Entitled Party may file a legal claim to a District Court to challenge the compensation value, and the decision of the District Court is subject to final appeal at the Supreme Court.

Corruption

Corruption has been a long standing problem in Indonesia. Decentralization and the shift of the governmental system from a purely Presidential system to a parliamentary-like one, has made corruption appear to be more widespread than before. In addition to that, generally, investors continue not to believe that the court system in Indonesia practices fairness and impartiality, and there is skepticism that the judicial system will enforce their contractual property rights. For this reason, many business contracts choose arbitration (including foreign arbitration) for settlement of disputes.

HOW TO IMPROVE INVESTMENT LAWS HARMONIZATION IN ASEAN

Given the above, it is clear that the goal of harmonization is not a simple one and is affected by many factors and conditions. Generally however, certain steps and measures can be taken to ensure the achievement of harmonization:

1. Create a "level playing field" so that at the minimum infrastructure, financial institutions, and courts in each ASEAN member state can meet on a level of parity with the most developed ones. ①

This is a process which will take time but is critical to be done, especially Indonesia which is an archipelago of over 17,000 islands.

2. Ensure there is political support and unified view on matters of law to be harmonized in each ASEAN member state.

Translating principles of harmonization into a law can be challenging for countries where politically, they may not have a unified view on the matter.

---

① In the case of Indonesia, there is a significant catch up to be made. The Indonesian government must be firm in providing key infrastructures particularly modern airports in key cities. However, if the other ASEAN countries which have similar problems fail to also address them, then this disparity will continue to be a challenge to effective legal harmonization.

If there is a national political support in each country, then a Model Law format can be used to harmonize investment laws and regulations.

3. Improve and empower relevant government bureaucracy and agencies to deliver efficient processes.

To what extent investment procedures can be harmonized, simplified and facilitated, would be depended on the readiness of each country's bureaucracy to handle such procedures. It also depends on whether the agency overseeing foreign investment has been given adequate authorization in all areas of law, or just in certain business sectors. Furthermore, agencies that handle investments must be modern, responsive, and logical. To the extent certain authorities remain vested in the technical ministries, it is possible, there may be differences in policies/opinions between the investment board and the technical ministries leading to uncertain and slow process.

4. Strengthen the one-stop service and ASEAN Single Window system.

The one-stop investment center is essential to attract and support the potential investment. One-stop service is a concept that relates to the decentralization of authorities from the central government with respect to any investment decisions. To ensure this works, then concerns pertaining to decentralization issues in general must first be addressed by the respective countries. The One-Stop Service among the ASEAN countries must be linked so there is sufficient clear and adequate of information between the investment coordinating boards in each ASEAN countries.

5. Improve coordination in supervising areas of investment which may fall under the temporary exclusion list (TEL) or may be considered sensitive list (SL).

By having the TEL and SL lists harmonized, it may further emphasize the liberalization of ASEAN's foreign investment regime, as each ASEAN countries will likely have the TEL and SL lists that are substantially similar.

6. Enhance harmonization of incentive policies between ASEAN countries.

Research has shown that several ASEAN member countries compete with each other in competitive bidding wars relating to costly incentive systems for attracting and maintaining foreign investment.

7. Ensure that double taxation arrangements between ASEAN countries are fully completed between all member states.

8. Create a mutual surveillance system among ASEAN countries to ensure all ASEAN country will be in an equal status and position.

9. Establish a common ASEAN institution having the duty to receive performance report from all ASEAN countries with respect to their respective achievements or obstacles in fulfilling the action plans determined under the ACIA agreement, AEC Blueprint.

10. Involve private sector participation in harmonization efforts.

Harmonization cannot be effective if the process does not sufficiently involve private sector participation and comments. While not all private sectors' feedbacks are relevant or appropriate, getting practitioners involved in resolving various issues faced by foreign investors may give the government officials more accurate perspectives to push harmonization.

11. Communicate the policies so there is no ambiguity or uncertainty and discrepancy between what is regulated and what is enforced.

Harmonization implies liberalization. Each Government needs to better appreciate the market, that it will only be confused if in the name of national interest, the Government implies that they may apply certain restrictive policies retroactively. When the Government later ends up not applying it, it would not mean that some declining investment had not already occurred due to the uncertainty.

12. Implement zero tolerance policy to corrupt practices in licensing processes and judicial administration.

Corruption in licensing processes must be reduced as it adds up transaction costs and generally create uncertainty particularly where different authorities to issue permits or approvals based their actions not merely on what is permitted by the law, but due to corruption. There must be zero tolerance to such practices, especially when they relate to licensing processes and judicial administration.

13. Specifically for Indonesia, amend the Mandatory Tender Offer rules on forcing 20% sell-down after acquiring more than 80% as this regulation does not exist in any other jurisdiction.

If the intention is to ensure there is sufficient number of quality listed companies whose shares are liquid, then the obligation to undertake the mandatory tender offer should be adjusted accordingly, instead of requiring a mandatory purchase from all public but then requiring the investors to sell again within 2 years.

While there is no quick solution to achieving harmonization, the writer believes that if the above were implemented, there would be a more successful harmonization process of the investment laws among the ASEAN countries.

To what extent it can be implemented depends on the political will of each member state and to what extent there is national political support to adopt those laws and policies.

REFERENCES

Carbonara, E. &Parisi, F., The Paradox of Legal Harmonization. *University of Minnesota School of Law and University of Bologna Department of Economics Working Paper*, 2007.

Crettez, B., Deffains, B., &Deloche R., On the Optimal Complexity of Law and Legal Rules Harmonization. *University of Paris Ouest and University of Paris Descartes*, 2008.

Faria, J. A. E., Future Directions of Legal Harmonisation and Law Reform: Stormy Seas or Prosperous Voyage, 2009.

Florijn, N. A., Quality of Legislation: A Law and Development-Project., in Arnscheidt, J., Van Rooij, B. & Otto, J. M (ed.). Lawmaking for Development. Leiden University Press, 2008, pp. 75～89.

Government Regulation No. 76, 2007 regarding The Criteria and Establishment of Closed Business Line and Open Business with Conditions in respect of Capital Investment.

Jarvis, D. S. L., Foreign Direct Investment and Investment Liberalization in Asia: Assessing ASEAN's Initiatives1. *Lee Kuan Yew School of Public Policy National University of Singapore*, 2010.

Newton, S., Law and Development, Law and Economics, and The

Fate of Legal Technical Assistance. , in Arnscheidt, J. , Van Rooij, B. & Otto, J. M (ed.). Lawmaking for Development. *Leiden University Press*, 2008, pp. 23～52.

Pistor, K. , The Standardization of Law and Its Effect on Developing Economics. *G-24 Discussion Paper*, 2000, 4.

Thanadsillapakul, Lawan, Framework Agreement on the ASEAN Investment Area (AIA), accessed on 17 December 2011 at http://www.thailawforum.com/articles/lawanaia.html.

Various laws and regulations of Indonesia and materials pertaining to ASEAN.

白礁岛主权争议案及其借鉴意义

钟庭辉*

2008年5月23日,海牙国际法庭一锤定音,将白礁岛判决归新加坡所有,解决了新加坡与马来西亚多年来的领土纠纷问题。由于历史、地缘政治等原因,新加坡和马来西亚对白礁岛的主权归属已经争夺了长达29年。新马两国对白礁岛主权归属的争端对新马双边关系和东盟的发展造成了一定影响。同时,双方对白礁岛主权的争端过程和争端通过海牙国际法院得以解决也给了我们一定的启示。

一、白礁岛的地理和历史

白礁岛位于柔佛海峡东部,两端长度137米,平均宽度60米,低潮时面积约8560平方米。白礁岛位于马来西亚柔佛州东南13公里,距新加坡东部海岸有60多公里,距印尼宾坦岛14公里。这座小岛虽然很小,但是其在新加坡国际水道的重要位置,历史上曾经有很多船只在这里发生意外,具有重要战略意义。英国殖民政府在1840年占领了白礁岛,并于1851年在岛上建了霍士堡灯塔。有关灯塔随后交由新加坡管理,并一直处于新加坡实际管辖之下。

中岩礁则位于白礁岛以南零点六海里,它由两块礁石组成,南礁则距离白礁岛以南二点一海里,它只有在低潮时才露出海面。

二、白礁岛主权争议的开端

从1847年至1979年的130年间,新加坡一直都在没有任何国家反对的情况下对白礁岛行使主权,并负责管理与维修岛上的霍士堡灯塔,而马来西亚

---

* 钟庭辉,新加坡钟庭辉律师事务所创始人,著名律师。

在 1979 年之前所出版的地图上，也都把它标为新加坡领土。1953 年 6 月 12 日，新加坡英殖民地秘书曾经致函柔佛州苏丹的英籍顾问以询问有关白礁岛的主权状况，以确定殖民地（新加坡）的海域。结果在同年 9 月 21 日，柔佛代州秘书回函说，柔佛州政府并未拥有白礁岛的主权。

1978 年 4 月，新加坡驻马来西亚参赞向新加坡外交部发了一个报告，报告中指出，马来西亚正在收集证据，要证明当年只是允许英国殖民政府修建和维护白礁岛上的霍士堡灯塔，白礁岛的主权应当归属马来西亚。虽然马来西亚政府并没有向新加坡政府发出正式的信函，但在 1979 年马来西亚突然单方面在所出版的新地图中首次把白礁岛划入它的领土范围，以此宣布开始与新加坡争夺白礁岛主权。对于马来西亚政府的行为，新加坡政府感到异常震惊，随即向马来西亚递交外交照会，抗议马来西亚在地图中把白礁岛列为其岛屿。

1980 年开始，不断有携带武器的马来西亚海军船只在白礁岛附近挑衅，新加坡驻白礁岛海军严格控制自己的行为，以防止形势进一步升级。尽管如此，两国局势依然日趋紧张。

随后的几年中，新加坡政府通过各种外交途径向马来西亚政府表示了对两国形势的担忧，并且在 1989 年的几次外交会议中向马来西亚政府提交了第三方文件，以证明白礁岛的主权；同年，两国的总检察长会面并交换了文件。之后，马来西亚的海军逐渐减少了在白礁岛附近的挑衅行为。为加强对白礁岛的控制，新加坡随后在岛上兴建了一座两层楼的建筑物，1989 年装置了雷达系统，1991 年建造了直升机降落坪及军事通信设备，同时派驻军舰巡逻，阻止马来西亚渔民在附近捕鱼。

可是，白礁岛的主权问题依然逐渐上升为一个政治问题，并引起一些马来西亚国内政治团体的注意。1992 年 5 月 21 日，据媒体报道，马来西亚伊斯兰政治党打算在白礁岛上插马来西亚国旗，新加坡外交部随即发布了严厉的警告，马来西亚政府及时阻止了他们的行动计划。

三、新马两国谈判以及达成特别协定

由于白礁岛主权问题的政治敏感性，在此后多次的两国总理会面中，两国达成了要交换证据文件共同解决白礁岛主权问题的共识。但是这样的共识却因为 20 世纪 80 年代中期三个事件使得新马两国关系恶化而被搁置。这三个事件分别是对 1986 年 11 月以色列总理哈伊姆·赫尔佐格访问新加坡的抗议、1987 年国防部部长李显龙对新加坡军队中的马来人作出的评价以及马来

西亚对新加坡4名士兵侵入马来西亚领土的指控。

1992年1月,在新马两国总理再次会面之后,新加坡正式向马来西亚发去了关于白礁岛的外交照会和支持性文件。1992年6月马来西亚也向新加坡发来了外交照会。在之后的两国磋商中,双方互换了证据文件。虽然在两次磋商中两国充分交换了意见、进行了辩论,但并不能得出令人满意的结论。于是在1994年新马两国总理会晤中,新加坡总理提出了由第三方如国际法庭来解决争议。很快,马来西亚同意将白礁岛主权争议交由国际法庭来处理。

因为新加坡和马来西亚均没有接受国际法庭强制性管辖权的声明,那么若要国际法庭来审理此案,新马两国的首要任务就是达成一个特别协定来约定此案由国际法庭裁决。而这个特别协定经过了3轮谈判、足足花了两国4年的时间才确定下来,主要是因为两国对几个问题迟迟无法达成一致,一是"白礁岛"和"蒲牢巴图普特岛"(马来西亚对白礁岛的称呼)在特别协定中的次序;二是需要裁决的争议中是否应该包括中岩礁和南礁岛;最后一点是在国际法庭裁决白礁岛主权之后,是否由国际法庭来决定另一方的应得权利。

在双方拟定好特别协议之后,由于新加坡国务资政回忆录的出版、马来西亚海关的迁址等等事务的影响,新加坡和马来西亚迟迟没有对特别协议进行签字和认可。直到2003年2月6日,两国才在吉隆坡正式签署并认可了这份特别协定。

四、为国际法庭审判做准备

早在1989年新加坡就从律政部、外交部、国防部、法律部、交通部、海事局以及口述历史和档案局抽调了相关工作人员组成了白礁岛委员会,委员会紧密合作,广泛收集材料和证据,其中包括最重要的证据:柔佛代州秘书回函。

与此同时,委员会的重要成员还亲临白礁岛进行实地考察,其中包括首席大法官陈锡强、特别法官许通美等等。

根据国际法庭相关法律规定,如果当事国在国际法庭中没有本国法官,可以委任指派一名特别临时法官参与特定案件。新加坡和马来西亚均没有本国法官在国际法庭中,因此都可以委派特别临时法官。新加坡白礁岛委员会最初选择许通美为这名特别临时法官,因为许通美国际外交经验丰富,而且因其主持联合国关于海事法律的会议而拥有广泛的知名度,并且他已经参与了很多白礁岛主权争议之案的准备工作。大家都认为他是不二人选。但是1995年,一名来自法国的国际法律师提出了异议,根据国际法庭第17条规定,国际

法庭法官的人选不应当同时以任何身份介入国际法庭审理的案件中。即使许通美只是参与了一些准备工作，并没有在委员会中有实际的身份，白礁岛委员会不愿冒任何风险，于是着手另立特别临时法官人选。印度籍国际法专家劳巫，是一名了解英国殖民制度的法律专家，曾代表印度参与了很多联合国关于海事法律的谈判，也是联合国属下国际法委员会委员，被最终敲定为特别法官的人选。

白礁岛委员会的成员陈锡强于2006年被任命为新加坡的首席大法官，而另一成员赵锡燊则被任命为新的总检察长。虽然在国际法庭中，在任首席法官出席法庭辩论史无前例，但由于陈锡强自1993年就一直在白礁岛委员会中担任顾问并做出了杰出贡献，所以在无异议的情况下他一直担任顾问直到案子终结。

白礁岛案件历时30多年，其间，新加坡政府三届政府总理李光耀、吴作栋和李显龙以及内阁都给予白礁岛委员会充分的支持，提供了政治、外交、法律方面的诸多建议。

虽然新加坡曾经在国际海事特别法庭有过一个关于填海开发的案子，白礁岛一案却是其参与国际法庭诉讼的第一案。虽然新加坡政府为白礁岛案件做了大量的准备工作，但由于新加坡缺少国际法的实战经验，而且国际法庭的官方语言是英语和法语，所以寻找有经验的国际法律师和法语系国际法律师组成新加坡国际律师团被提上了白礁岛委员会的日程。挑选过程首先由律政部展开，律政部先列出了一份名单，委员会委托一位前国际法庭法官进行筛选，并咨询了一位资深国际法律师后，作出了最终决定，即邀请四位国际法专家加入新加坡国际律师团。他们是英国牛津大学执教的女皇律师布朗利、法国巴黎第十大学的国际法教授佩莱、在巴黎执业的专攻国界与领土纠纷问题的律师邦迪及律师兼地图专家马林托皮。

五、国际法庭听证会

2007年11月6日星期二上午，白礁岛案件在国际法庭口头辩论阶段开始。听证会辩论阶段，双方的辩护团就白礁岛、中岩礁和南礁岛的归属问题向国际法庭作了历时3个星期的口头陈词。新加坡声称从1847年至1979年这130年期间，新加坡是在“公开、连续而又众所周知”的情况下占有白礁，从来没有人挑战新加坡的主权。在1953年，当柔佛在国际法律下还是个自主国时，邦秘书便以这个公职身份写信通知新加坡政府，柔佛政府并不拥有白礁。

按照国际法律,这样的说明对柔佛后来加入的马来西亚,是有法律约束力的。同时,新加坡还向法庭出示了1980年马来西亚总理谈及白礁岛时的一段录音,在录音中,马来西亚总理表示马来西亚对白礁岛主权也存疑。另外,新加坡还出示了在1962年至1975年之间马来西亚先后出版的6份把白礁归入新加坡版图的地图,以证明马来西亚曾认同白礁岛属于新加坡的事实。

在马来西亚的陈词中,马来西亚强调,白礁岛自古就属于马来西亚,马来西亚只是授权英国殖民地政府建造和管理霍士堡灯塔,但是并没有提出很有利的证据。

2008年5月23日经位于荷兰海牙的国际法院裁决,由16名多国法官组成的聆审团以12票对4票判决白礁岛主权归新加坡,以15票对1票判决白礁岛南部的中岩礁归马来西亚,而南礁主权则归拥有它所处海域主权的一方。

国际法院经审理认为,尽管新加坡主张在19世纪时白礁岛是无主地,但是,一系列的证据表明白礁岛本属于柔佛苏丹王朝。然而1844年后情况发生了变化,特别是1852年至1853年间,英国殖民当局在白礁岛修建霍斯堡灯塔,对其进行了一系列行使主权的行为,这些活动均未公开进行,且直到1979年并未为马来西亚所反对,因此表明了其对该岛的主权。

六、新加坡赢得白礁岛一案的原因以及判决的影响

是什么能让新加坡赢得白礁岛这个案子?这不仅仅是律政部、外交部的努力,最重要的是新加坡全体政府部门的齐心协力、紧密合作。同时,新加坡的国际律师团也对此案做出了杰出的贡献。

白礁岛争议的解决,不仅使新加坡增强了国际法方面经验,对于改善新加坡和马来西亚的双边关系有着重要的意义,同时也为东盟其他国家地区通过第三方审判解决领土纠纷作出表率。

七、白礁岛一案对中国解决领土纠纷的借鉴意义

从白礁岛一案我们可以看出,通过国际法庭解决领土纠纷,不仅为未来解决一些区域领土纠纷提供了借鉴,而且也是安抚一些拒绝谈判并且尚武的邻邦的手段。总之,它所提供的是一种促使国际社会和平发展的解决方案。

值得注意的是,并非所有的个案都符合国际法庭的解决模式。对于有领土纠纷案件的国家,应当先挑选一些从国际法角度胜算把握比较大的案件提

交到国际法庭来解决，以此挑选并建立一支优秀的国际法律师团队和积累解决领土纠纷案件的经验。

此外，白礁岛一案也说明了，在国际法庭受理前，这个案子可能要花费十年甚至更长的时间做准备工作。

与此同时，我们应该如何做呢？

以下是笔者的几点建议：

1. 对公众进行普法教育。除了培养优秀的国际法律师，对公众的法律教育也很重要。一个社会的文明程度与公众对法律这一游戏规则的接受度是相辅相成的。即使一个判决不符合当事人的意愿或选择，判决结果不符合他的期望，他也应当接受这样的判决结果，而不能借此上街示威游行。也许一个国家最大的尴尬莫过于大部分公众在这样的情况下选择上街示威游行，侵犯本国公民的人身和财产利益。

2. 加强档案管理。所有国家都有档案管理，但如何做得更好却不是一件简单的事。要想在国际法庭上赢得这些领土纠纷案件，应尽可能地组织好相关档案证据，且将最有力的档案证据展示出来。要实现这些，就需要一些有过专业培训并且诉讼经验非常丰富的人才。因此发现、培养这类人才也是十分重要的。

3. 此外，无论是通过国际法庭诉讼还是其他方式赢得这样的领土纠纷案件，政府机构之间的密切合作至关重要。特别是一个大国，其内部的机构组织纷繁复杂，人员结构和权力范围交叠重合，如何合作更为重要。事实上，很多国际分析人士对此表示忧虑：在中国的一些领土纠纷案件中，政府可能并非出于自身意愿，而是由于众多政府机构的介入，在缺乏明细的分工和无间的合作的情况下，而使得政府最终还是沦陷于军事泥潭之中。因此，在牵涉国际法庭案件诉讼的时候，国家宜出台相关法令来明晰各国家机关的职责和权力范围。

Case Study on the Sovereignty Dispute of Pedra Branca and its Significance

Zhong Tinghui

On 23 May 2008, International Court of Justice delivered its judgment, and determined that Singapore held the sovereignty over Pedra Branca, solving the territorial dispute between Singapore and Malaysia. The case can use for reference.

Pedra Branca, located at 1° 19′ 48″ N and 104° 24′ 27″ E, is an island with an area of about 8,560 square metres (92,100 sq ft). It is approximately 24 nautical miles (44 km; 28 mi) to the east of Singapore; 7.7 nautical miles (14.3 km; 8.9 mi) south of Johor, Malaysia; and 7.6 nautical miles (14.1 km; 8.7 mi) north of Bintan, Indonesia.

On 21 December 1979, the Director of National Mapping of Malaysia published a map entitled Territorial Waters and Continental Shelf Boundaries of Malaysia showing Pedra Branca to be within itsterritorial waters. Singapore argued in a diplomatic note of 14 February 1980 and asked for the map to be corrected.

The dispute was not resolved by an exchange of correspondence and intergovernmental talks in 1993 and 1994. In the first round of talks in February 1993 the issue of sovereignty over Middle Rocks and South Ledge was also raised. Malaysia and Singapore therefore agreed to submit the dispute to the International Court of Justice (ICJ), signing a Special Agreement for this purpose in February 2003 and notifying the Court of it in July 2003.

The case was heard at the Peace Palace in The Hague between 6 and 23 November 2007. The International Court determined that Singapore held the sovereignty over Pedra Branca, and Malaysia retained sovereignty over

Middle Rocks. As for South Ledge, it belonged to the state which owned the territorial waters in which it is located.

The efforts of the Justice Secretary and the Ministry of Foreign Affairs contributed to the victory of Singapore, as well as the sincere cooperation of all government departments and the international lawyers' group. This case sets a good example to solve territorial dispute by the trail of third party.

To sum up, it provides a solution to promote the peaceful development of international society. We can also get a lesson from this case that it may take ten or much longer years to prepare before the international court accepts a case. So what shall we do? Here are some advices:

(1) Strengthen the education of law, raise public awareness;

(2) Scientifically utilize existing resources to enhance the management of archives;

(3) Close cooperation between government departments is of vital importance.

云南农特产品加工业对东盟贸易中的专利战略初探

杨 静[*] 高崇慧[**]

内容摘要 云南与东盟国家在农特产品加工领域的专利技术方面各具特点和优势,在对东盟贸易中,农特产品行业应当根据东盟相关产业的专利现状和竞争态势,制定实施专利战略,以提升产业竞争力,形成区域特色和竞争优势。

关键词:农特产品加工业;东盟;专利战略

农特产品加工业在云南省对外贸易中占据重要地位。近年来,云南积极参与中国—东盟自由贸易区建设,"蔬菜换石油"、"鲜花换水果"、"冷果换热果"的贸易进展顺利,对外开放势头强劲。随着 2010 年 7 月云南桥头堡建设战略的启动实施,又给云南省农特产品加工业带来重大利好。拓展贸易离不开知识产权的保护,专利战略为行业发展保驾护航,本文拟从专利信息分析的角度探讨云南农特产品加工业对东盟贸易中的基本策略。

一、云南农特产品加工业专利申请现状

《云南省新型工业化重点产业发展纲要》提出重点发展以农产品为原料的糖、茶、畜禽、果蔬等栽培及实施技术等四个领域的农特产品加工业。该四个技术领域国际专利分类号分别为 C13(糖类产品制备技术)、A23F(茶叶产品制备技术)、A22(畜禽产品制备技术),以及 A01G(果蔬等栽培及实施技术)。通过对国家知识产权局专利数据库进行检索,截至 2009 年,云南省在这四个领域的专利申请及构成状况如下表:

---

* 杨静,云南财经大学法学院副教授,同济大学博士研究生。

** 高崇慧,云南财经大学法学院教授。

表 1　云南省农特产品加工领域的专利申请及构成

农特产品加工	C13(糖类产品制备技术)	A23F(茶叶产品制备技术)	A22(畜禽产品制备技术)	A01G(果蔬等栽培及实施技术)
发明申请	16	205	0	280
实用新型	21	45	3	202
总数	37	250	3	482

云南省 2000—2009 年农特产品加工各领域专利年度申请趋势如下：

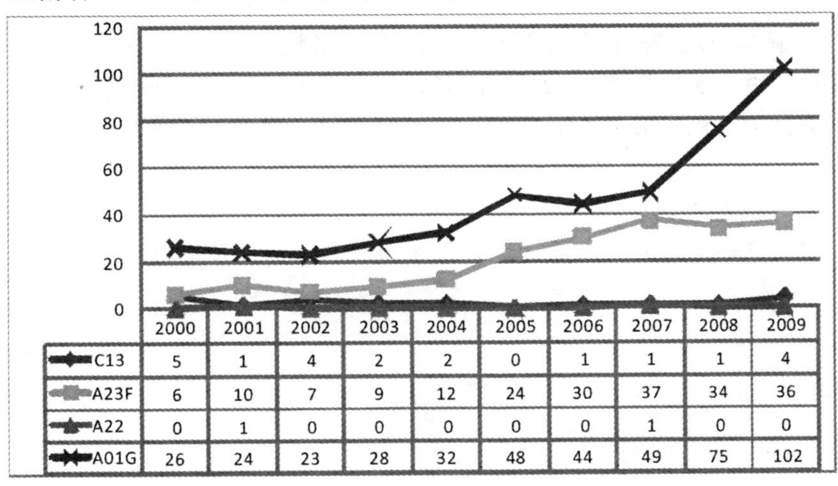

	2000	2001	2002	2003	2004	2005	2006	2007	2008	2009
C13	5	1	4	2	2	0	1	1	1	4
A23F	6	10	7	9	12	24	30	37	34	36
A22	0	1	0	0	0	0	0	1	0	0
A01G	26	24	23	28	32	48	44	49	75	102

图 1　云南省农特产品加工各领域专利(包括发明和实用新型)年度申请趋势

数据显示，截至 2009 年，云南省上述四领域发明专利申请数分别为糖类制备(C13)16 件，茶叶制备(A23F)205 件，畜禽产品加工(A22)0 件，果蔬等栽培及实施(A01G)280 件，其中果蔬等栽培及实施和茶叶制备的申请量最大。糖类制备、茶叶制备及果蔬等栽培设施农业发明申请占专利申请总数分别为 43.2%，82%和 58.1%，表明茶叶制备专利申请的技术含量较高。从专利年度申请趋势上看，果蔬等栽培及实施技术和茶叶产品制备技术自 2005 年以来专利申请量大幅上升，犹以果蔬等栽培及实施技术上升趋势明显，两领域均呈现出明显的朝阳产业趋势，说明云南省在果蔬栽培设施农业及茶叶产品技术上具有较好的技术基础，相关主体也对专利技术给予高度重视，近年来加大了专利申请的力度；而糖类和畜禽产品类加工技术专利申请增长不明显，专利申请少，多年来一直在低位徘徊，尤其是畜禽产品加工技术没有一件发明专利申请，截至 2009 年全省仅有 3 件实用新型专利申请，说明在这两个领域云南省知识产权市场控制和技术竞争力较弱；另据资料显示，云南省申请农特产

品加工技术领域专利的单位主要是科研院所,企业专利申请数量少,不利于专利技术的转化实施。

二、东盟五国农特产品加工业专利分析①

(一)新加坡②

1. 新加坡农特产品加工领域发明专利申请数

新加坡只保护发明,不保护实用新型专利,因而该国专利申请均为发明专利。通过数据检索发现,截至 2009 年,新加坡申请数为:糖类制备(C13)32 件、茶叶制备(A23F)71 件、畜禽产品加工(A22)14 件、果蔬等栽培及实施(A01G)76 件。

图 2 是新加坡农特产品加工技术领域专利申请的年度趋势。

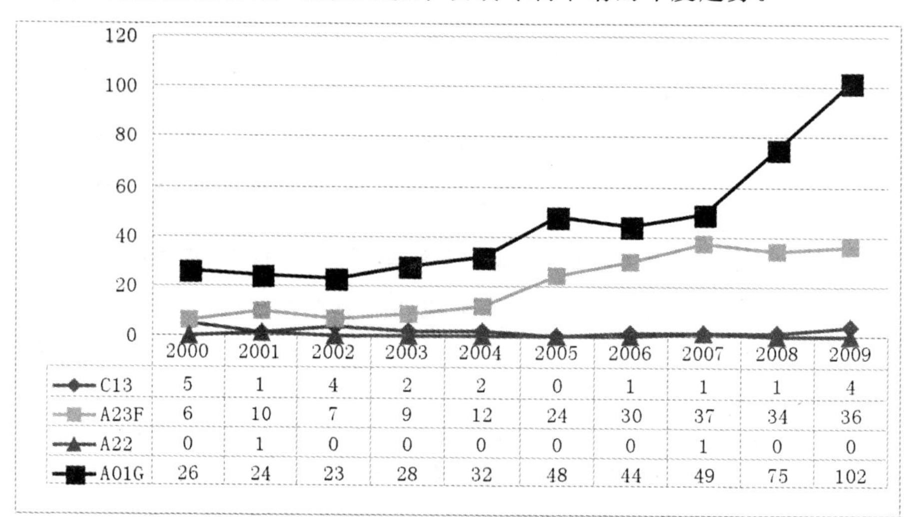

	2000	2001	2002	2003	2004	2005	2006	2007	2008	2009
C13	5	1	4	2	2	0	1	1	1	4
A23F	6	10	7	9	12	24	30	37	34	36
A22	0	1	0	0	0	0	0	1	0	0
A01G	26	24	23	28	32	48	44	49	75	102

图 2　新加坡农特产品加工技术领域专利申请年度趋势

---

① 目前东盟十国中只有新加坡、泰国、菲律宾、印度尼西亚、越南等五国建立起比较完备、方便的本国专利申请的数据库,故本文相关数据仅涉及上述 5 个国家,并且由于专利申请文件公开时间的延迟,未能获取 2009 年以后的专利申请数据。

② 新加坡数据来源:http://www.ipos.gov.sg/topNav/hom/,访问日期:2010 年 12 月。

2. 新加坡农特产品加工技术领域专利形势分析

新加坡农特产品加工领域专利申请数与其他技术领域动辄上千的申请数相比，数量较小，与新加坡作为城市国家，农业基础薄弱的国情相符。数据显示，1995—2007 年，C13 领域除 1998—2001 年申请量为 0 外，其他年份每年均有少量申请，申请人主要来自美国，其他国家在近年的申请量很少，表明制糖业在新加坡并非重点产业，发展受限，技术发展日趋成熟，近年来没有大的突破。A23F 领域多年来平稳发展，但 2005 年申请量有所增加，达到峰值 11 件，主要来自于日本的申请（当年有 8 件），说明日本看好新加坡的茶产品市场。瑞士雀巢公司在该领域的申请量达 21 件，分布于 1999—2006 年，表明该公司一直关注新加坡茶叶产品制备领域。A22 领域的申请 1995 年 2 件，1999 年 3 件，2004 年 2 件，呈点状分布，说明新加坡畜禽产品制备业并不发达。A01G 申请量较为平均，每年都有但数量都很少，同样说明新加坡该领域的竞争并不激烈。中国在新加坡农特产品加工领域尚无专利申请。

综上，农特产品加工业不是新加坡的重点产业，专利申请总量少，不过在 A23F 和 A01G 领域具有一定的技术优势，这种技术优势主要为瑞士、美国、日本等发达国家所把持。

（二）印尼[①]

1. 印尼农特产品加工技术领域专利申请数

截至 2009 年，印尼农特产品加工领域申请量为糖类制备（C13）126 件（其中发明 125 件），茶叶制备（A23F）64 件（发明 63 件），畜禽产品加工（A22）13 件（发明 11 件），果蔬等栽培及实施（A01G）34 件（发明 32 件），与新加坡相比，C13 申请量较大，A23F 和 A22 相差不多，A01G 的申请量少。印尼各项申请中发明专利占绝大部分，说明申请的技术水平较高。

图 3 是印尼农特产品加工领域专利申请年度趋势。

2. 印尼农特产品加工技术领域专利形势分析

从 1995—2007 年各领域专利申请的年度趋势上看，C13 领域 2002 年以前每年均有一定的申请数，数量有起伏但变化不大，自 2003 年起，申请量逐年增加，并在 2006 年达到峰值 19 件，表明近年来印尼制糖业的竞争加剧，跨国公司专利申请的力度加大。A23F 领域的专利申请 2003 年以前在低位徘徊，

---

① 印尼数据来源：http://www.dgip.go.id/ebscript/publicportal.cgi?.ucid=2715，访问日期：2010 年 12 月。

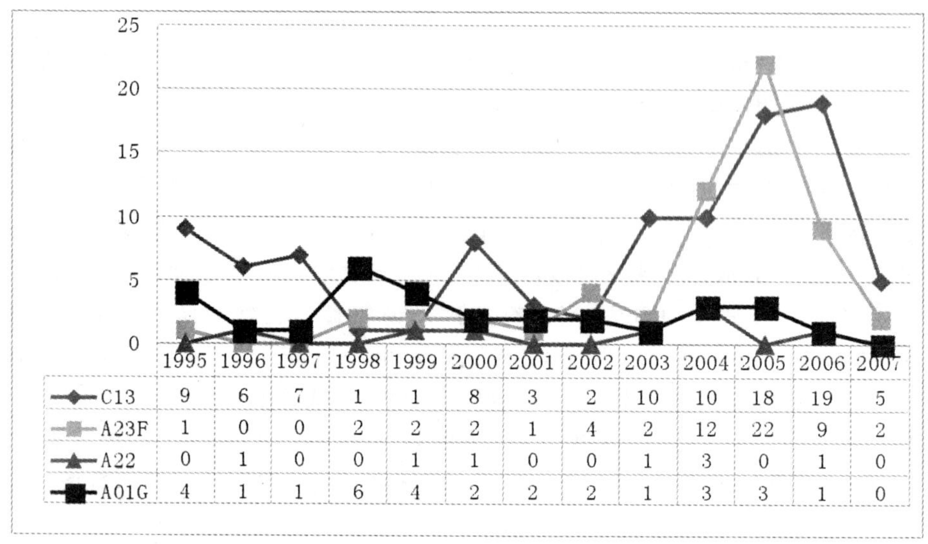

	1995	1996	1997	1998	1999	2000	2001	2002	2003	2004	2005	2006	2007
C13	9	6	7	1	1	8	3	2	10	10	18	19	5
A23F	1	0	0	2	2	2	1	4	2	12	22	9	2
A22	0	1	0	0	1	1	0	0	1	3	0	1	0
A01G	4	1	1	6	4	2	2	2	1	3	3	1	0

图 3　印尼农特产品加工领域专利申请年度趋势

但自 2004 年开始专利申请大幅增加,2005 年达到 22 件,此后有所回落。A22 领域多年来的专利申请均在低位徘徊,表明印尼畜禽产品制备业并不发达。A01G 领域 1995—2006 年每年均有一定数量的申请,但件数不多,变化不大,表明相关产业平稳运行,技术优势并不明显。

综上,印尼在糖类产品制备技术和茶叶产品制备两个领域具备一定的产业基础,拥有一定的技术领先优势,而畜禽产品制备技术及果蔬等栽培及实施业专利申请数少,竞争不激烈,对于这个人口众多的农业大国来说,这两个产业仍然有较大的发展空间。

(三)菲律宾①

1. 菲律宾农特产品加工技术领域专利申请及授权统计

截至 2009 年,菲律宾农特产品加工领域申请量为糖类制备(C13)88 件(其中发明 72 件),茶叶制备(A23F)86 件(发明 56 件),畜禽产品加工(A22)43 件(发明 33 件),果蔬等栽培及实施(A01G)98 件(发明 49 件),与印尼相比,除了 C13 申请量少于印尼外,A23F、A22 和 A01G 领域的申请量都较高,尤其是 A22 和 A01G 领域的申请量比较大。其中发明申请比例最高的是

① 菲律宾数据来源:http://ipophil.gov.ph/,访问日期:2010 年 12 月。

C13，占 81.82%；发明授权比例最高的是 A22，占 90.91%，说明该领域专利申请的技术水平较高。

图 4 是菲律宾农特产品加工技术领域专利申请年度趋势。

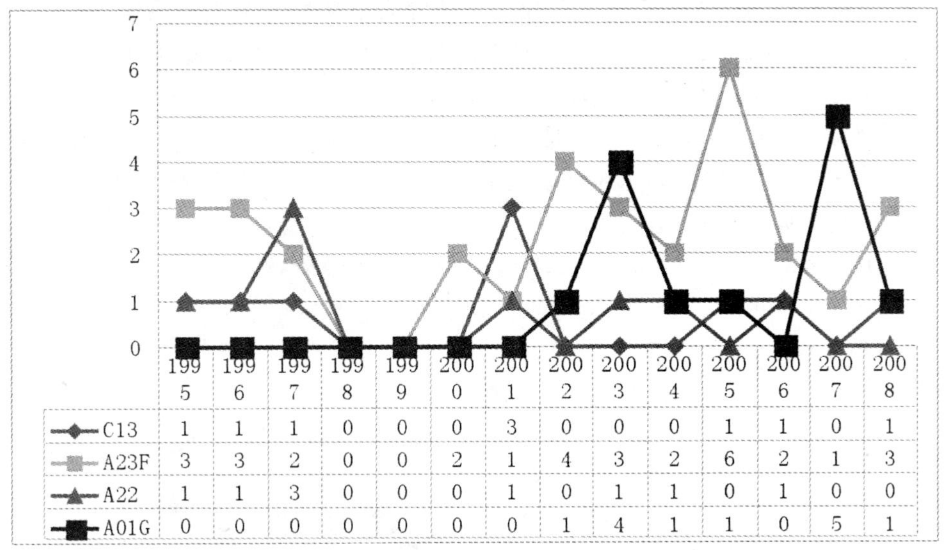

	1995	1996	1997	1998	1999	2000	2001	2002	2003	2004	2005	2006	2007	2008
C13	1	1	1	0	0	0	3	0	0	0	1	1	0	1
A23F	3	3	2	0	0	2	1	4	3	2	6	2	1	3
A22	1	1	3	0	0	0	1	0	1	1	0	1	0	0
A01G	0	0	0	0	0	0	0	1	4	1	1	0	5	1

图 4　菲律宾农特产品加工领域专利申请年度趋势

2. 菲律宾农特产品加工领域专利形势分析

从 1995—2007 年各领域专利申请的年度趋势上看，C13 和 A22 领域多年来的申请量均很少，在 0～3 件之间徘徊，表明菲律宾制糖业和畜禽产品制备业技术趋于成熟，缺乏创新。A01G 除 2003 和 2007 年申请量有所突破外（2003 年 4 件，2007 年 5 件），其余年份申请量多为 0 或仅有 1 件，该领域虽然申请总数有 98 件，但大部分是 1995 年以前的申请，并且发明申请仅占 50%，因而从总体上看，菲律宾在该领域的技术优势也并不明显。A23F 领域多年来基本每年均有一定数量的申请，表明跨国公司（主要是瑞士雀巢公司）一直关注菲律宾茶叶产品制备业，注重该领域的技术开发和保护。

综上，菲律宾在茶叶产品制备领域具备一定的产业基础，拥有一定的技术领先优势，而制糖业、畜禽产品制备业及果蔬等栽培及实施业近年来专利申请数少，表现平淡，产业趋于成熟。

(四)泰国[①]

1. 泰国农特产品加工领域发明专利申请数

截至2009年,泰国农特产品加工领域发明申请量为糖类产品制备(C13)256件,茶叶制备(A23F)70件,畜禽产品加工(A22)28件,果蔬等栽培及实施(A01G)116件,与其他几个东盟国家相比,A23F和A22的申请量相差不大,但C13和A01G领域的申请量是几个国家中最大的,尤其是C13领域,申请量达256件,是申请量第二位的印尼的两倍还多,表明泰国在制糖领域拥有明显的技术优势。

图5是泰国农特产品加工领域专利申请年度趋势。

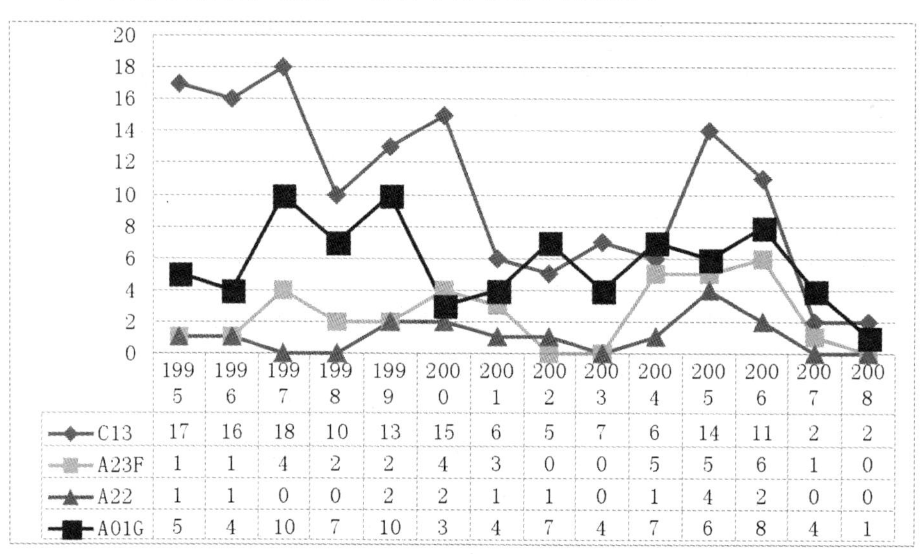

	1995	1996	1997	1998	1999	2000	2001	2002	2003	2004	2005	2006	2007	2008
C13	17	16	18	10	13	15	6	5	7	6	14	11	2	2
A23F	1	1	4	2	2	4	3	0	0	5	5	6	1	0
A22	1	1	0	0	2	2	1	1	0	1	4	2	0	0
A01G	5	4	10	7	10	3	4	7	4	7	6	8	4	1

图5 泰国农特产品加工技术领域专利申请总量年度趋势

2. 泰国农特产品加工技术领域专利形势分析

从1995—2007年各领域专利申请的年度趋势上看,C13制糖业专利申请2000年以前在高位运行,2001—2004年申请量有所下降,2005年后申请量又有所增加,表明制糖业仍然是泰国重要产业,不断有创新技术出现,行业知识产权保护意识强。A23F和A22领域多年来的申请量均很少,在0~6件之间徘徊,表明泰国制茶业和畜禽产品制备业技术趋于成熟,缺乏创新。A01G(果

① 泰国数据来源:http://www.ipthailand.org/,访问日期:2010年12月。

蔬等栽培及实施技术)除1997年和1999年申请量有所突破，达到10件外，其余年份差别不大，显示该行业平稳发展。

综上，泰国在制糖业具备较好的产业基础，拥有较强的技术领先优势，果蔬等栽培及实施业也具备一定的技术基础，稳步发展，而茶产品制备业、畜禽产品制备业技术趋于成熟，近年来专利申请数少，表现平淡。

(五)越南[①]

1. 越南农特产品加工技术领域专利申请数

截至2009年，越南农特产品加工领域申请量为糖类制备(C13)16件，茶叶制备(A23F)38件，畜禽产品加工(A22)8件，果蔬等栽培及设施(A01G)43件，与其余东盟四国相比，除A01G申请量超过印尼外，其他领域的申请量都是最少的。

图6是越南农特产品加工领域专利申请年度趋势。

	1995	1996	1997	1998	1999	2000	2001	2002	2003	2004	2005	2006	2007	2008
C13	0	0	2	1	4	0	0	0	0	0	0	1	4	1
A23F	0	3	2	0	0	0	1	0	1	0	0	10	16	1
A22	1	1	0	0	1	3	0	0	0	0	0	0	0	1
A01G	0	1	5	4	2	2	1	1	0	2	1	7	6	6

图6 越南农特产品加工领域专利申请年度趋势

2. 越南农特产品加工领域专利形势分析

越南C13和A22领域的专利申请多年来在一致在低位徘徊，表明越南制

① 越南数据来源：http://www.s-i-asia.com/，访问日期：2010年12月。

糖业和畜禽产品制备业技术不强,产业发展成熟,缺乏创新。A23F 领域 1995—2005 年的专利申请量在 0～3 件之间徘徊,但 2006 年和 2007 年申请量增幅明显,分别为 10 件和 16 件,表明竞争者看好越南该行业的发展,加大了技术研发和专利申请的力度,获得了技术领先优势。A01G 领域自 1996 年以来每年均保持一定的申请数,数量有起伏但变化不大,表明行业发展平稳,竞争者一直予以关注。

综上,越南除了 A01G(果蔬等栽培及实施业)领域具有一定的专利申请量外,其余几个农特产品加工领域的专利申请量少,技术优势不明显,竞争不激烈。

三、云南农特产品加工业对东盟贸易中的专利战略

东盟五国数据显示,在农特产品加工领域,新加坡专利申请总量较少;印尼在糖类产品制备技术和茶叶产品制备两个领域具备一定的产业基础,拥有一定的技术领先优势,而畜禽产品制备技术及果蔬等栽培及实施业专利申请数少,竞争不激烈;菲律宾在茶叶产品制备领域具备一定的产业基础,拥有一定的技术领先优势,而制糖业、畜禽产品制备业及果蔬等栽培及实施业近年来专利申请数少,表现平淡,产业趋于成熟。泰国在制糖业具备较好的产业基础,拥有较强的技术领先优势,果蔬等栽培及实施业也具备一定的技术基础,稳步发展,而茶产品制备业、畜禽产品制备业技术近年来专利申请数少。越南除了 A01G(果蔬等栽培及实施业)领域具有一定的专利申请量外,其余几个农特产品加工领域的专利申请量少,技术优势不明显,竞争不激烈。另外,截至 2010 年 12 月,云南省农特产品加工业未在东盟五国申请过专利。

下表是截至 2009 年云南与东盟五国农特产品加工领域专利申请量比较[①]:

① 由于专利申请数是一个动态变化的数字,并且基于专利申请公开的滞后性,因此,上述数据会有一定的变化,但是能反映各方基本情况。

表 2　云南与东盟五国农特产品加工领域专利申请数比较

国别	云南		新加坡（发明）	印尼（发明）	菲律宾（发明）	泰国（发明）	越南（发明＋实用新型）
类型	发明	实用新型					
C13	16	21	32	125	72	256	16
A23F	205	45	71	63	56	70	38
A22	0	3	14	11	33	28	8
A01G	280	202	76	32	49	116	43
总数	501	271	193	231	210	470	105

总体上看，与东盟五国相比，目前云南省农特产品加工业在茶叶制备和果蔬等栽培及实施业技术领域的专利申请量大，已经具备一定的技术基础，应当进一步提升技术水平，但在糖类产品和畜禽产品领域的知识产权市场控制和技术竞争力较弱。根据目前的情况，在对东盟贸易中，云南省农特产品加工业应当采取下列专利战略：

1. 进攻型专利战略

进攻型专利战略是指企业积极主动地将开发出来的技术及时申请专利并取得专利权，利用专利权保护手段抢占、垄断市场。它是利用专利制度建立并扩大自己的专利阵地，取得市场竞争主动权，避免受制于人的前提和条件。对于已经掌握了一批专利技术、具备技术比较优势的云南省茶叶制备及果蔬等栽培及实施业，在对东盟贸易中可以采取进攻型专利战略，加紧在目标市场申请专利，为将来占领市场铺平道路，同时还要注意申请外围专利筑起专利保护网。

2. 引进消化吸收再创新战略

引进消化吸收再创新模式是指通过转让或授权，引进现有的专利技术，然后再加以改造，变成自己的技术。此种创新模式主要针对云南省目前技术实力较弱，而东盟部分国家具有较好基础和技术领先优势的产业，如泰国、印尼的糖类制备业，菲律宾、泰国的畜禽加工业等。云南省相关产业在今后一段时期，可以走引进与创新相结合战略，引进相关技术，同时注重消化吸收和再创新，形成自主知识产权。

3. 技术创新专利战略

面对东盟各国农特产品在自贸区市场的竞争，云南省农特产品加工业应当采取积极措施，加强技术创新，加大在农产品深加工技术领域的技术创新力

度,尽快形成更多的核心专利技术,提升产品竞争力。

例如,在茶叶深加工方面,可从茶饮料加工、新型茶饮料开发及制备新技术、茶叶天然产物的提取及利用技术方面加强研发,开发类黄酮化合物、茶多糖、茶氨酸等天然产物的提取技术及其新产品;在糖加工方面,加强蔗糖及其衍生物深加工技术,糖蜜酒精废液处理技术,糖蜜制乙醇技术,蔗渣造纸及纤维素生产技术的研发工作;在畜禽产品深加工技术领域,加强畜禽产品深加工技术的研发和畜禽副产品的综合开发利用,开辟产品深加工新用途的专利,适应市场需求;在果蔬深加工领域,大力发展果蔬深加工、贮藏保鲜以及"最少量加工"技术,开展果蔬功能成分提取技术、特色果蔬新型贮藏保鲜技术与设备、冻干果蔬、果蔬粉加工、果酒等果蔬发酵制品的技术攻关①。

4."产学研"合作创新战略

资料显示,云南省申请农特产品加工技术专利的单位主要是科研院所,包括中科院植物研究所,云南省农业科学院茶叶研究所及生物技术研究所,云南农业大学,云南轻工业科学研究所等科研单位。应当注重采用"产学研"合作创新战略,一方面可以促使科研院所及高校的科研资源得到有效利用,科研与市场有效结合,提高科研成果转化实施率,另一方面可以使企业获得有利的持续性的技术支撑,比如在茶叶深加工技术领域,即可以通过科研机构提供技术支撑,联合具有茶叶深加工实力的合作企业,拉长产业链。

5. 专利利用战略

专利文献上记载的专利信息是提供各种技术信息的最佳信息源。农特产品加工业应当加强对东盟贸易伙伴专利申请文献的监测,了解其专利申请态势,把握其技术发展方向,以便采取相应对策;在技术创新的过程中,应当积极查阅专利文献中已公开的、详细的技术信息,从中找到可资借鉴的信息或解决问题的方法,从而收到迎刃而解,事半功倍的效果;再有,在采取引进消化吸收再创新的过程中,对专利信息的调查和研究也非常重要,可以避免风险和盲目投入。

专利权具有时间限制,另外,国内不少农特产品加工机构和个人申请的专利存在期满前已失效现象,其中有很多是因为未缴年费而导致专利权终止。有技术需求的企业完全可以通过调研后对仍有价值的失效专利和期满专利加以利用。再有,专利除了具有时间性外,还具有地域性,只在授权的国家或地区才有效。据此,对于超过优先权期在我国没有申请专利的国外技术,完全可

---

① 李义敢:《云南省知识产权战略研究》,云南民族出版社 2006 年版,第 139 页。

以在我国使用，不构成专利侵权。

6. 建立专利联盟，推行“绿色”专利标准

云南一些大型的农特产品企业，如茶叶加工业，三七产业，花卉产业，橡胶产业，可以通过强强联合的方式，建立专利联盟，既能充分发挥集体协作的优势，又能加强成员运用知识产权战略的能力；同时还可推行“绿色”专利标准，采用环保、绿色的生产工艺流程，提升产品的档次，提高市场竞争力，实现最佳经济效益。

总之，云南与东盟国家在农特产品加工领域的专利技术方面各具特点和优势，面临自由贸易区快速发展及云南桥头堡建设启动的历史性机遇，面对贸易伙伴的合作与竞争，农特产品加工业亟须加快实施专利战略，培育核心技术，形成明显区域特色和竞争优势，以实现更快更好的产业发展，获取自由贸易区市场竞争中的有利地位。

Probe into the Patent Strategy of Yunnan Agricultural Product Processing Industry in its Trade with ASEAN

Yang Jing* Gao Chonghui**

Abstract: Yunnan and ASEAN countries have characteristics and advantages respectively in the patented technology of agricultural products processing field. In trade with ASEAN, agricultural products industry should develop patent strategy based on the patent status and competitive situation of ASEAN-related industries so as to enhance industrial competitiveness and form regional features and competitive advantages.

Keywords: Agricultural Products Processing Industry; ASEAN; Patent Strategy

The agricultural products processing industry occupies an important position in the Foreign Trade of Yunnan Province. In recent years, Yunnan actively participates in the construction of China-ASEAN Free Trade Area, and the trade of "vegetable for oil", "flowers for fruit" and "cold fruit for hot fruit" are progressing smoothly with strong opening-up momentum. With the implementation of Yunnan gateway strategy in July 2010, it has brought a great benefit for agricultural product processing industry in Yunnan Province. Expansion of trade cannot be separated from the protection of

---

* Yang Jing, associate professor of law school of Yunnan university of finance and economics, PhD student of Tongji University.

** Gao Chonghui, professor of Law School of Yunnan University of Finance and Economics.

intellectual property rights, and patent strategy escorts the development of the industry. This paper intends to explore the basic strategy of Yunnan agricultural products processing industry in its trade with ASEAN from the perspective of patent information analysis.

I. THE STATUS QUO OF PATENT APPLICATION OF YUNNAN AGRICULTURAL PRODUCTS PROCESSING INDUSTRY

"Program for the Development of the new industrialization key industries in Yunnan Province" focuses on the development of agricultural products processing industry in four areas of sugar, tea, livestock and poultry, fruit and vegetable cultivation and implementation technology with agricultural products as raw materials. The International Patent Classifications of these four technical areas are C13 (carbohydrate product preparation technology), A23F (tea products preparation technology), A22 (livestock and poultry products preparation technology) and A01G (fruit and vegetable cultivation and implementation technology). By retrieval of the patent database of State Intellectual Property Office, Yunnan patent application and constituting condition in the four areas are shown in the following table as of 2009:

Table 1: Patent Application and Constitution in Yunnan Agricultural Products Processing Field

agricultural products processing	C13 (carbohydrate product preparation technology)	A23F (tea products preparation technology)	A22 (livestock and poultry products preparation technology)	A01G (fruit and vegetable cultivation and implementation technology)
Invention application	16	205	0	280
Utility model	21	45	3	202
Sum	37	250	3	482

Annual patent application trends of Yunnan agricultural products pro-

cessing fields from 2000 to 2009 are as follows:

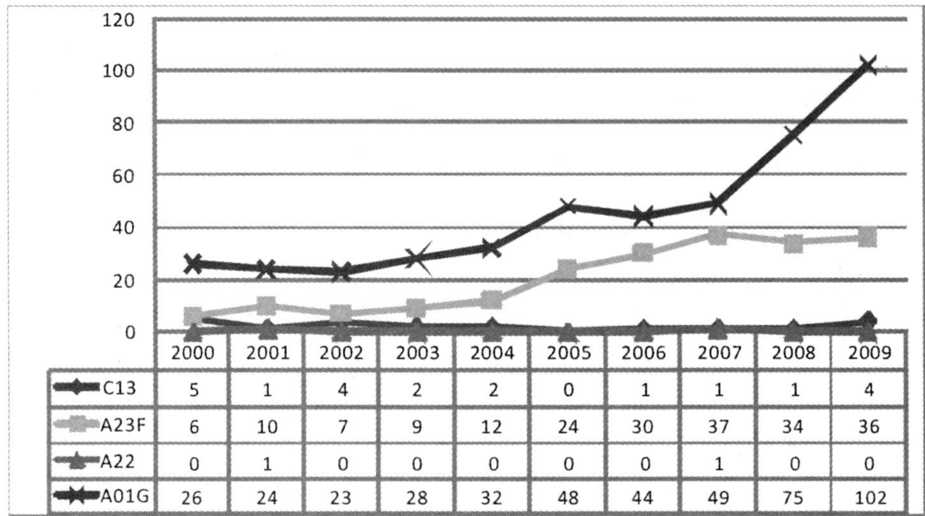

	2000	2001	2002	2003	2004	2005	2006	2007	2008	2009
C13	5	1	4	2	2	0	1	1	1	4
A23F	6	10	7	9	12	24	30	37	34	36
A22	0	1	0	0	0	0	0	1	0	0
A01G	26	24	23	28	32	48	44	49	75	102

Figure 1: Annual Patent Application Trends of Yunnan Agricultural Products Processing Fields (including the invention and utility model)

The above data show that Yunnan invention patent applications in the above four areas are 16 carbohydrate preparations (C13), 205 tea preparations (A23F), no livestock and poultry products processing (A22) and 280 fruits and vegetables cultivation and implementation (A01G) respectively as of 2009, during which fruits and vegetables cultivation and implementation, and tea preparation have maximum applications. Agriculture invention application of sugar preparation, tea preparation and fruit and vegetable cultivation facilities account for 43.2%, 82% and 58.1% in the total number of patent applications respectively, which indicates that the technical content of tea preparation patent application is higher.

From annual patent application trends, patent application of fruit and vegetable cultivation and implementation technology and tea products preparation technology have surged obviously since 2005, among which fruits and vegetables cultivation and implementation technology rises more remarkably. The two areas are showing the obvious sunrise-industry trend, which reflects that Yunnan Province has a good technical base in the fruit and vegetable cultivation and implementation and tea products technology. In addition, rele-

vant departments also attached high priority to the patented technology and increased the strength of patent application in recent years.

However, the growth of patent application in sugars and livestock products processing technology is not obvious. Patent applications in these two fields are less and have been at low levels over the years, and livestock products processing technology has no invention patent application. As of 2009, the province only had three utility model patent applications indicating weaker intellectual property market control and technological competitiveness of Yunnan Province in these two areas; according to the data, the applicants that apply for patents in the agricultural products processing technology field in Yunnan Province are mainly scientific research institutes, while corporate patent applications are less, which is not conducive to the transformation and implementation of the patented technology.

Ⅱ. ANALYSIS OF AGRICULTURAL PRODUCTS PROCESSING INDUSTRY PATENT OF FIVE ASEAN COUNTRIES①

A. Singapore②

1. Invention patent application numbers of Singapore agricultural products processing field

Singapore only protects the invention but does not protect utility model patents, and thus its patent applications are all invention patents. Through data retrieval, as of 2009, Singapore applications were 32 carbohydrate preparations (C13), 71 tea preparations (A23F), 14 livestock and poultry products processing (A22) and 76 fruits and vegetables cultivation and implementation (A01G).

---

① Only five countries , Singapore, Thailand, Philippines, Indonesia and Vietnam in ten ASEAN countries have established complete and convenient database for their patent applications currently, so related data of this paper only refer to the above five countries. Besides, due to the delay of the public time of patent application documents, it fails to obtain patent application data after 2009.

② Singapore data sources: http://www. ipos. gov. sg/topNav/hom/, visited in December 2010.

The following figure shows the annual trend of patent applications of Singapore agricultural products processing technology field.

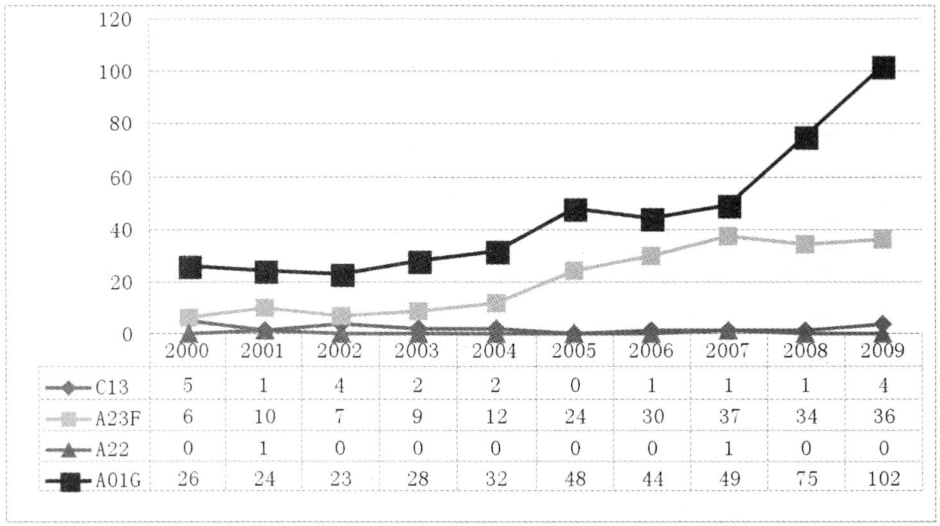

	2000	2001	2002	2003	2004	2005	2006	2007	2008	2009
C13	5	1	4	2	2	0	1	1	1	4
A23F	6	10	7	9	12	24	30	37	34	36
A22	0	1	0	0	0	0	0	1	0	0
A01G	26	24	23	28	32	48	44	49	75	102

Figure 2: Annual patent application trend of Singapore agricultural products processing technology field

2. Situation analysis of the patents in Singapore agricultural products processing technology field

Compared to hundreds of thousands of applications in other technical fields, Singapore patent applications in the agricultural products processing field are less, which is consistent with the national conditions of weak agricultural foundation in Singapore as a city state. The data show that from 1995 to 2007, C13 field had a small amount of applications every year in addition to zero application from 1998 to 2001, and the applicants mainly come from the United States while other countries have few applications in recent years, which show that the sugar industry is not a key industry in Singapore. The development is limited, the technologies have matured increasingly, and there has been no major breakthrough in recent years.

A23F field has stable development for many years and the applications in 2005 increased to peak 11 which mainly came from the application of Japan (8), and it shows that Japan is optimistic about Singapore's tea products

market. Swiss Nestle Company's application amounted to 21 in the field which is distributed from 1999 to 2006, and it shows that the company has been concerned about the field of tea products preparation in Singapore. The application in the A22 field was 2 in 1995, 3 in 1999 and 2 in 2004 with punctiform distribution, which shows that livestock and poultry products preparation industry is not developed in Singapore. The A01G application is quite average and it has a small number every year, which also shows that the competition in the field is not fierce in Singapore. China still has no patent application in Singapore agricultural products processing field.

In summary, agricultural products processing industry is not a key industry in Singapore and it has less patent applications, but A23F and A01G fields have certain technical advantages which are mainly dominated by Switzerland, the United States, Japan and other developed countries.

B. Indonesia①

1. Patent Application Numbers in Indonesian Agricultural Products Processing Technology Field

As of 2009, applications in Indonesian agricultural products processing field were 126 carbohydrate preparations (C13) (125 inventions), 64 tea preparations (A23F) (63 inventions), 13 livestock products processing (A22) (11 inventions) and 34 fruits and vegetables cultivation and implementation (A01G) (32 inventions). Compared with Singapore, C13 has a bigger application number, and A23F and A22 are close to each other while A01G has fewer applications. Invention patents account for the vast majority in Indonesia applications indicating that the application has a higher technology level.

The following figure is the annual trend of patent applications in Indonesian agricultural products processing field.

① Indonesian data sources: http://www. dgip. go. id/ebscript/publicportal. cgi?. ucid=2715, visited in December 2010.

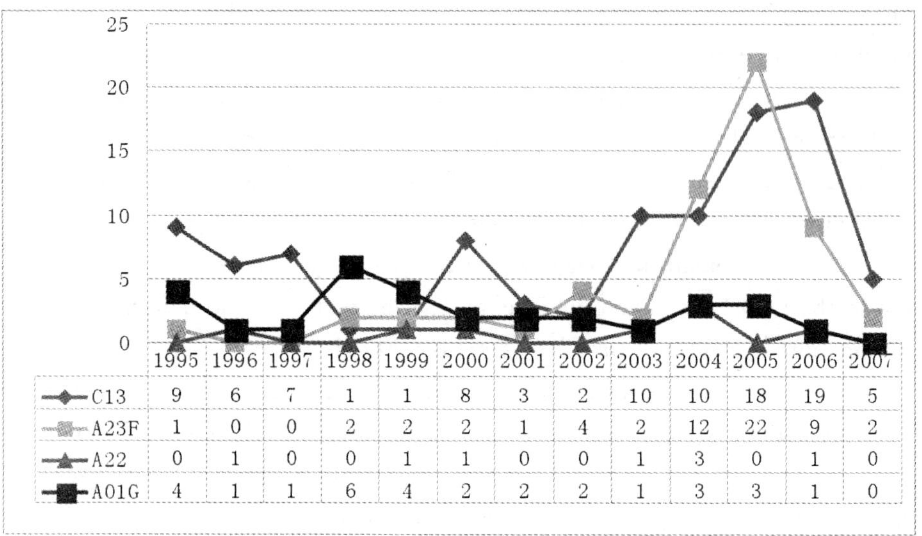

	1995	1996	1997	1998	1999	2000	2001	2002	2003	2004	2005	2006	2007
C13	9	6	7	1	1	8	3	2	10	10	18	19	5
A23F	1	0	0	2	2	2	1	4	2	12	22	9	2
A22	0	1	0	0	1	1	0	0	1	3	0	1	0
A01G	4	1	1	6	4	2	2	2	1	3	3	1	0

Figure 3: Annual Trend of Patent Applications in Indonesian Agricultural Products Processing Field

2. Situation Analysis of the Patents in Indonesian Agricultural Products Processing Technology Field

The annual trend of patent applications in various fields from 1995 to 2007 indicates that C13 field had a certain number of applications each year before 2002, and there were ups and downs but little change in the number. Since 2003, the application numbers have been increased year by year, and reached a peak of 19 in 2006, which indicates that the competition in sugar industry has been increasing in Indonesia in recent years and multinational corporations have strengthened the efforts in patent applications.

The patent application in the A23F field remained at low levels before 2003, but it showed a substantial increase since 2004 and reached to 22 in 2005 and then fell back thereafter. Patent applications have been at low levels in the A22 field over the years indicating that the livestock and poultry products preparation industry is not developed in Indonesia. A01G field had a certain number of applications each year from 1995 to 2006, but it has a few cases and little change, which indicates that the related industries run smoothly, and the technical advantage is not obvious.

In summary, Indonesia has certain industrial base in the two areas of sugar products preparation technology and tea products preparation with certain technical leading advantages, but the livestock and poultry products preparation technology and fruit and vegetable cultivation and implementation have fewer patent applications and less intense competition. For the populous agricultural country, these two industries still have larger development space.

C. Philippines①

1. Patent Applications and Authorization Statistics in Philippine Agricultural Products Processing Technology Field

As of 2009, the applications in Philippine agricultural products processing field were 88 carbohydrate preparations (C13) (including 72 inventions), 86 tea preparations (A23F) (56 inventions), 43 livestock products processing (A22) (33 inventions) and 98 fruit and vegetable cultivation and implementation (A01G) (49 inventions). Compared with Indonesia, except that the C13 application is less than Indonesia, applications in A23F, A22 and A01G fields are high, especially it has a larger application number in the A22 and A01G fields, among which C13 has the highest proportion of invention applications accounting for 81. 82%; A22 has the highest proportion of invention authorization accounting for 90. 91%, which shows that this field has a higher technical level in the patent applications.

The following figure(Figure 4) is the annual trends of patent applications in Philippine agricultural products processing technology field.

2. Situation Analysis of Patents in Philippine Agricultural Products Processing Field

The annual trend of patent application in various fields from 1995 to 2007 shows that the applications were fewer in the C13 and A22 fields over the years which hovered between 0 and 3, and it indicates that Philippine technology in sugar industry and livestock products preparation industry trends to be mature with a lack of innovation. The A01G application amount is 0 or 1 in the rest years in addition to the breakthrough of applications in

① Philippine data sources: http://ipophil. gov. ph/, visited in December 2010.

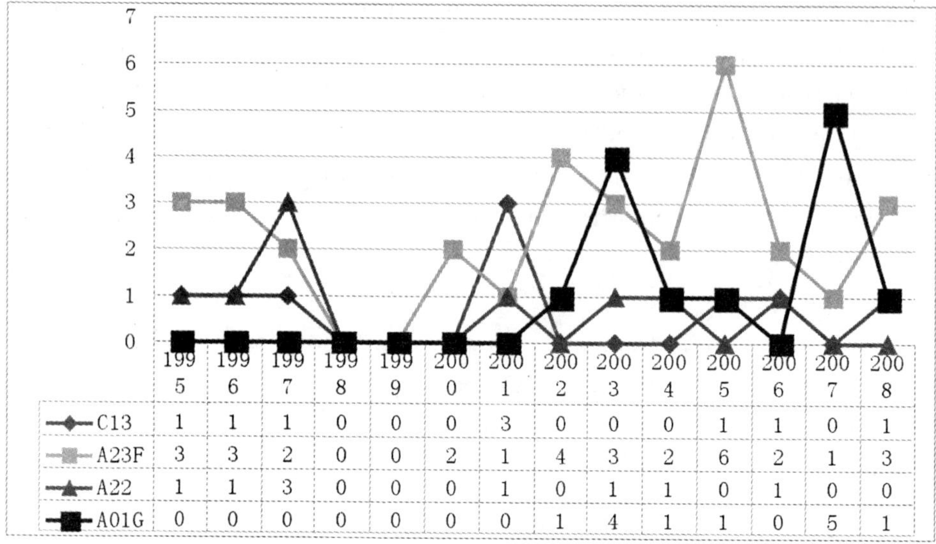

	1995	1996	1997	1998	1999	2000	2001	2002	2003	2004	2005	2006	2007	2008
C13	1	1	1	0	0	0	3	0	0	0	1	1	0	1
A23F	3	3	2	0	0	2	1	4	3	2	6	2	1	3
A22	1	1	3	0	0	0	1	0	1	1	0	1	0	0
A01G	0	0	0	0	0	0	0	1	4	1	1	0	5	1

Figure 4: Annual Trends of Patent Applications in Philippine Agricultural Products Processing Field

2003 and 2007 (2003:4; 2007:5). Although the total number of applications is 98 in this field, they were mostly applications before 1995, and the invention application only accounted for 50%. Therefore, Philippine technical advantage is not obvious in the field as a whole. A23F field basically has a certain number of applications each year over the years indicating that the multinational companies (mainly Swiss Nestle) have been concerned about the tea products preparation industry in Philippines and focus on the technology development and protection in this field.

In summary, the Philippines has certain industrial basis in the tea products preparation field and owns certain technical leading advantages, while the patent applications are fewer in the sugar industry, livestock and poultry products preparation industry and fruit and vegetable cultivation and implementation industry in recent years with lackluster development and the industries tend to be mature.

D. Thailand①

① Thai data sources: http://www.ipthailand.org/, visited in December 2010.

1. Invention Patent Applications in Thai Agricultural Products Processing Field

As of 2009, invention applications in Thai agricultural products processing field were 256 sugar products preparations (C13), 70 tea preparations (A23F), 28 livestock and poultry products processing (A22) and 116 fruit and vegetable cultivation and implementation (A01G). Compared with several other ASEAN countries, A23F and A22 applications are more or less, but the applications in the C13 and A01G fields are maximum in several countries, especially applications in the C13 field amount to 256, which is more than twice of Indonesia which is the second place in applications, and it indicates that Thailand has a clear technological advantage in the sugar field.

The following figure(Figure 5) is the annual trend of patent applications in Thai agricultural products processing field.

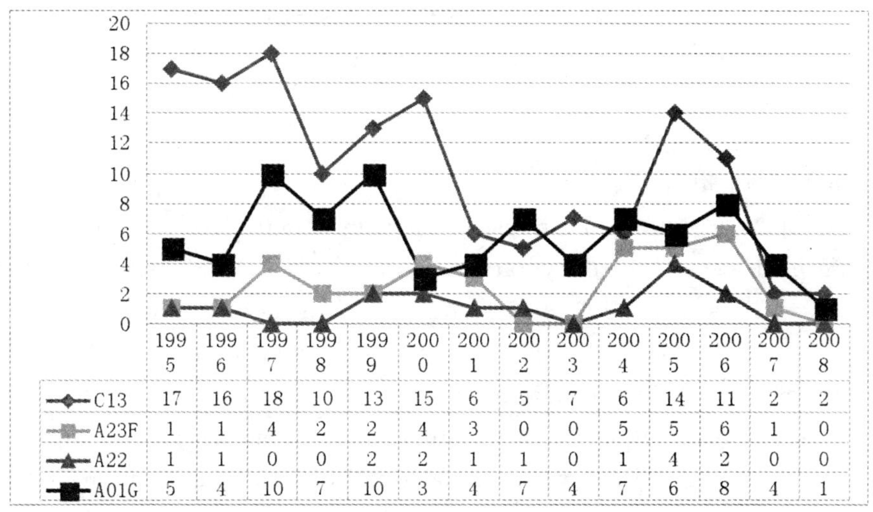

	1995	1996	1997	1998	1999	2000	2001	2002	2003	2004	2005	2006	2007	2008
C13	17	16	18	10	13	15	6	5	7	6	14	11	2	2
A23F	1	1	4	2	2	4	3	0	0	5	5	6	1	0
A22	1	1	0	0	2	2	1	1	0	1	4	2	0	0
A01G	5	4	10	7	10	3	4	7	4	7	6	8	4	1

Figure 5: Annual Trend of Patent Applications in Thai Agricultural Products Processing Technology Field

2. Situation Analysis of the Patents in Thai Agricultural Products Processing Technology Field

The annual trend of patent applications in various fields from 1995 to 2007 shows that the patent applications in C13 sugar industry kept a high

level before 2000 and declined from 2001 to 2004 and then increased after 2005, which indicates that the sugar industry is still an important industry in Thailand. The innovative technology appears constantly and the industry IPR protection awareness is strong. The applications in A23F and A22 fields are less over the years hovering between 0 to 6, which indicates that the tea industry and livestock and poultry products preparation technology in Thailand are getting mature and thus lacking innovation. A01G (fruits and vegetables cultivation and implementation technology) had less differences in rest years in addition to the application breakthrough (reaching 10) in 1997 and 1999, which shows the smooth development of the industry.

In summary, Thailand has a good industrial basis in the sugar industry and a strong technical leading advantage, fruit and vegetable cultivation and implementation industry also has certain technical basis with the steady development, while the technology in tea products preparation industry and livestock and poultry products preparation industry tends to be mature in recent years with less patent applications and lackluster achievement.

E. Vietnam①

1. Patent Applications in Vietnamese Agricultural Products Processing Technology Field

As of 2009, the applications in Vietnamese agricultural products processing field were 16 carbohydrate preparations (C13), 38 tea preparations (A23F), 8 livestock and poultry products processing (A22) and 43 fruit and vegetable cultivation and facilities (A01G). Compared with the abovementioned four ASEAN countries, all the applications of Vietnam in other areas are the fewest besides that its A01G applicationsurpasses Indonesia.

The following figure is the annual trend of patent application in Vietnamese agricultural products processing field.

2. Situation Analysis of Patents in Vietnamese Agricultural Products Processing Field

Vietnamese patent applications in C13 and A22 fields have kept at low levels over the years indicating that the technology of Vietnamese sugar in-

① Vietnamese data sources: http://www.s-i-asia.com/, visited in December 2010.

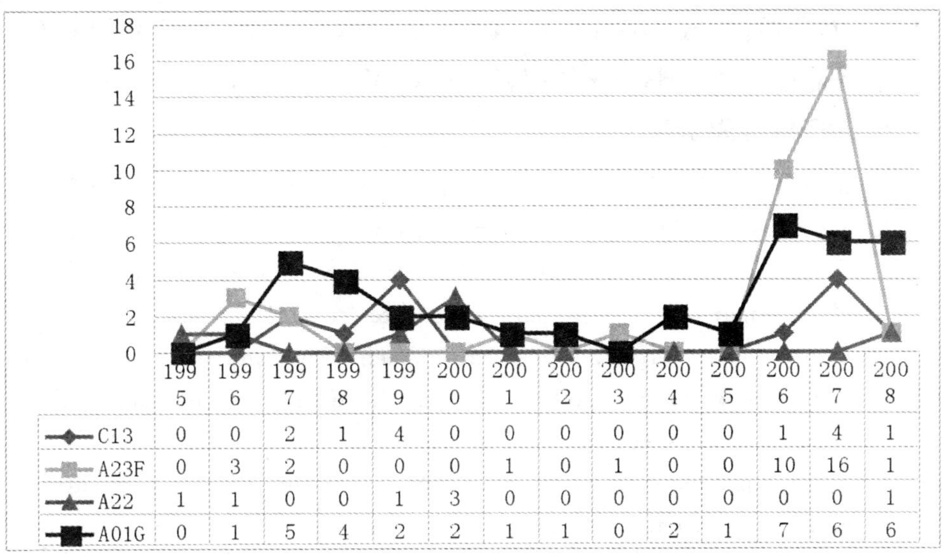

	1995	1996	1997	1998	1999	2000	2001	2002	2003	2004	2005	2006	2007	2008
C13	0	0	2	1	4	0	0	0	0	0	0	1	4	1
A23F	0	3	2	0	0	0	1	0	1	0	0	10	16	1
A22	1	1	0	0	1	3	0	0	0	0	0	0	0	1
A01G	0	1	5	4	2	2	1	1	0	2	1	7	6	6

Figure 6: Annual Trend of Patent Application in Vietnamese Agricultural Products Processing Field

dustry and livestock products preparation industry is not strong and the industries are mature with a lack of innovation. Patent applications in A23F field hovered between 0 to 3 from 1995 to 2005, but the applications in 2006 and 2007 were 10 and 16 respectively with obvious increase, which indicates that the competitors are optimistic about the development of this industry in Vietnam, strengthen the efforts in technology R & D and patent applications and obtain the technical leading advantage. A01G field maintains a certain number of applications every year since 1996, there are ups and downs but little change in the number, which indicates the steady development of the industry and competitors keep paying attention to them.

In summary, Vietnamese has a certain amount of patent applications in the A01G field (fruit and vegetable cultivation and implementation industry) , while the patent applications in the rest agricultural products processing fields are fewer, technical advantages are not obvious and the competition is not fierce.

Ⅲ. PATENT STRATEGY OF YUNNAN AGRICULTURAL PRODUCT PROCESSING INDUSTRY IN ITS TRADE WITH ASEAN

The data of the five ASEAN countries show that in the agricultural products processing field, Singapore has fewer total patent applications; Indonesia has certain industrial basis and technology leading advantage in the two fields of sugar products preparation and tea products preparation, while livestock and poultry products preparation technology and fruit and vegetable cultivation and implementation industry have fewer patent applications and the competition is not fierce. Philippines has certain industrial base in the field of tea products preparation and certain technical leading advantage, while the number of patent applications is small in the sugar industry, livestock and poultry products preparation industry and fruit and vegetable cultivation and implementation industry in recent years with lackluster development and increasingly mature industry.

Thailand has a good industrial base in the sugar industry and a strong technical leading advantage, fruit and vegetable cultivation and implementation industry also has certain technical basis with the steady development, while the tea product preparation industry and livestock and poultry products preparation industry have smaller number of patent applications in recent years. Vietnam has a certain amount of patent applications in the A01G field (fruit and vegetable cultivation and implementation industry) , while the patent applications in the rest agricultural products processing fields are fewer, technical advantage is not obvious and the competition is not fierce. In addition, as of December 2010, Yunnan agricultural products processing industry had not applied for patents in the five ASEAN countries. ①

The following table is the comparison of patent applications between Yunnan and five ASEAN countries in agricultural products processing field

---

① The number of patent applications is dynamically changing, and the publication of patent applications lags, so the above data will have some changes, but they can reflect the basic situation of the parties.

as of 2009:

Table 2: The Comparison of Patent Applications betweenYunnan and Five ASEAN Countries in Agricultural Products Processing Field

Country / type	Yunnan Invention	Yunnan Utility model	Singapore (Invention)	Indonesia (Invention)	Philippines (Invention)	Thailand (Invention)	Vietnam (Invention+Utility model)
C13	16	21	32	125	72	256	16
A23F	205	45	71	63	56	70	38
A22	0	3	14	11	33	28	8
A01G	280	202	76	32	49	116	43
Sum	501	271	193	231	210	470	105

Overall, compared with the five ASEAN countries, Yunnan agricultural product processing industry has the large amount of patent applications in the technology fields of tea preparation and fruits and vegetables cultivation and implementation industry. It already has some technical basis and should further enhance the technical level. However, the intellectual property rights market control and technical competitiveness in the fields of carbohydrate products and livestock products are weaker. According to the current situation, in its trade with ASEAN, Yunnan agricultural products processing industry should take the following patent strategies:

1. Offensive Patent Strategy

Offensive patent strategy means that the enterprises take the initiative to apply patents for the technology that they develop timely and obtain patents, and then use patent protection means to seize and monopolize the market. It uses the patent system to establish and expand their patent positions, gain the competitive initiative and avoid passive premise and conditions. For Yunnan tea preparation and fruit and vegetable cultivation and implementation industry with a number of patented technologies and comparative technology advantages, they can take the offensive patent strategy in its trade with ASEAN, step up to apply for patents in the target market and pave the way for the future occupation of market. At the same time, they should apply for peripheral patent to build patent protection network.

2. Introduction, Digestion, Absorption and Re-Innovation Strategy

Introduction, digestion, absorption and re-innovation mode is the introduction

of existing patented technology through transfer or authorization and then transformation to turn into its own technology. This innovative mode mainly focuses on industries in which Yunnan Province has weaker technology currently while some ASEAN countries have better foundation and leading-edge technology, such as Thai and Indonesian sugars preparation industry and Philippine and Thai livestock and poultry processing industry. The related industries in Yunnan can carry out the strategy of the combination of introduction and innovation in the future period to introduce related technologies and focus on the digestion and absorption and re-innovation so as to form independent intellectual property rights.

3. Technological Innovation Patent Strategy

In the face of the competition of agricultural products of ASEAN countries in the FTA market, Yunnan agricultural products processing industry should take active measures, strengthen technological innovation, increase the technology innovation in agricultural deep processing technology fields, form the core patented technology as soon as possible and enhance the competitiveness of their products.

For example, in the deep processing of tea, they could enhance research and development from the tea beverage processing, new tea drinks development and preparation of new technology, tea natural products extraction and use technology, but also develop the extraction technology of the natural products such as flavonoid compounds, tea polysaccharide and theanine as well as their new products;

In sugar processing, they could strengthen the research and development work in deep-processing technology of sucrose and its derivatives, molasses, alcohol and waste processing technology, molasses for ethanol technology, bagasse for paper and cellulose production technology; in the deep processing field of livestock and poultry products, they could strengthen the research and development of livestock products deep processing technology and their integrated development and use, but also open up the patent of new uses of the product deep processing to meet the market demand; in fruit and vegetable deep processing field, they could vigorously develop the fruit and vegetable deep processing, storage and fresh-keeping as well as "the minimum processing" technology, and carry out fruits and vegetables function ingredients extraction technology, the new storage and fresh-keeping techniques and equipment of specialty fruits and vegetables as well as technical breakthrough of freeze-dried fruits and vegetables, fruit and vegetable powder processing, fruit wine and other

fruits and vegetables fermented products. [①]

4. "Produce-Learn-Research" Cooperative Innovation Strategy

The data show that the units to apply for the agricultural product processing technology patents in Yunnan Province are mainly scientific research institutes including Institute of Botany of Chinese Academy of Sciences, Tea Research Institute and the Institute of Biotechnology in Yunnan Academy of Agricultural Sciences, Yunnan Agricultural University, Yunnan Light Industry Research Institute and other research units. They should focus on the "produce-learn-research" cooperative innovation strategy. On the one hand, it could promote the efficient use of scientific research resources in scientific research institutes and universities as well as the effective combination of scientific research and market so as to improve the transformation and implementation rate of scientific research results. On the other hand, it could make enterprises obtain favorable and sustained technical support. For example, in the tea deep processing technical field, it could provide technical support through research institutions, combine with enterprises of tea deep processing strength and lengthen the industry chain.

5. Patent Utilization Strategy

Patent information recorded in the patent literature is the best information source to provide a variety of technical information. Agricultural product processing industry should strengthen the monitoring of patent application literature of ASEAN trading partners, understand the trend of patent applications and grasp their direction of technology development in order to take appropriate countermeasures; in the process of technological innovation, they should actively inspect disclosed and detailed technical information in the patent literature and find the information for reference or problem-solving methods so as to obtain the double effects with half efforts; moreover, in the introduction, digestion, absorption and re-innovation process, surveys and studies of patent information are also very important, which could avoid risks and blind investment.

The patent has a time limit, in addition, many patents applied by domestic agricultural products processing institutions and individuals have become invalid before

① Li Yigan, On Intellectual Property Strategy in Yunnan Province, Yunnan Nationality Publishing House in 2006, p. 139.

expiration, and among them many patent rights are terminated because of unpaid annual fee. Enterprises of technology needs can take advantage of the valuable invalid patents and expiration patents through research. In addition, patents not only have timeliness but also have regionalism, and they are only effective in authorized countries or regions. Accordingly, foreign technology which exceeds the priority period and has no patent in our country can be used in our country, which does not constitute patent infringement.

6. The Establishment of Patent Union and the Implementation of "Green" Patent Standards

Some large enterprises of agricultural products in Yunnan Province could establish patent alliance through the powerful combination such as tea processing industry, Panax industry, flower industry and rubber industry, which not only gives full play to the advantages of collective collaboration, but also enhances members' abilities to use intellectual property strategies; at the same time, they could implement the "green" patent standards, adopt environment-friendly and green production process, improve product quality, increase market competitiveness and then achieve the best economic benefits.

In short, both Yunnan and ASEAN countries have characteristics and advantages in the patented technology of agricultural products processing field. Faced with the rapid development of Free Trade Area and the historic opportunity of Yunnan gateway construction as well as the cooperation and competition of trade partners, agricultural products processing industry has an urgent need to speed up the implementation of patent strategy, nurture core technology and form the obvious regional specialties and competitive advantage in order to achieve better and faster industry development and obtain an advantageous position in the market competition of Free Trade Area.

学术综述

ACADEMIC SUMMARY

第五届"中国—东盟法律合作与发展高层论坛"学术综述

中国—东盟法律研究中心秘书处*

摘要：第五届"中国—东盟法律合作与发展高层论坛"吸引了来自中国和东盟国家的100多位法律界人士就中国—东盟自由贸易区的发展问题展开讨论。本届论坛以"合作共赢"为主题，充分体现了自贸区内各国对通过开展和加强区域合作寻求共同发展的期望与信心。各国代表们围绕"中国—东盟自由贸易区条约争端"、"中国—东盟自由贸易区内的仲裁机构——机遇与挑战"、"中国—东盟自贸区货物、服务和投资贸易现状与未来趋势"和"中国—东盟自由贸易区下的法律服务自由化"四个分主题畅所欲言，为中国—东盟自由贸易区的发展建言献策。本次论坛在促进各国代表关于巩固和加强中国—东盟国家间的法学法律合作，推动区域经济一体化朝向纵深发展等方面达成广泛共识。

关键词：中国—东盟自由贸易区；条约争端；仲裁机构；法律服务自由化

2011年9月26日至27日，由中国法学会主办，马来西亚律师公会、东盟法律协会马来西亚分会以及吉隆坡区域仲裁中心承办的第五届"中国—东盟法律合作与发展高层论坛"在马来西亚吉隆坡召开，200多位来自中国和东盟国家法学法律界人士参加了本届论坛。在本届论坛的开幕式上，东盟法律协会会长，敦拿督斯里查基·敦阿兹米和中国法学会代表团团长、中国法学会副会长胡忠先后致辞。论坛期间还举行了"中国—东盟自由贸易区(重庆)商事调解中心"，"中国—东盟自由贸易区(海口)法律服务中心"成立仪式。

本届论坛是继2006年越南下龙湾高层论坛之后，又一次由东盟国家承办举行的高层论坛，这也充分体现了中国—东盟各国间互相交流，彼此尊重、互利共赢的意旨。本次论坛的主题是"合作共赢"，就"中国—东盟自由贸易区条

* 由中国—东盟法律研究中心秘书处张晓君、宋继瑛编辑整理。

约争端"、"中国—东盟自由贸易区内的仲裁机构——机遇与挑战"、"中国—东盟自贸区货物、服务和投资贸易现状与未来趋势"和"中国—东盟自由贸易区下的法律服务自由化"四个分主题进行讨论。研讨发言和讨论的内容反映了中国—东盟自由贸易区法制建设与研究领域的最高水平。

本届论坛上共有20位中国和东盟国家的代表发言,其中有5位代表进行论坛的主旨发言。分别是来自马来西亚联邦法院首席大法官丹·斯里·阿里芬·查卡拉,中国法学会副会长、北京大学常务副校长吴志攀、联昌国际伊斯兰银行有限公司首席执行官巴德里·萨阿都·甘尼和菲律宾首席大法官雷纳托·克罗纳和马来西亚皇家雪兰莪锡器公司董事总经理/PEMUDAH促进业务特别工作小组联席主席丹斯里杨宝康。其中,吴志攀副会长从中国人深层次心理及文化的层面剖析中国高额储蓄率存在的根源与初衷,有助于东盟和其他国家消除对中国高额储蓄的误解和恐惧。他还介绍了中国金融法律的最新发展,强调近几年中国与东盟的金融市场合作日益紧密,双方应加强金融领域的法律交流,促进金融合作持续健康发展。

现将本届论坛研讨的内容按照专题单元综述如下,以飨读者。

一、中国—东盟自由贸易区条约争端

这一单元由文莱法学会会长潘基兰·伊萨德·瑞恩·巴哈林主持。马来西亚总检察长办公室国际事务司司长阿扎里沙·宾蒂·穆赫德·阿哈德和马来西亚祖吉菲·拉菲克律师事务所合伙人丹·斯里·塞西尔·亚伯拉罕以及泰国外交部条法司国际法发展处处长维拉万·芒克拉坦纳库和中国外交部条法司马新民参赞先后做了发言。

条约作为当代国际法最主要的依据,不仅是国家交往与合作的保障,更是现代国际秩序重要组成部分,而由条约引起的争端也成为国际社会中主要的争端形式。有效解决条约争端对于国际社会的经济一体化和全球化发展具有十分重要的意义。中国—东盟自由贸易区的成立和发展在很高程度上就是中国—东盟自由贸易区内国家间条约及法律相互协调和博弈的过程。

阿扎里沙·宾蒂·穆赫德·阿哈德探讨了国际争端的出现及其司法解决方面的问题。以国际贸易领域的争端解决为视角,分析了以WTO为代表的多边争端解决机制与经常包含WTO"超义务"条款在内的双边协定的争端解决机制的异同,并就日趋增加的双边协定对多边争端解决机制以及国际法的发展带来的挑战进行了思考,诸如争端避免程序的改进以及国际法的碎片化

等问题。他认为，在国际交往中国家应尽量谨慎应对其所承担的国际义务以避免冲突的发生。不过，他也承认在复杂的国际社会中，很多时候争端及冲突是无法避免的。因此，各国就应尽量寻求以和平的方式来解决国家间的争端。

丹·斯里·塞西尔·亚伯拉罕则从东盟与中国的视角审视了投资争议的仲裁问题。他从解决国际投资争议中心(ICSID)的存在及运行入手，探究未经 ICSID 定义的"国际投资"一语的内涵，从双边投资协定(BIT)及相关案例中寻求国际投资的认定路径。进而分析了东盟国家投资争议的主要情况，认为目前东盟国家发生的投资争议主要集中在投资者对当地法律的触犯以及国家在先同意的投资两个方面。他认为投资者表现出扩大和突破 BIT 以及 ICSID 关于投资范畴的倾向值得中国和东盟国家的关注，同时中国和东盟国家也应通过其相应国家机构使其关于投资保护的规定更加明确并具可预见性，从而有助于减少投资者对当地法律的背离，并进而促进国际投资的健康运行。

维拉万·芒克拉坦纳库认为经济全球化的影响，使得各种争端也呈现出国际性的特征。争端解决机制的存在则一定程度上确保了法律的确定性并进而维护着国际贸易体系的稳定性和可预见性。他在发言中探讨了国际贸易与投资领域不同类型的条约争端及其解决机制，着重审视了 WTO 争端解决机制和 CAFTA 下的争端解决机制以及在两种机制下的国家间争端和跨国公司与国家间争端的运行情况。他认为，在中国—东盟自由贸易区向法治化迈进的道路上，条约争端已不再局限于传统认知的国家间及其各自政策层面上的争端。在此时代背景下，唯交流与合作才是自贸区和投资得以不断发展和成熟的条件及前提。

马新民在其发言中主要介绍了中国的条约争端解决机制及实践。着重讨论了中国参加或缔结的条约对条约争端解决的规定以及中国条约争端解决的特征和基本精神。他认为，中国除采用谈判和协商办法外，也注意采用仲裁、选择性的斡旋、调停与和解等第三方介入的解决办法，使中国的条约争端机制逐步形成多种争端解决办法并存的局面。受"和为贵"传统文化思想影响的中国，在条约争端解决领域更倾向于采用"非对抗性方式"解决分歧与争端。换言之，中国的条约争端解决显示出以谈判协商为核心，以仲裁为补充，并辅之以调停与和解等第三方介入的争端解决机制的特征。

二、中国—东盟自贸区内的仲裁中心——机遇和挑战

这一单元由新加坡盛德国际律师事务所合伙人杨炎龙主持。吉隆坡区域

仲裁中心总监孙达·拉铢和西南政法大学副校长刘想树教授以及印度尼西亚布迪嘉加联合律师事务所首席兼执行合伙人托尼·布迪嘉加各自就该议题作了发言。

中国—东盟自由贸易区自建成以来,有力地促进区域贸易总量稳步增长,不但在促进自贸区内国家的经济发展和社会进步方面成效显著,更有利于自贸区内法学及相关法律层面的交流与沟通。伴随经济发展的大力推进,自由贸易区内的法律冲突及争议等副产品也开始出现,如何有效应对并合理解决这些法律纠纷和争议,成为中国—东盟自由贸易区发展中不可回避的问题。多名与会专家不约而同地将仲裁视为中国—东盟自由贸易区内解决争端的有效手段。

孙达·拉铢在其发言中主要关注中国—东盟自由贸易区在产生及未来发展过程中所面临的机遇与挑战。他认为一个仲裁中心的成功运行与否很高程度上依赖于国家政府层面的支持,以及司法部门和同业者的认可与评价。仲裁机构发展的制约因素很多,处于发展过程中的仲裁机构,一般都面临资金、设施、法制环境等问题的困扰。他认为,透明的程序、良好的法治,以及完善的机制是吸引国际投资者采用仲裁方式来解决国际争端的必要元素。

刘想树认为,在当前形势下,设立中国—东盟自贸区仲裁中心的可能性及机遇已经具备。他认为中国—东盟自贸区仲裁中心的建立和发展具有良好的政治基础和经济支持,同时中国与东盟各国间"互相尊重,求同存异"的文化交流态势,也有助于构筑双方对于仲裁机制的理解及共识。就中心的运行问题,刘教授认为仲裁中心应在服务自贸区发展的目标下明确其定位,广泛选聘高素质仲裁员,加强制度创新,强化其裁决的执行力。

托尼·布迪嘉加则在其发言中主要就印度尼西亚的仲裁机制进行了讨论。荷兰殖民时期就已经存在的仲裁制度直到上世纪90年代都很少被用到,随着印度尼西亚经济的不断开放发展,仲裁才逐渐受到关注并主要被国际商业合同采纳为争端解决的方式。以印度尼西亚国家仲裁委员会(BANI)为代表的印尼仲裁机构受理的仲裁案件数量不断上升,所涉主题多样化。根据印尼仲裁法律规定,在印尼作出的仲裁裁决必须在管辖该地区的法院进行登记并由该院院长以授权形式签署执行命令。印尼法律中对于仲裁裁决执行问题历来存在很多争议。在他看来,这主要源于印尼法律对诸如"公共秩序"及仲裁裁决的承认标准等问题的解释及适用方面存在法律上的不确定性。同时,法官对于仲裁制度和程序的不熟悉以及对国际商事交往的非专业性也成为制约仲裁制度充分发展的因素之一。

三、CAFTA 货物、服务和投资贸易现状与未来趋势

本单元由来自菲律宾瑞嘉拉及克鲁兹律师事务所资深合伙人、律师阿维利诺维·克鲁兹主持。新加坡瑞德律师事务所合伙人许丽霞和马来西亚国际贸易及工业部东盟经济合作司司长拉文德兰·帕拉尼亚潘以及菲律宾阿克拉律师事务所联合执行合伙人、律师弗朗西斯科·爱得林和中国广西师范大学法学院杨丽艳教授作了发言。

《中国—东盟全面经济合作框架协议货物贸易协定》,《中国—东盟全面经济合作框架协议服务贸易协议》,以及《中国—东盟全面经济合作框架协议投资协议》构成了中国—东盟自由贸易区成立的基本法律文件的重要组成部分,在中国—东盟自由贸易区的发展过程中发挥着十分重要的作用。建成后的自贸区,在货物贸易、服务贸易以及投资贸易领域表现出怎样的发展现状,在自贸区不断深化发展的过程中,又将呈现怎样的发展态势,就成了代表们关注的热点。

许丽霞女士的发言主要涉及有关投资领域的现状与发展。中国—东盟自由贸易区内的投资,从双方互相投资现状为基础,对各自的政治、经济、政策等领域的优势和缺陷进行分析,认为中国的全球投资战略、中国公司以及中产阶级财富处理方式连同自由贸易区内生性的发展和技术领域促进因素等都会影响到未来中国—东盟自由贸易区的发展趋势。中国和东盟各国应尽量消除自贸区内市场准入门槛和限制,并朝着促进贸易自由化的方向共同努力,同时提高法律、规则和政策的透明度及执行力从而建立一个更为强大和融洽的亚洲。

拉文德兰·帕拉尼亚潘认为,中国—东盟国家间的区域一体化在某种程度上是由市场驱动的,中国和东盟国家政府通过建立自贸区的法律框架来进一步增强彼此关系。中国以及东盟国家的大量承诺使彼此关系变得更加紧密。他着重讨论了自贸区在货物贸易、服务贸易以及投资领域的成就,推进更加深入的战略性伙伴关系所面临的挑战以及自贸区未来方向及路径。他提出,加快各方可接受的兼容性评估结果的推进,彼此承认对方对法律和一致性问题的评估,包括使其国内标准与国际标准一致性的合作是非常接近现实而必要的措施。

弗朗西斯科·爱得林则从全球竞争的角度探讨中国与东盟国家在自贸区内发展及需应对的挑战,并对制度、司法独立性、法律框架在争端解决中的效能、政府规定的负效应以及法律框架与政府规定协调性等方面都进行了比较

分析,认为中国和东盟多数国家都存在比较明显的问题。就货物市场而言,中国的当地竞争以及市场主导度都表明了其强大的内部政策功效,另外在反垄断方面相比一些东盟国家也更为有效。但在鼓励创业方面却由于繁琐的设立程序及较长的期限而有所不足。金融市场的发展领域,大多数东盟国家在此方面表现都好于全球平均水平,中国的风险资金位于世界前列,有助于鼓励和帮助中小型企业的发展。他提出,中国和东盟国家应在增强效能和激励创新领域不断深入和完善,以充分发挥其潜在市场和经济效应,并最终谋利于自贸区内的各国人民。最后他认为律师应在自贸区内关于司法独立性、争端解决中法律框架效能的发挥以及通过法律促使政府规定更趋合理等领域发挥应有的作用。

杨丽艳教授的发言主要涉及中国—东盟合作领域扩大及其机制的分析。在分析了中国—东盟自由贸易区发展的现状的基础上提出扩大中国—东盟合作领域的必要性。双边国家和人民的福利需要、国际社会发展的需要、地区安全和繁荣发展的需要共同决定了中国—东盟自由贸易区应该进一步扩大的合作领域,主要是在知识产权、海洋合作、能源环境合作以及在非传统安全、跨境犯罪、劳工和人权等领域通过多种方式进行。

四、中国—东盟自由贸易区下的法律服务自由化

本单元专题由中国对外经济贸易大学法学院副院长丁丁教授主持。马来西亚再依易卜拉欣律师事务所执行合伙人周成国和越南法学会阮成秀博士以及中国商务部条约法律司副司长杨国华和中国司法部司法研究所所长王公义就法律服务自由化问题先后进行了发言。

中国—东盟自由贸易区成立以来发展势头良好,在经济交往良好运行的情况下,也给相关的法律服务行业带来新的发展机遇和广阔的市场空间。法律服务自由化成了广大法律服务从业者的核心追求。实务界的法律从业者们对该单元的关注充分体现了各方对中国—东盟自由贸易区的发展与未来的积极认同,代表们对法律自由化的发展提出了很多切实可行的对策及建议。

周成国的发言主要涉及中国—东盟自由贸易区内法律服务自由化所面临的问题与挑战。他认为在开展中国—东盟自由贸易区的法律服务自由化之前应先完成东盟国家的法律自由化。但是东盟服务框架内的法律服务自由化进程实施面临诸多问题:自由化承诺透明度不够并伴随着各种限制和条件、各国法律实务和标准的差异以及共享机制的缺乏、各国专业机构的内在观念和排

他性规定等都在一定程度上制约着东盟内部法律服务自由化的推进。他认为,推进法律服务自由化是当务之急,同时应该大力推动法律服务的资产化使其保障性作用得以发挥。

阮成秀主要从越南的视角来讨论法律服务行业的现状及法律要求。他梳理了越南在中国—东盟自贸区框架和WTO框架下的法律服务承诺及规则以及2006年律师法的规定。他详细分析了WTO四种服务模式在越南服务承诺和国内法律上的具体操作和差异化要求。他认为,开放法律服务行业既是WTO成员国所需遵从的服务承诺,同时又是创造一个竞争性的法律服务市场的必然要求。加强法学教育与交流促进本地区的法律服务自由化水平,必须使本地区内国家关于开放法律服务行业的承诺得到区域化呈现。

杨国华认为WTO《服务贸易总协定》为实现法律服务贸易自由化奠定了规则层面的基础。就中国—东盟自贸区而言,应该有更高程度的法律服务贸易开放水平。具体而言,法律服务的属地性、一定程度上的政治性使各国在开放法律服务领域采取较为谨慎的态度,但是过多过细的限制,在一定程度上将形成贸易壁垒,阻碍法律服务贸易自由化的发展,同时也会对经济全球化和本国经济繁荣造成不利影响。GATS为国际法律服务贸易设定的多边规则如最惠国待遇原则、具体承诺、市场准入以及国民待遇等规则的影响最为直接和深远。GATS的有关规定有助于法律服务贸易限制措施的削减,形成法律服务贸易自由化的持续推动力,使发展中国家在法律服务自由化进程中获得更多的发展机会。在中国—东盟自贸区实现服务贸易自由化,将在GATS规则的框架下进行。而《服务贸易协议》的内容,也正是基于GATS下的各项义务和承诺而制定的。自贸区的法律服务贸易自由化也应当在GATS、《框架协议》和《服务贸易协议》确定的原则、目标和义务下进行推进。

王公义的发言集中于国际社会尤其是自贸区内国家关注的中国法律服务行业开放问题。根据中国的入世承诺和《外国律师事务所驻华代表机构管理条例》的规定,外国律师事务处在中国境内开展业务的范围越来越广泛,可就本国法、第三国法和国际法提供咨询服务,也可通过订立合同的形式与中国律师事务所建立长期的委托关系,开展业务合作,较好地满足了外国律师事务所适应经济全球一体化趋势,提供跨法域法律服务的实际需求。中国也将进一步推动中外(包括内地与港、澳)律师事务所和律师的交流与合作,特别是加强与东盟法律服务行业的合作,为促进中国与其他国家和地区特别是东盟的经贸往来和民商事交往做出贡献。与此同时,他也认为一国法律服务领域的开放应与其国情及国内律师业的发展状况相适应。循序渐进地开放服务业,有

助于维持开放要求与国内律师行业发展状况间的良性平衡。

小　　结

本届论坛上共有二十多位来自中国和东盟成员国的专家、学者和法律实务界代表做了精彩发言,多位中国和东盟国家代表参与主持和点评。研讨期间代表们高瞻远瞩,提出的一些创新观点极具现实意义和可行性,如各方代表广泛支持并响应有关设立"中国—东盟自由贸易区仲裁中心"的设想。代表们普遍认为,增强多元市场主体争端解决机制建设,加强自由贸易区协议的执行力度对于中国—东盟自由贸易区的健康稳定运行意义深远。中国与东盟国家间的法学和法律领域的交往应进一步加强,充分利用现代文明的法律手段来增进彼此理解与沟通。中国—东盟法律合作与发展论坛适逢其时,充分发挥了其对中国—东盟自由贸易区发展不可或缺的助推作用。而合作共赢的论坛主题则为解决代表们共同关心的问题提供了很好的思路——自贸区内的各国及其市场主体,应立足于在合作的前提下共谋社会与经济利益的发展,在共同发展的基础上开展更加真诚而互信的合作。论坛代表们在巩固和加强中国—东盟国家间的法学法律合作,推动区域经济一体化朝向纵深发展方面具有广泛共识。

Academic Summary for the Fifth China-ASEAN Top Forum on Legal Cooperation and Development

The Sechetariat of China-ASEAN Legal Research Center*
Translated by Li Xiaoyu (Isabel)

Abstract: More than one hundred legal professionals from China and ASEAN countries attended the Fifth China-ASEAN Forum on Legal Cooperation and Development in Kuala Lumpur. The theme "cooperation and common prosperity" fully conveys the good expectation and confidence of China-ASEAN countries to the future development of the China-ASEAN Free Trade Area. The representatives from China and ASEAN countries deeply exchanged their opinions and observations concerning the Treaty Disputes and Arbitral Institutions in CAFTA region as well as the present and future trends of CAFTA Trade in Goods, Services and Investment and the liberalization of CAFTA Legal Services. In the end, the representatives gained common opinions on the importance of the consolidation and improvement of the legal cooperation, so as to promote the profound development of the regional economic integration.

Key Words: CAFTA; Treaty Disputes; Arbitral Institutions; Liberalization of Legal Service

At September 26th to 27th, 2011, hosted by Chinese Law Society and undertaken by Malaysia Bar Council, the Malaysia Branch of ASEAN Law As-

---

* The Sechetariat of China-ASEAN Legal Research Center, Southwest University of Political Science and Law Edited by Zhang Xiaojun & Song Jiying.

sociation as well as KLRCA, the fifth China-ASEAN Forum on Legal Cooperation and Development is hosted in Kuala Lumpur, the capital of Malaysia with more than one hundred legal professionals from China and ASEAN countries attended. The president of the Malaysia Branch of ASEAN Law Association and the vice chairman of Chinese Law Society deliver speeches and the Commercial Mediation Center (Chongqing) and Legal Service Center (Haikou) of China-ASEAN Free Trade Area are established in the ceremony.

Representing the mutual communication, respect and benefit, this forum is hosted again by ASEAN countries since the 2006Vietnam's. With the theme of win-win cooperation, the discussion mainly contains four parts: China-ASEAN free trade area treaty dispute, Arbitration-opportunities and challenges, Current situation and future trends of product, Service and investment as well as legal service liberation, which reflect the frontier of legal construction and academic research.

Totally 20 representatives made their speeches among which 5 gave keynote speeches. Wu Zhipan, vice president of Chinese Law Society, analyzed the root of China's high savings rate deeply from Chinese people's psychology and culture, which may eliminate to some degree the misunderstanding and worry among other countries. He also introduced the newly development of Chinese financial law and emphasized that China and ASEAN countries should enhance the close relationships in financial market through legal cooperation and exchange approaching sustainable development.

Now, I'll divide the main content into four units and talked in detail for the readers.

1. The Treaty Dispute of China-ASEAN Free Trade Area

As the main sources of international law, treaties are not only the guarantee of the communication and cooperation between states, but also an important part of modern international orders as well. Treaty-caused conflicts urge to be solved for the globalization and economic integration. The establishment and development of CAFTA, to a large degree, is the process of treaties and laws' coordination and conflicts in this area.

Datuk Azailiza Mohd Ahad, head of International Affairs Division Attorney General's Chambers probed into the reasons why international conflicts emerge and the judicial way to solve them. He also explained the differences between multilateral dispute settlement mechanisms represented by WTO and bilateral agreement including WTO-plus commitments. Moreover, he talked about the improvements of avoiding conflicts, the fragmentation of international law and so on. He reckoned that countries should be mindful of their own obligations to avoid conflicts but many conflicts are unavoidable. Then we need to seek for a peaceful and effective settlement to solve them.

Tan Sri Cecil Abraham, partner of Malaysia law firm analyzed the situation of investment conflicts and sought for identification path from BIT as well as the related cases. He held the opinion that according to the situation that disputes happened in breaking the local law and investors felt secure merely because some organs of Government has considered and approved the investment, countries should in turn make their rules more clear.

Vilawan Mangklatanakul from Thailand specifically examined dispute settlement process under WTO's Understanding on Rules and Procedures governing the Settlement of Disputes (DSU) and the CAFTA. He held the opinion that a developed free trade area should use intensive informal and discreet discussions behind the scenes to work out the general consensus which then acts as the starting point around which the unanimous decision is finally accepted in more formal meetings, rather than across-the-table negotiations involving bargaining and give-and-take that results in deals enforceable in a court of law.

Mr. Ma Xinmin, counselor from Ministry of Foreign Affairs of China mainly introduced China's mechanism and practice of treaty dispute settlement. He reckoned that influenced by the traditional culture that peace is more precious than anything else, Chinese prefer solving disputes through non-confrontational means. The treaty dispute settlement mechanism in China has the following features: negotiation and consultation as the priority, arbitration as supplement, conciliation and reconciliation as subsidiary.

2. The Arbitration Center of CAFTA-opportunities and challenges

Since establishment, trading in CAFTA is promoted steadily. Nevertheless, conflicts and disputes arouses as well. Arbitration is regarded as the most efficient way of solving the problems above.

Director of KLRCA, Sundra Rajoo held the view that whether an arbitral institution running well or not relies on government's support as well as the approval and comments from legal department and the same field. There are many factors restraining a developing institution such as expenses, lack of facility and favorable legal environment. Moreover, transparency, good governance and infrastructure are necessary to attract the international investors.

Liu Xiangshu, vice-chancellor of SWUPL, pointed out the possibility and opportunities of establishing the Arbitration Center of CAFTA under the present situation. The Center should clear its positioning based on the goal of stimulating the development of CAFTA, hire arbitrators of high quality, promote systematic innovations, and strengthen the enforcement of arbitral awards.

Tony Budidjaja, chief partner from Indonesia law firm talked about the arbitration bodies of Indonesia representing by BANI. At the same time, challenges appeared. For instance, Many Indonesian judges are not really familiar with arbitration and lack of experience as well as guidance in handling arbitration related issues. Enforcement of arbitral awards is still uncertain due to Legal uncertainly in the interpretation and application of "public policy" and annulment standards.

3. Current Situation and Future Trends of Product, Service and Investment in CAFTA

The representatives focused on the current situation and future trends of product, service and investment in CAFTA in this part.

Josephine Koh, partner from Singapore indicated that China's global investment strategy, wealth and sophistication of Chinese companies and middle class, relaxation of foreign exchange controls and so on will affect the future trends of CAFTA. Liberalization and elimination of restrictions and thresholds on market access, increased transparency and enforcement efforts in laws, rules and policies are a necessity in creating a more cohesive and stronger Asia.

Mr. P. Ravidran, senior director of ASEAN Economic Cooperation Division from Malaysia talked about achievements on trade in goods, services and investments, challenges to form a deeper ASEAN-China strategic economic partnership and the ways to go forward including accelerating work on establishing mutual acceptance of the results of compatibility assessment procedures, mutually recognizing each other's system and conformity assessment and so on.

Francis Lim, co-managing partner from Philippines law offices held the opinion that while there are 2 or 3 ASEAN countries that score very well across all indices in the rankings, many ASEAN economies still need to improve to be globally competitive. Secondly, China's growth in the last decade or more has been nothing short of extraordinary, but yet its economy still has much more room to improve. Thirdly, there is an existing legal framework in the form of various agreements between the ASEAN and China. Last, pursuing concrete projects under the various agreements will not only address each one's weaknesses, but also further solidify their respective strengths, in the world arena of competition.

Professor Liyan Yang from Guangxi Normal University of China mainly talked about analysis of the enlarging cooperation of China-ASEAN's and its mechanism. The necessity lies in the need of the welfare of China and ASEAN's people, the development of international society and the safety and development of the east Asia.

4. The Liberalization of Legal Service in CAFTA

In this part, representatives put up with many suggestions of liberation of legal service in CAFTA. The sound development momentum of CAFTA brings new opportunities and markets for legal service.

Chew Seng Kok, managing partner from Malaysia law firm emphasised that legal services in ASEAN must be liberalized before liberalization of legal services in CAFTA. Meanwhile, liberalization within ASEAN is hardly making any progress for the reason that inward looking and exclusive regulation by national professional bodies has not facilitated liberalization of legal services and so on. He advocated managing the liberalization of legal services to capitalize on economic growth.

Dr. Nguyen Thanh Tu from Vietnam talked about this topic in Vietnam's perspective. In the first place, he gave the audience an overview of liberalization of trade in legal services in CAFTA. Later, regulation of trade in legal services in Vietnam and efforts in CAFTA is explained.

Yang Guohua, deputy director of treaty and law division in China's Ministry of Commerce held the view that countries take on discreet attitude towards liberalization of legal service due to regional and political factor of it. However, too many restraints will form trade barriers. The liberalization needs to be promoted under the framework of GATS, Outline Agreement and Service and Trade Agreement.

Wang Gongyi, director of Private Law Research Center of Ministry of Justice in China reckoned that according to the promise when China joined WTO and the Regulations on the Administration of Foreign Law Firms' Representative Offices in China, the scope of law business in China of the Foreign Law Firms' Representative Office has been more and more widespread. What's more, every countries' opening of legal services could be step by step, should be adjusted with its national conditions and the development of inner lawyers' industry.

Summary

Totally 20 representatives made their speech on this forum, which put up with some creative and practical points including the establishment of an arbitration center. It is widely believed that enhancing the construction of

dispute settlement mechanism and enforcement of agreement is good for stable and healthy operation in CAFTA. This forum has irreplaceable functions that it will promote the cooperation of legal research and practice between China and ASEAN countries, and give solutions to the problems concerned, which can push forward economic integration both in scope and in depth.

附 录

APPENDIX

中国—东盟高端法律人才培养基地简介

为强化中国与东盟国家在制度建设领域的合作，加深对国际法准则、中国—东盟自由贸易区规则、中国和平发展政策和中国法律制度的了解，2012年10月，中国法学会批准创设了"中国—东盟高端法律人才培养基地"。该基地设在西南政法大学，与中国—东盟法律研究中心实行一套人马、两块牌子，是中国—东盟法律研究中心实体化建设的重要内容。

依托学校办学条件等各种优势资源，基地将通过开展高层次的学历和非学历教育，为中国与东盟社会经济交往培养高层次的法律人才。通过开展访问学者项目、硕博士项目以及培训项目，面向东盟国家，每年资助若干名高层次的官员和专家学者到基地进行项目合作研究和硕博士学位或进入博士后流动站究。同时，基地也将积极开展与东盟国家高校合作办学与硕博士项目，为东盟国家和中国的企业界、行业协会、司法界和政府部门提供培训项目。

"中国—东盟高端法律人才培养基地"将努力建成为国内有影响力、培养涉外东盟高端法律人才的基地，为中国—东盟自由贸易区及其经济发展提供制度建设的高层次法律人才支持。

An Introduction of the China-ASEAN Training Center for High-Level Legal Talents

In order to enhance the cooperation between China and ASEAN Member States in the field of institution building, and to make understand on the norms of international law, the legal rules of China-ASEAN Free Trade Area (CAFTA), the Policies of China's peaceful development as well as the legal system of China, *China-ASEAN Training Center for High-Level Legal Talents* has been set up by the China Law Society. The Base is located in SWUPL, and is a concrete construction for China-ASEAN of China-ASEAN Legal Research Center (CALRC), which shares the same personnel with CALR CALRC.

Supported by advantageous resources for high-level education in SWUPL, through offering high-level academic and non- academic education, more and more high-level legal talents will be trained for social and economic exchanges and development between China and ASEAN in Center. Moreover, Scholars Program, Master and doctor degree projects and Professional training programs Opening to officers, experts and students for ASEAN member states will be launched. The Center will actively launch the possibility for cooperative education and Master's and PhD project with ASEAN Member States' University, aiming to provide training programs for both China and ASEAN member states' business community , industry associations , the judiciary and the government departments.

China-ASEAN Training Center for High-Level Legal Talents will take any efforts to be an influential foreign-related training center for high-level legal talents of ASEAN, and supply more high-level legal talents for CAFTA.

《中国—东盟法律评论》稿约

作为第四届"中国—东盟法律合作与发展高层论坛"的重要成果,"中国—东盟法律研究中心"集聚了中国与东盟国家法学法律界的相关研究资源,开展对中国与东盟法律的系统性、基础性和前瞻性的研究,为"中国—东盟自由贸易区"的可持续发展保驾护航。

经研究,由"中国—东盟法律研究中心"组织出版《中国—东盟法律评论》法学学术刊物,通过以书代刊的形式按年分期连续公开出版。《中国—东盟法律评论》将会秉承会通中外和而不同的传统精神,发扬宽容为本的组稿理念,提倡多元交流、学术争鸣,鼓励创新性学术成果。

本刊主要特色在于:既注重法学理论的分析和研究,也兼顾对法律实践问题的探索与讨论。刊物研究内容主要涵盖:东盟国家的法律制度及与中国法律制度的比较研究,中国与东盟国家相关的立法及其实践研究、东盟组织法律制度研究、中国—东盟自贸区法制建设研究等;开展对国别法、组织法、比较法等领域的具体专题研讨,并将结合相关的学术焦点问题组织稿件、专刊出版。

《中国—东盟法律评论》将以中国及东盟国家外商投资法为主题,内容包括中国—东盟自贸区投资规则及其争端解决机制与实践等。现诚挚地邀请邀请国内外各界专家、学者赐稿,为中国—东盟法律合作与法学交流奉献力量。

为提高刊物质量,就相关投稿事宜说明如下:

1.《中国—东盟法律评论》投稿文章请以 Word 文档(英文或中文)电子版发至以下编辑电子邮箱:edofcalr@supsl. cn,并请注明"《中国—东盟法律评论》投稿"字样。为便于中英文双语出版,本刊鼓励论文以中英文两种语言版本投稿。

2.文章注释采用脚注,每页重新编号,以阿拉伯数字加圆圈标识的形式。英文注释依其注释习惯。来稿需有文章摘要及关键词(中英文);并请注明作者姓名、单位、职称(或职务)、学位、研究方向、通讯地址、邮政编码、联系电话

和电子邮箱等。

3.稿件原则上不支付稿酬,一经采用,寄送样刊两本以示谢意。

4.本刊反对抄袭,来稿文责自负,请勿一稿多投,在三个月内未收到用稿通知,可自行处理稿件。来稿均应为未在公开出版物发表之成果。

5.《中国—东盟法律评论》编辑部有权对来稿做适当文字修改。拥有对在《中国—东盟法律评论》上发表的作品出版权,任何转载、收录等须事先获《中国—东盟法律评论》编辑部书面许可。任何来稿视为作者、译著者已同意本《中国—东盟法律评论》约稿条件。

6.《中国—东盟法律评论》新一期投稿截止时间为2013年9月15日。

《中国—东盟法律评论》编委会

2012年12月

Call for Papers

As an important outcome of the fourth China-ASEAN Forum on Legal Cooperation and Development, the China-ASEAN Legal Research Center highly enjoys corresponding research and study resources both home and abroad, especially the law sectors from the ASEAN countries and Chinese government. Accordingly, the China-ASEAN Legal Research Center would like to develop and explore the China-ASEAN Legal Research to a systematic way, making a good balance between the theoretical academic topics and the foresighted importance frontiers. With such a solid research foundation, the China-ASEAN Free Trade Area will be possibly in good operation and maintain a sustainable development.

Pursuant to relevant consideration, the China-ASEAN Law Review is in publication under the administration and management of the China-ASEAN Legal Research Center. The China-ASEAN Law Review is publicly in circulation yearly continuously with the means of book instead of periodical. And it will stick to the traditional spirit of "he er bu tong" and cordially welcome the diverse ideas and concepts home and abroad. The Law Review calls for papers in the conception of tolerance and advocates the collision and merger of different viewpoints as well as encourage the creative and original academic research works.

The contents of the China-ASEAN Law Review have a wide coverage, mainly including the legal system of the ASEAN nations and the comparative research between Chinese law and the former. Besides, the contents also contain the relative legislation and practice study in the China-ASEAN area; legal system of ASEAN organizations; legal construction research under the

framework of China-ASEAN FTA etc. Moreover, the China-ASEAN Law Review also develops many specific discussions concerning the national law, organizational law as well as the comparative law and so on. Meanwhile, the China-ASEAN Law Review much concerns the academic focus and concentrations , considering to organize excellent papers and publish in special volume of great importance. It enjoys very clear characteristic—giving emphasis on the analysis and research of the theoretical legal principles and jurisprudence, as well as showing wide compatibility to the discussions of the topics of strategic importance in practice.

The theme of the China-ASEAN Law Review, is about foreign investment law, which includes China-ASEAN Free Trade Area Investment Rules and Dispute Settlement Mechanism and Practice. Now, We sincerely calls the professionals and scholars from different sectors home and abroad for good papers, making great contributions for the legal exchange of China-ASEAN legal research.

To guarantee the academic quality of the China-ASEAN Law Review, the editor notes the corresponding information as follows:

I. Please email the electronic version of your paper (in English or Chinese) in file of word to the China-ASEAN Law Review editor's mailbox respectively:

Editorial Board of China-ASEAN Law Review, *edofcalr@supsl.cn*

Please note clearly the words "the China-ASEAN Law Review paper ". For the convenience of bilingual publication, the editor encourages the authors providing papers both in Chinese and English.

II. The China-ASEAN Law Review requires all the papers to use footnotes each page by new Arab No. repeat with circle around. English notes uses according to the customer. Each paper is expected to be complete with abstract and key words both in Chinese and English. For communication convenience, information such as author's full name, unit, professional title (or work status),degree, major and research orientation, telephone, post address, code No, and email address shall be clear noted.

III. Oncerecruited, the editor would post two samples to the author for gratitude. No capital profit in principle.

IV. The China-ASEAN Law Review is against any form of academic piracy. Author's self-responsibility is the only means for any piracy-related issues. The editor reminds that one paper shall not be provided for more than once at the same time . Not receiving recruit letter within three months, the author could deal with the paper freely. Furthermore, each paper should be the unpublished work of the author in public.

V. The editor of the China-ASEAN Law Review has the right to properly revise the paper. Besides, the editor has the right to publish the works that have published in the China-ASEAN Law Review. Any form of trans-publishing, paper recording should get the consent permission of the China-ASEAN editor in written form in prior. Each paper emailed to the editor's mailbox shall be regarded as a consent of agreement from the author to the calling requisition for paper of this Law Review.

VI. The deadline for the submission of next volume of the China-ASEAN Law Review is September 15, 2013.

The China-ASEAN Law Review Commission

图书在版编目(CIP)数据

中国—东盟法律评论.第2卷.第1期/张晓君主编.—厦门:厦门大学出版社,2013
ISBN 978-7-5615-4563-8

Ⅰ.①中… Ⅱ.①张… Ⅲ.①法律-中国、东南亚国家联盟-文集
Ⅳ.①D92-53②D933-53

中国版本图书馆CIP数据核字(2013)第029648号

厦门大学出版社出版发行
(地址:厦门市软件园二期望海路39号 邮编:361008)
http://www.xmupress.com
xmup @ xmupress.com
厦门市明亮彩印有限公司印刷
2013年6月第1版 2013年6月第1次印刷
开本:720×970 1/16 印张:19.5 插页:2
字数:339千字 印数:1~1 200册
定价:42.00元